Language Hub

ELEMENTARY
Student's Book

PETER MAGGS
CATHERINE SMITH

A2

Contents

	LESSON • OBJECTIVES	GRAMMAR	VOCABULARY	PRONUNCIATION	READING • LISTENING	SPEAKING • WRITING
U1	**ARRIVALS**					
1.1	**People and places** (p2) Talk about countries and nationalities	**present simple** *be*: positive and negative	countries and nationalities	syllable stress	listen to people meeting for the first time	introduce yourself say where you are from
1.2	**Where are you?** (p4) Ask and answer questions about a place	**present simple** *be*: questions	big numbers	similar numbers	read text messages about a city listen to someone talking about a city	talk about distances describe a place
1.3	**What's in your bag?** (p6) Talk about everyday items	*a/an* and plural nouns; *this, that, these, those*	everyday items	vowel sounds: /ɪ/, /æ/, /iː/, /əʊ/	listen to a conversation at an airport read an article about hand luggage **KEY SKILL** Reading for gist	**SPEAKING HUB** talk about what's in your bag
1.4	**Café Hub** **Good morning** (p8) Greet people and make introductions		greet people and make introductions	word stress	▶ watch someone introduce a friend	give a personal presentation
	UNIT REVIEW p10	**WRITING** (p160) Fill in a form with personal details | **KEY SKILL** Capital letters				
U2	**PEOPLE**					
2.1	**Family** (p12) Talk about your family	**possessive adjectives and apostrophes**	family	/ə/ 'schwa'	read an article about a famous family	talk about famous families describe your family tree
2.2	**The same, but different** (p14) Talk about appearance	*have/has got*	describing appearance	contracted *have*	read an article about family appearance listen to someone describing their brother	describe a family member's appearance compare and contrast family members
2.3	**Friends** (p16) Describe family members and friends	**using adjectives**	personality adjectives	syllable stress: adjectives	listen to a conversation about university friends read an email about flatmates **KEY SKILL** Reading for organisation	describe someone's personality **SPEAKING HUB** choose a flatmate for a friend
2.4	**Café Hub** **Café chaos** (p18) Make and respond to requests		make and respond to requests	stress and intonation	▶ watch someone order food in a café	order in a café
	UNIT REVIEW p20	**WRITING** (p161) Write an email to a friend | **KEY SKILL** *and, but* and *or*				
U3	**DAYS**					
3.1	**A typical day** (p22) Talk about daily routines	**present simple positive**	everyday activities	third person *-s*	listen to a radio interview about a typical day	talk about someone's typical day talk about jobs and routines
3.2	**All day, every day** (p24) Discuss daily activities	**adverbs of frequency**	prepositions of time	word stress	read about daily essentials listen to people talk about screen-free week	talk about how often you do things list your top ten daily essentials
3.3	**A special day** (p26) Describe a special day	**present simple negative**	big celebrations	sentence stress	read a blog post about a festival listen to a conversation about big celebrations **KEY SKILL** Listening for detail	**SPEAKING HUB** give a short presentation about a special day
3.4	**Café Hub** **Finding Neena** (p28) Make and respond to suggestions		make and respond to suggestions	stress and intonation	▶ watch people making and responding to suggestions	make plans with your classmates
	UNIT REVIEW p30	**WRITING** (p162) Write a blog post about your day | **KEY SKILL** Sequencing words				

II CONTENTS

Contents

	LESSON · OBJECTIVES	GRAMMAR	VOCABULARY	PRONUNCIATION	READING · LISTENING	SPEAKING · WRITING
U4	**WORK AND EDUCATION**					
4.1	**What do you do?** (p32) Talk about jobs	present simple *yes/no* questions; short answers	work and jobs	linking sounds: *do/ does*	read an interview about someone's job	talk about your job ask questions to guess someone's job
4.2	**Good job!** (p34) Talk about the perfect job	*have to / don't have to*	time expressions	connected speech: *have to*	read an article about good and bad jobs listen to a conversation about someone's job	talk about the pros and cons of a job talk about the perfect job
4.3	**Learn something new** (p36) Talk about adult education and career development	question words	education collocations	word stress: questions	read an FAQ page about a distance learning university listen to a conversation at a careers fair **KEY SKILL** Listening for gist	talk about education in your country **SPEAKING HUB** plan a course for adults who want to retrain
4.4	**Café Hub** **Busy day** (p38) Ask for someone and leave a message		ask for someone and leave a message	stress and intonation	▶ watch someone leaving a message with a receptionist	talk on the phone
	UNIT REVIEW p40	**WRITING** (p163) Write an email asking for information	**KEY SKILL** Punctuation: question marks, commas and full stops				
U5	**PLACES**					
5.1	**There's no place like home** (p42) Describe a home	*there is/are*	rooms and furniture; prepositions of place	/b/, /d/ and /g/	listen to a conversation about a house swap	talk about your home write an advert for a house swap
5.2	**My neighbourhood** (p44) Describe a neighbourhood	*can*	places in a town or city	weak forms: *can/ can't*	read online comments about a neighbourhood	talk about what makes a good neighbourhood talk about your neighbourhood
5.3	**Amazing buildings** (p46) Describe an interesting building	imperatives	adjectives to describe the appearance of things	word stress: adjectives	read an article about interesting buildings **KEY SKILL** Reading for specific information	practise giving instructions **SPEAKING HUB** describe famous buildings
5.4	**Café Hub** **Moving in** (p48) Ask for and give directions		ask for and give directions	stress and intonation	▶ watch someone asking for directions in the street	tell someone how to get somewhere
	UNIT REVIEW p50	**WRITING** (p164) Write a description of a place	**KEY SKILL** Using adjectives				
U6	**THAT'S ENTERTAINMENT**					
6.1	**Let's go out** (p52) Talk about likes and dislikes	likes and dislikes	entertainment	word stress: noun patterns	read a city guide about events	talk about your free time talk about your likes and dislikes
6.2	**It was fun** (p54) Talk about entertainment in the present and the past	*was/were*	past time expressions	weak forms: *was/ were*	listen to a conversation about TV	talk about TV talk about entertainment now and in the past
6.3	**Life stories** (p56) Talk about your life	past simple regular and irregular verbs	life events	past simple regular endings	read an article about inspiring people **KEY SKILL** Scanning for names	talk about what you did last year **SPEAKING HUB** describe important events in your life
6.4	**Café Hub** **Love hate** (p58) Ask for and give opinions		ask for and give opinions	stress and intonation	▶ watch a group of friends talking about music	make a playlist for a road trip
	UNIT REVIEW p60	**WRITING** (p165) Write a review of an event	**KEY SKILL** Using narrative sequencers				

Irregular Verbs (p121)   **Grammar Hub** (p122)   **Vocabulary Hub** (p146)   **Communication Hub** (p154)   **Audioscripts** (p172)

CONTENTS   III

	LESSON • OBJECTIVES	GRAMMAR	VOCABULARY	PRONUNCIATION	READING • LISTENING	SPEAKING • WRITING
U7	**TRAVEL AND TRANSPORT**					
7.1	**Getting around** (p62) Talk about transport in a city	*could*	transport	/eɪ/ and /əʊ/	read a quiz about transport in different cities	talk about a past ability talk about transport in a city you know well
7.2	**A love of adventure** (p64) Talk about a journey	**past simple negative**	travel phrases	word stress: cities	read an article about a famous journey	talk about transport you used last year play a transport vocabulary game
7.3	**A trip to remember** (p66) Talk about a holiday	**past simple questions**	verb phrases	connected speech	listen to a conversation about an unusual trip **KEY SKILL** Guessing the meaning of unknown words	**SPEAKING HUB** tell a story about an unusual or funny holiday
7.4	**Café Hub** **New York** (p68) Check in and out of a hotel		check in and out of a hotel	intonation in questions	▶ watch someone checking in and out of a hotel	ask and answer questions at a hotel
	UNIT REVIEW p70	**WRITING** (p166) Write a short article about a travel experience | **KEY SKILL** *So* and *because*				
U8	**FOOD AND DRINK**					
8.1	**I'm hungry!** (p72) Talk about the food you eat	**countable and uncountable nouns;** *some* **and** *any*	food and drink	plurals	listen to a conversation about a diet	talk about diets discuss food habits
8.2	**What we eat** (p74) Talk about the food your family eats	*much, many, a lot of*	containers	short and long vowel sounds	read an article about food around the world	compare diets in other countries interview your partner about their diet write a paragraph about your partner's diet
8.3	**Yes, chef!** (p76) Talk about ingredients and recipes	*a/an, the,* **no article**	food preparation	consonant clusters	read an advert about a food business **KEY SKILL** Decoding	**SPEAKING HUB** present a recipe
8.4	**Café Hub** **More cheese** (p78) Order food in a restaurant		order food in a restaurant	stress and intonation	▶ watch two friends ordering a meal in a restaurant	ask and answer questions to order food
	UNIT REVIEW p80	**WRITING** (p167) Write an online restaurant review | **KEY SKILL** Pronoun referencing				
U9	**SHOPPING**					
9.1	**People watching** (p82) Talk about clothes and what people are doing	**present continuous**	clothes	/ɜː/	listen to a conversation about clothes	talk about interesting clothes talk about what you're doing describe someone in a picture
9.2	**Job swap** (p84) Talk about what people do at different times	**present simple vs present continuous**	present time expressions	/ŋ/	listen to an announcement read social media posts about job swaps	talk about job swaps talk about your life now and in general interview your partner about their job/studies
9.3	**Shop till you drop** (p86) Talk about shopping habits and tastes	**object pronouns**	shops and services	/tʃ/ and /ʃ/	read an article about marketing a business **KEY SKILL** Reading for genre	talk about your shopping preferences **SPEAKING HUB** conduct a survey about shopping habits
9.4	**Café Hub** **Meeting Milly** (p88) Shop for clothes		shop for clothes	connected speech	▶ watch someone shopping for clothes	talk about clothes in a shop
	UNIT REVIEW p90	**WRITING** (p168) Write a social media post | **KEY SKILL** Checking your work				

IV CONTENTS

Contents

	LESSON · OBJECTIVES	GRAMMAR	VOCABULARY	PRONUNCIATION	READING · LISTENING	SPEAKING · WRITING
U10	**THE GREAT OUTDOORS**					
10.1	**The right location** (p92) Talk about and compare outdoor places	comparatives	landscape features	weak forms: /ə/ in *than*	listen to an interview about film locations	talk about the landscape in your country compare countries, landscapes or films
10.2	**Where on Earth?** (p94) Talk about places around the world	superlatives	seasons and weather	/əʊ/ and /aʊ/	read an article about extreme places	talk about weather in your country complete a geography quiz
10.3	**Survival** (p96) Talk about living outdoors	**verb + *to* + infinitive**	phrasal verbs	weak forms: /tuː/ and /tə/	read an article about surviving in the wild listen to an interview with a survival expert **KEY SKILL** Identifying fact and opinion	rank survival items by importance **SPEAKING HUB** write a survival plan
10.4	**Café Hub** **Party invitation** (p98) Make and respond to invitations		make and respond to invitations	stress and intonation	▶ watch a group of friends inviting people to a party	make plans with your classmates
	UNIT REVIEW p100	**WRITING** (p169) Write a product review | **KEY SKILL** Adverbs of manner				
U11	**THE BODY**					
11.1	**Health tips** (p102) Talk about the body and health	*should* and *shouldn't*	the body	sentence stress	listen to a conversation about health tips	discuss healthy/unhealthy activities practise giving advice
11.2	**In it to win it** (p104) Talk about your experiences	**present perfect**	irregular past participles	past participles	read an article about a TV show	interview your classmates about their life experiences
11.3	**Move it** (p106) Talk about sports and hobbies	**present perfect vs past simple**	sports	contractions	read a text about an ultra-runner **KEY SKILL** Understanding the sequence of past events	discuss extreme sports **SPEAKING HUB** interview your classmates about sports and hobbies
11.4	**Café Hub** **Get fit** (p108) Ask for information		ask for information	stress and intonation	▶ watch someone booking a yoga lesson	ask for information about a class and book lessons
	UNIT REVIEW p110	**WRITING** (p170) Write a recommendation on a forum | **KEY SKILL** Adding information with *too*, *also* and *as well*				
U12	**MODERN LIVES**					
12.1	**Life's too busy** (p112) Talk about future plans	*going to*	future time expressions	*going to*: weak and strong *to*	listen to a conversation about being organised	discuss time management talk about future plans and intentions
12.2	**Everything will be shiny** (p114) Make predictions	*will* for predictions	collocations with *get*	contractions: *'ll*	read an article about life in the future	make predictions about the world in 2050
12.3	**Communication** (p116) Talk about social media habits	*might*	internet communication	diphthongs	listen to people talking about social media **KEY SKILL** Predicting	**SPEAKING HUB** interview your classmates about their social media use
12.4	**Café Hub** **Party time** (p118) Show interest in something		show interest in something	stress and intonation	▶ watch friends giving compliments, responding to bad news and apologising	make small talk at a party and give compliments
	UNIT REVIEW p120	**WRITING** (p171) Write a formal email | **KEY SKILL** Structuring emails				

Irregular Verbs (p121)   **Grammar Hub** (p122)   **Vocabulary Hub** (p146)   **Communication Hub** (p154)   **Audioscripts** (p172)

CONTENTS   **V**

Welcome

GREETINGS

A Read and listen to three conversations. Match conversations (1–3) with pictures (a–c).

1 ___

Marc: Hi, Luca.
Luca: Hi, Marc. How are you?
Marc: Fine, thanks.

2 ___

Emily: Good morning.
David: Hello. Nice to meet you.
Emily: You, too.

3 ___

Gudrun: Bye, Clara.
Clara: Bye, Gudrun. See you.

B Complete the table with the words and phrases in the box.

> Bye.   Fine, thanks.   Good afternoon.   How are you?
> Good morning.   Goodbye.   Hi.   Good night.
> I'm very well, thank you.   Good evening.
> Not too bad.   See you.

Say hello	Ask a question	Answer	Say goodbye
Good afternoon.	How are you?	Fine, thanks.	Bye.

C Complete the conversations with words from Exercise B.

1 A: How are you?   B: Not too _____.
2 A: Goodbye.   B: _____ night.
3 A: How are you?   B: I'm very _____, thanks.
4 A: Bye.   B: _____ you.

NUMBERS 0–100

A Listen and repeat the numbers.

> 0 1 2 3 4 5 6 7 8 9 10 11 12 13 14 15 16 17 18 19 20 21
> 30 40 50 60 70 80 90 100

B Listen and write the numbers you hear.

a ___   c ___   e ___   g ___
b ___   d ___   f ___   h ___

DAYS OF THE WEEK

Write the days of the week in the correct order. Then listen and repeat.

> Friday   Monday   Saturday   Sunday
> Thursday   Tuesday   Wednesday

1 _Monday_   5 _____
2 _____   6 _____
3 _____   7 _____
4 _____

THE ALPHABET

A Listen and repeat the letters of the alphabet.

a b c d e f g h i j k l m n o p q r s t u v w x y z

B Circle the letter in each group that has a different sound. Then listen and check.

1 b g (m)   2 a f k   3 j i y   4 l m r   5 i e t

C Listen and write the colours.

1 _____   4 _____
2 _____   5 _____
3 _____   6 _____

D SPEAK Work in pairs. Spell these things for your partner to write.

- your name
- your surname

CLASSROOM INSTRUCTIONS

Match questions (1–5) with replies (a–e). Then listen and check.

1 What does _book_ mean?
2 What's _libro_ in English?
3 I don't understand.
4 Could you repeat that, please?
5 Could you write it down, please?

a That's OK. I'll explain it again.
b Yes, sure.
c It means _libro_.
d It's _book_.
e Of course – _book_.

1 ARRIVALS

I am a citizen of the world.

Socrates

A traveller watching the sun rise over a new city.

OBJECTIVES

- talk about countries and nationalities
- ask and answer questions about a place
- talk about everyday items
- greet people and make introductions
- fill in a form with personal details

Work with a partner. Discuss the questions.

1 Where are you from?
2 Look at the picture. Where is it?
3 What's your favourite city?

1.1 People and places — Talk about countries and nationalities

V countries and nationalities **P** syllable stress **G** present simple *be*: positive and negative

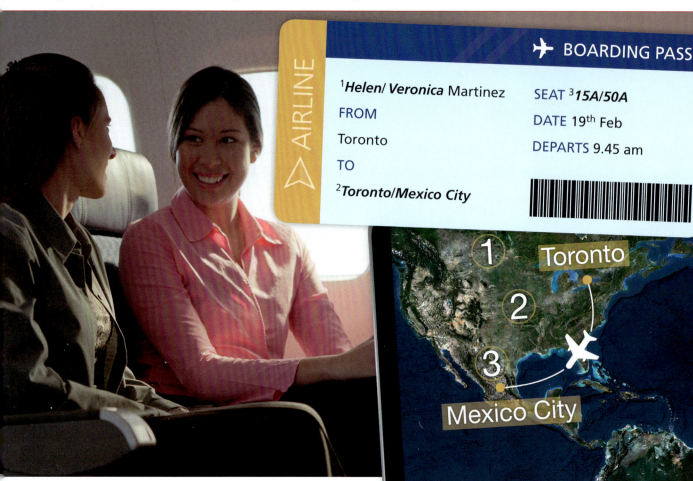

LISTENING

A LISTEN FOR GIST Look at the picture and listen. Are the two women friends?

B LISTEN FOR DETAIL Choose the correct options to complete the boarding pass. Then listen again and check.

C LISTEN FOR KEY WORDS Listen again. Choose the correct words to complete the sentences.

| Canadian   Mexico   Mexico City   names |

1 Helen likes Spanish _____.
2 Veronica is from _____.
3 Helen is _____.
4 Helen's company is in _____.

D SPEAK Work in pairs. Introduce yourself to your partner.
A: *Hi. I'm Anton.*
B: *Nice to meet you, Anton. I'm Katie.*

VOCABULARY
Countries and nationalities

A Work in pairs. Look at the flight map. Match the numbers on the screen (1–4) with the countries in the box.

| ___ Brazil   ___ Canada   ___ Mexico   ___ the USA |

B Go to the Vocabulary Hub on page 146.

PRONUNCIATION
Syllable stress

A A syllable is a word or a part of a word that has only one vowel sound. Listen and repeat the words.

One syllable words	Two-syllable words	Three-syllable words	Four-syllable words
France French	Japan China Chinese	Canada Mexico Mexican Japanese	Canadian

B Add the words in the box to the table in Exercise A. Then listen, check and repeat.

| Brazil   Brazilian   India   Indian   Spain   Spanish |

C Underline the stressed syllables in the table in Exercise A. Use the information box to help you.

Syllable stress
In words with multiple syllables, one syllable is stressed more than others. ●● Ja<u>pan</u>   ●● <u>Chi</u>na   ●●● <u>In</u>dian

ARRIVALS

1.1

GRAMMAR
Present simple *be*: positive and negative

A Listen to the conversation between Helen and Veronica again. Complete the conversation with *'m, 's* or *'m not*.

Helen: Excuse me, is this row 15?
Veronica: Yes. I'm in seat 15A.
Helen: My seat is 15B. Hi, I¹_____ Helen.
Veronica: Nice to meet you. I'm Veronica Martinez.
Helen: That ²_____ a nice name. I like Spanish names.
Veronica: Thanks, but I ³_____ Spanish. I'm Mexican. I'm from Mexico. Where are you from?
Helen: I ⁴_____ Canadian, but I live in Mexico. My company's office is in Mexico City.
Pilot: Good morning, ladies and gentlemen. This is the 9.45 flight to Mexico City …

B **WORK IT OUT** Choose the correct options to complete the rules. Use the conversation in Exercise A to help you.

> **Present simple *be***
> 1 We use *'m, 's* and *'re* to make **positive** / **negative** sentences with *be*.
> 2 We use *'m not, isn't* and *aren't* to make **positive** / **negative** sentences with *be*.

C Go to the Grammar Hub on page 122.

D Listen to Chloe introducing herself. Complete the introduction with the correct forms of *be*.

E Write three sentences about nationality – two true, and one false.

I'm Japanese. I'm not Chinese. My mother is Japanese.

F **SPEAK** Work in pairs. Read your sentences from Exercise E. Guess which sentence is false.

A: I'm Japanese. I'm not Chinese. My mother is Japanese.
B: You're Japanese. That's true. But your mother isn't Japanese. She's French!

SPEAKING

A **THINK** Imagine you are on an aeroplane. Choose the country you are from.

B **PLAN** You are going to introduce yourself to another passenger. Look at the model conversation and make notes on what you are going to say.

A: Hello, is this seat 14B?
B: Yes, it is. I'm in seat 14A. Hi, I'm Frederic by the way.
A: Nice to meet you, Frederic. I'm Sonia. I'm from Italy.
B: Nice to meet you, too, Sonia! I live in Italy, too. But I'm French. My wife is Italian.
A: Oh, great! I'm Italian, but my family isn't. They're Spanish.

C **SPEAK** Work in pairs. Practise your conversation.

Hi, I ¹_____ Chloe.
I ²_____ from France.
I often go to Germany to see my friend, Camille. We ³_____ old friends. Camille lives in Berlin, but she ⁴_____ German.
She ⁵_____ French like me. Her boyfriend, Luc ⁶_____ German, but his mother and father ⁷_____.
They ⁸_____ French.

○─ Talk about countries and nationalities

ARRIVALS 3

1.2 Where are you?

● Ask and answer questions about a place

V– big numbers   P– similar numbers   G– present simple *be*: questions

READING

A Work with a partner. Look at the picture in the text message below. Where is it?

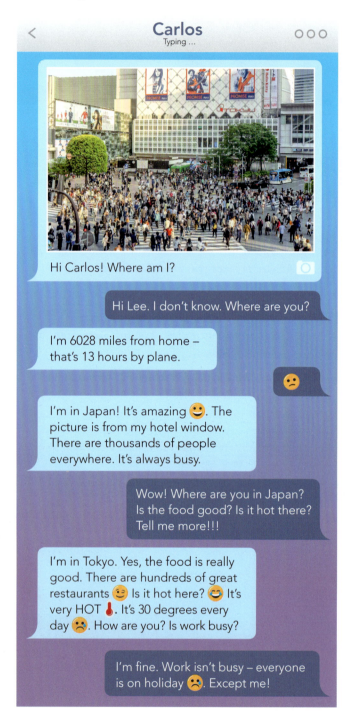

Carlos
Typing ...

Hi Carlos! Where am I?

Hi Lee. I don't know. Where are you?

I'm 6028 miles from home – that's 13 hours by plane.

I'm in Japan! It's amazing 😃. The picture is from my hotel window. There are thousands of people everywhere. It's always busy.

Wow! Where are you in Japan? Is the food good? Is it hot there? Tell me more!!!

I'm in Tokyo. Yes, the food is really good. There are hundreds of great restaurants 😋 Is it hot here? 😄 It's very HOT 🌡. It's 30 degrees every day 😓. How are you? Is work busy?

I'm fine. Work isn't busy – everyone is on holiday 😟. Except me!

B READ FOR GIST Read the messages between Carlos and Lee. Where is Lee?

C READ FOR DETAIL Read again. Are the sentences true (T) or false (F)? Correct the false sentences.

1 Japan is far from where Carlos and Lee live.   T / F
2 The picture is from Carlos's work.   T / F
3 It isn't hot where Lee is.   T / F
4 Lee likes Japanese food.   T / F
5 Carlos is very busy at work.   T / F

VOCABULARY
Big numbers

A Match numbers (1–5) with the words (a–e).

1 100   a one million
2 1000   b ten thousand
3 10,000   c one hundred thousand
4 100,000   d one thousand
5 1,000,000   e one hundred

🔊 **B** Listen and write the numbers you hear.
1.5
1 _____
2 _____
3 _____

C SPEAK Work in pairs. How far is Lee from home?

D SPEAK Work in pairs. Student A – say how far a city is from Paris. Student B – name the city. Then swap.

Paris → New York	3625 miles
Paris → Melbourne	10,427 miles
Paris → Seoul	5568 miles
Paris → Milan	529 miles
Paris → Cape Town	7965 miles

A: *This city is 5568 miles from Paris.*
B: *It's Seoul. This city is ...*

PRONUNCIATION
Similar numbers

🔊 **A** Listen to part of a phone call between Carlos and Lee.
1.6 Which number does Lee say?

a thirteen (13)
b thirty (30)

🔊 **B** Listen and repeat. <u>Underline</u> the stressed syllables in the
1.7 numbers in Exercise A.

🔊 **C** Listen and tick (✓) the number you hear.
1.8
a 17 ☐   70 ☐   e 16 ☐   60 ☐
b 19 ☐   90 ☐   f 14 ☐   40 ☐
c 15 ☐   50 ☐   g 18 ☐   80 ☐
d 12 ☐   20 ☐   h 13 ☐   30 ☐

🔊 **D** Listen again and repeat the numbers.
1.8

4   ARRIVALS

GRAMMAR
Present simple *be*: questions

A **WORK IT OUT** Look at the text conversation between Lee and Carlos again. Complete the table with words from the text.

Wh- questions	Yes/No questions
A: Where [1]_____ you? B: I [2]_____ in Tokyo.	A: [5]_____ the food good? B: Yes, the food [6]_____ really good.
A: How [3]_____ you? B: I [4]_____ fine.	A: [7]_____ it hot there? B: It [8]_____ very hot.

B Look at the table in Exercise A and complete the rules.

> **Present simple *be*: questions**
> 1 We put question words *before* / *after* be.
> 2 We put the subject *before* / *after* be.
> 3 When we answer *yes*/*no* questions, we put the subject *before* / *after* be.

C Go to the Grammar Hub on page 122.

D **PRACTISE** Match the questions (1–5) with the answers (a–e).

1 Where are you?
2 How far is Mumbai from there?
3 Is your city big?
4 Are you Egyptian?
5 What's your flight number?

a It's 10 hours by plane.
b It's J230.
c No, I'm not.
d Yes, it is.
e I'm at the hotel.

E **SPEAK** Work in pairs. Write questions, adding the correct form of *be*. Take turns to ask and answer questions.

1 Where / from? _____
2 food good / your country? _____
3 your hometown / big? _____
4 your hometown / hot or cold? _____
5 How far / your home / from here? _____

LISTENING

A **LISTEN FOR GIST** Listen to Carlos and Lee talking on the phone. Where is Lee now? Choose the correct picture below.
1.9

B **LISTEN FOR DETAIL** Listen again. Number Carlos' questions in the order you hear them (1–6).
1.9

___ Are you still in Tokyo?
___ Is the food good?
___ What's it like there?
___ What's your next destination?
___ Where are you in China?
_1_ Where are you?

C Work in pairs. Answer the questions in Exercise B for Lee.

SPEAKING

A **PREPARE** Choose a place. It could be your home or another place that you know. Imagine you are in that place. What is it like? Think about:

- far from here?
- busy/quiet?
- hot/cold at the moment?
- what kind of food?

B **PLAN** Use the prompts in Exercise A to make questions to ask your partner about the place he/she is in.

C **SPEAK** Work in pairs. Take turns to ask and answer questions about your places. Guess where the place is.

Ask and answer questions about a place

ARRIVALS

1.3 What's in your bag?
▶ Talk about everyday items

V everyday items **G** a/an and plural nouns; this, that, these, those **P** vowel sounds: /ɪ/ /æ/ /iː/ /əʊ/ **S** reading for gist

What's in your **hand luggage?**

Three travel experts talk about the things in their hand luggage when they go on a plane.

Bruce I don't carry a lot of luggage when I go on a plane. My bag is very small. **I have a bottle of water and tissues.** That's it. I usually sleep when I'm on a plane.

Wei I never use a suitcase. I put everything in my hand luggage, so there's no need to wait at baggage reclaim. My hand luggage is very heavy, but that's OK. **I have two watches.** I wear one and I put one in my bag, so I always know what time it is at home. **I travel to lots of countries.** I just want to get off the plane and leave the airport as soon as I can.

Elif I always have a laptop and my phone in my hand luggage when I go on a plane. **I usually have an umbrella and my keys.** Flying is a good time to do my work. I can relax at home.

VOCABULARY
Everyday items

A Work in pairs. Look at the picture. Match the items in the picture (1–12) with the words in the box.

___ a bottle of water   ___ a credit card
___ headphones   ___ keys   ___ a laptop
___ a magazine   ___ a mobile phone
___ a bag   ___ tissues   ___ an umbrella
___ a wallet   ___ a watch

B SPEAK Work in pairs. Tell your partner what is in your bag.

A: *What's in your bag?*
B: *My keys, a bottle of water and an umbrella.*

READING

A READ FOR GIST Read *What's in your hand luggage?* What is the text about? Things people …

a take to work.
b take to a party.
c take on a plane.

Reading for gist
When you read a text for the first time, it is important to get a general idea of what it is about. To help you, think about:
- the title of the text and the pictures
- the general topic
- key words

B READ FOR DETAIL Read the text again. Are these sentences true (T) or false (F)? Correct the false sentences.

1 Bruce's bag is very big.   T / F
2 Bruce takes a bottle of water and tissues on the plane.   T / F
3 Wei never uses a suitcase.   T / F
4 Wei always has his watch and a wallet in his bag.   T / F
5 Elif usually has an umbrella and her keys in her hand luggage.   T / F
6 Elif likes to relax on the plane.   T / F

GRAMMAR
a/an and plural nouns

A WORK IT OUT Look at the bold sentences in *What's in your hand luggage?* Underline the nouns in each sentence.

B Look at the nouns you highlighted in Exercise A and complete the rules.

a/an and plural nouns
1 We use *a/an* with **plural / singular** nouns.
2 We use *a* with singular nouns that begin with a *consonant sound / vowel sound*.
3 We use *an* with singular nouns that begin with a *consonant sound / vowel sound*.
4 We add *-s / -es* to most nouns to make a plural.
5 We add *-s / -es* to nouns that end in *-s* or *-ch* to make a plural.
6 For nouns that end in consonant + *-y*, we cut the *-y* and add *-es / -ies*.

C Go to the **Grammar Hub** on **page 122**.

D SPEAK Work in pairs. Point to items in the picture in Vocabulary Exercise A. Your partner says what it is.

6 ARRIVALS

LISTENING

A SPEAK Work in pairs. Which of these items can you take in your hand luggage?

 B LISTEN FOR GIST Listen to two conversations at airport
1.10 security. Which items from Exercise A does:

1 the woman have in her bag?

2 the man have in his bag?

 C LISTEN FOR KEY WORDS Listen again. Complete the
1.10 sentences with the correct words.

1 **A:** Excuse me, madam. Is this your _____?

   B: Yes, it is.

2 **A:** OK. You can go. Oh, wait! Are these your _____?

   B: Oh, yes, they are! Thank you so much!

3 **A:** Excuse me, sir. Is that your _____?

   B: Yes, it is.

4 **A:** Are those your _____?

   B: No, they aren't. I think they belong to that family over there.

PRONUNCIATION
Vowel sounds: /ɪ/ /æ/ /iː/ /əʊ/

 A Listen carefully and notice the vowel sounds. Then listen
1.11 again and repeat.

| /ɪ/ | this, kiss, sit | /iː/ | these, key, tree |
| /æ/ | that, hat, cat | /əʊ/ | those, toes, nose |

B SPEAK Work in pairs. Practise the conversations in Listening Exercise C.

GRAMMAR
this, that, these, those

A WORK IT OUT Look at the pictures. Match the situations (1–4) from Listening Exercise C with the pictures (a–d).

B Choose the correct words to complete the rules.

this, that, these, those

1 We use **this** / **that** to talk about a singular noun that's near.
2 We use **this** / **that** to talk about a singular noun that isn't near.
3 We use **these** / **those** to talk about a plural noun that is near.
4 We use **these** / **those** to talk about a plural noun that isn't near.

C Go to the **Grammar Hub** on **page 122**.

SPEAKING HUB

A Work in pairs. Imagine you are going on holiday. Draw six everyday items to take with you.

B PLAN Work alone. Choose three of the items in Exercise A to take in your hand luggage.

C DISCUSS Imagine you are at airport security. Try to find out what is in your partner's hand luggage. Follow these steps:

Student A – Point to a picture in Exercise A and ask a question with *Is this / Are these your …?*

Student B – Answer Student A's question.

Student A – Keep asking questions until you know which three items are in your partner's bag.

○— Talk about everyday items

ARRIVALS

Café Hub

1.4 Good morning
- **F** greet people and make introductions
- **P** word stress

COMPREHENSION

A ▶ Watch the video. Complete the information about each person in the photo captions below.

B Write a question about each person in Exercise A.
1 *How old is Sam?*
2 *Where is Gaby from?*
3 *Is Milly married?*

C **SPEAK** Work in pairs. Close your books and ask each other your question from Exercise B.
A: *How old is Sam?*
B: *He's 34.*

FUNCTIONAL LANGUAGE
Greeting people and making introductions

A Complete the phrases with the words in the box.

bad   fine   Hi   meet   morning   See   too   you

Say hello	Greet people + reply
Hello.	How are you?
1 ___Hi___.	Not too 3 _____.
Hey!	I'm 4 _____, thanks.
Good 2 _____.	Very well, thanks.
Good afternoon.	
Good evening.	

Introduce people + reply	Say goodbye
This is …	Bye.
This is my friend …	See 7 _____.
It's nice to 5 _____ you.	See you soon.
Nice to meet you, 6 _____.	8 _____ you later.

B ▶ Watch the first part of the video again. Check your answers to Exercise A.

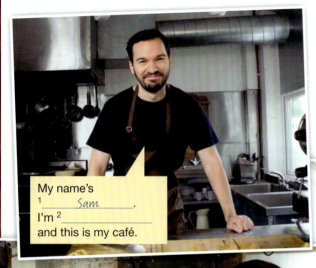

My name's 1 ___Sam___.
I'm 2 _____
and this is my café.

My name's 3 _____.
I'm a lawyer. There are 4 _____ free rooms in my flat.

My name's Zac.
I know 5 _____.
He's a good friend. I'm 6 _____ –
I'm from Seattle, but I live here in London.

I'm Gabriela, but my friends call me Gaby.
I love 7 _____, but I'm not from here. I'm 8 _____. I'm from a small town near Madrid.

I'm Milly. I'm 25. I'm 9 _____.
I'm American. I love clothes and I love 10 _____.

ARRIVALS

1.4

MILLY   **SAM**   **NEENA**   **ZAC**   **GABY**

USEFUL PHRASES

A Match the useful phrases (1–3) with the replies (a–c).

1 What would you like?
2 That's £2, please.
3 Take a seat.

a Thanks.
b Can I have a croissant to go, please?
c Here you go.

B ▶ 00:24–01:14 Watch part of the video again and check your answers to Exercise A.

PRONUNCIATION
Word stress

A ▶ 00:24–01:14 Watch part of the video again and read the conversation. Notice that the underlined words are stressed.

Neena: <u>Good</u> <u>morning</u>. How <u>are</u> you <u>Sam</u>?
Sam: <u>Not</u> <u>too</u> <u>bad</u>. How are <u>you</u>?
Neena: I'm <u>fine</u>, thanks. <u>This</u> is my <u>friend</u>, <u>Milly</u>.
Sam: <u>Hi</u> <u>Milly</u>. <u>Nice</u> to <u>meet</u> you.
Milly: <u>Nice</u> to <u>meet</u> you, <u>too</u>.

B ▶ 00:24–01:14 Watch again and repeat the conversation. Copy the word stress.

C SPEAK Work in groups of three. Practise the conversation in Exercise A. Remember to use the correct stress.

SPEAKING

A **PREPARE** Walk around the class. Introduce yourself to your classmates.

A: *Hello, I'm Andreas. It's nice to meet you.*
B: *It's nice to meet you, too.*

B **DISCUSS** Work in pairs. Walk around the class. Greet the people you know and introduce your partner.

A: *Hello, I'm Andreas. It's nice to meet you.*
B: *It's nice to meet you, too.*
A: *This is Nadia.*

C **PLAN** You're going to record a 'selfie' presentation. Make notes about what you want to say. Then record it.

Introducing	
Hi! My name's …	I'm …
My friends call me …	I'm from …
I'm single/married …	I'm a …

D **PRESENT** Work in groups. Compare your presentations.

○— Greet people and make introductions
➤ Turn to **page 160** to learn how to fill in a form with personal details.

ARRIVALS 9

Unit 1 Review

VOCABULARY

A Complete the table with the correct countries and nationalities.

Country	Nationality
Brazil	1 _____
2 _____	Chinese
3 _____	Egyptian
India	4 _____
Japan	5 _____
6 _____	Portuguese
Sweden	7 _____
The UK	8 _____

B Correct the mistakes in each sentence.

1 Tokyo is the capital of Japanese.

2 IKEA is a Sweden company.

3 My father's from Hanoi in Vietnamese.

4 I'm from New York, in USA.

5 I love Switzerland chocolate!

C Match the words (1–8) with the numbers (a–h).

1 one million   a 500,000

2 five hundred and ten   b 510

3 fifty-five thousand   c 5002

4 one thousand two hundred   d 1,000,000

5 five hundred thousand   e 1200

6 one hundred thousand   f 55,000

7 five thousand and two   g 250

8 two hundred and fifty   h 100,000

D Complete the everyday items with *a, e, i, o* or *u*.

1 h_e__a_dph_o_n_e_s

2 a cr__d__t c__rd

3 m__n__y

4 a m__b__l__ ph__n__

5 a b__ttl__ of w__t__r

6 a w__tch

7 a b__x of t__ss____s

8 a l__pt__p

9 a m__g__z__n__

10 a w__ll__t

E **SPEAK** Work in pairs. Discuss the questions.

1 Where are you from?

2 How old are you?

3 What nationality are your parents?

4 What's the capital of your country?

5 What's in your bag?

GRAMMAR

A Choose the correct words to complete the sentences.

1 I *'m* / *'s* from the USA.

2 We *'s* / *'re* Russian.

3 They *isn't* / *aren't* married.

4 You *'s* / *'re* my friend.

5 She *isn't* / *aren't* American.

6 He *'m* / *'s* 36 years old.

7 I *isn't* / *'m not* from Sweden.

B Write questions and short answers.

1 you / Japanese

   Are you Japanese (?)   _Yes, I am._ (+)

2 they / students

   _____ (?)   _____ (+)

3 he / German

   _____ (?)   _____ (-)

4 she / 18 years old

   _____ (?)   _____ (+)

5 you / married

   _____ (?)   _____ (-)

C Match the questions (1–4) with the answers (a–d).

1 What's your name?   a Oakland.

2 How old are you?   b It's in the USA.

3 Where are you from?   c Susan.

4 Where's that?   d 26.

D Complete the text with *a, an* or *–* (no article).

This is my bag. I usually carry [1]_____ apple, [2]_____ mobile phone and [3]_____ keys. Oh, and [4]_____ credit card!

E Choose the correct words to complete the sentences.

1 Is *this* / *these* your phone?

2 *That* / *Those* aren't my keys.

3 *That* / *Those* 's my book.

4 Are *this* / *these* your sunglasses?

FUNCTIONAL LANGUAGE

A Complete the conversation with the words in the box.

from   Good   Hi   meet   small   Where

A: [1]_____. I'm Andreas.

B: Nice to [2]_____ you, Andreas. I'm Tia.

A: [3]_____ to meet you, too, Tia.

B: [4]_____ are you from, Andreas?

A: Switzerland. I live in a [5]_____ village near Zurich.

B: Really? I'm [6]_____ Chicago, but I live in Paris.

B Work in pairs. Practise the conversation in Exercise A. Use your own information.

ARRIVALS

2 PEOPLE

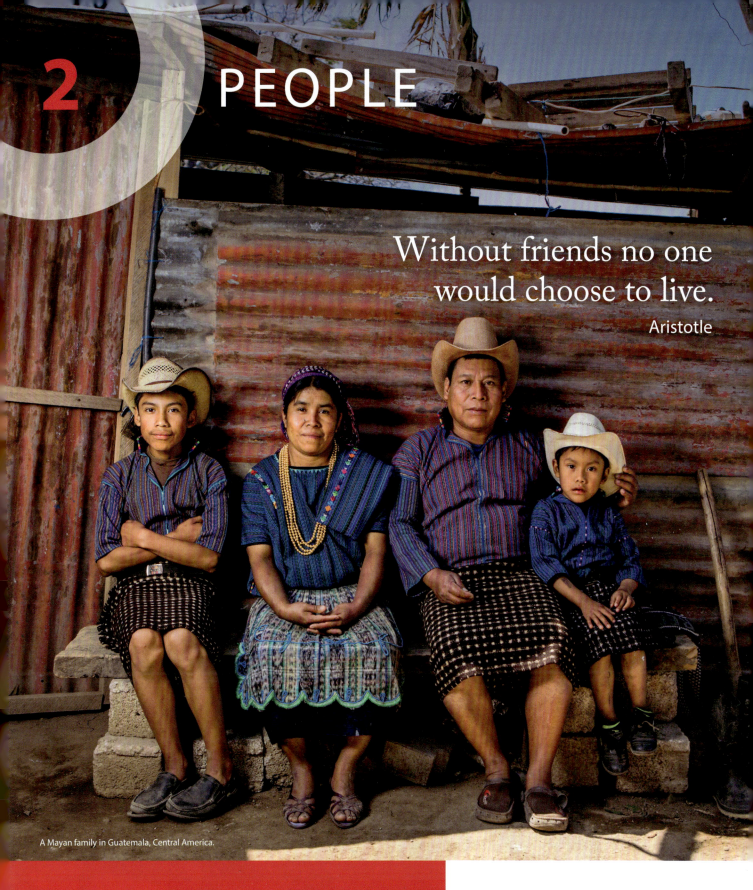

Without friends no one would choose to live.
Aristotle

A Mayan family in Guatemala, Central America.

OBJECTIVES

- talk about your family
- talk about appearance
- describe family members and friends
- make and respond to requests
- write an email to a friend

Work with a partner. Discuss the questions.

1. Do you have a big family?
2. Do you have any brothers or sisters?
3. What do you like doing with your friends?

PEOPLE   11

2.1 Family — Talk about your family

- V — family
- P — /ə/ 'schwa'
- G — possessive adjectives and apostrophes

READING

A Work in pairs. Look at the pictures in *Famous families*. Why are these people famous?

B READ FOR GIST Read *Famous families* and check your answers to Exercise A.

C Work in pairs. How many of the people do you know?

D READ FOR DETAIL Read *Famous families* again. Are the sentences true (T) or false (F)? Correct the false sentences.

1. Sofia is a famous actress. — T / F
2. Sofia's grandparents were Italian. — T / F
3. Sofia's brother is called Francis Ford Coppola. — T / F
4. Sofia's aunt was in the film *Rocky*. — T / F
5. Sofia and her husband, Thomas, live in Italy. — T / F

E SPEAK Work in pairs. What other famous families do you know?

FAMOUS ★ FAMILIES

This week, we continue our series on Hollywood families with a look at the Coppolas.

Sofia Coppola is an American film director. She's famous for directing the films *Marie Antoinette* and *Somewhere*. Sofia's family is famous, too. There are famous film directors, actors and musicians in her family.

Her grandparents, Carmine Coppola and Italia Pennino, were musicians from Italy. Sofia's father is the film director Francis Ford Coppola. He is the director of the three *Godfather* films. Sofia's brother, Roman Coppola, is also a film director.

Sofia's aunt is Talia Shire. She's an actress, and she was in the *Godfather* and the *Rocky* films. Talia's son is the actor Jason Schwartzman. Jason is Sofia's cousin. The actor Nicolas Cage is her cousin, too. Nicolas' father was August Coppola. He was Francis Ford Coppola's brother.

Sofia's husband is Thomas Mars, the singer of the rock band Phoenix. Sofia and Thomas live in New York City, and they have two daughters. Their daughters' names are Romy Mars and Cosima Mars.

Thomas Mars

Francis Ford Coppola · Talia Shire · Sofia Coppola

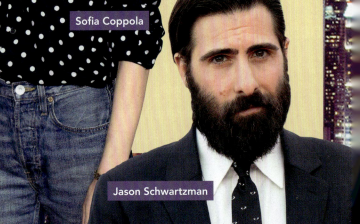
Jason Schwartzman

VOCABULARY
Family

A Look at the word in **bold** in the sentence below. Find and underline seven other words for family members in *Famous families*.

*Her **grandparents**, Carmine Coppola and Italia Pennino, were musicians.*

B Read the text again. Complete the family tree.

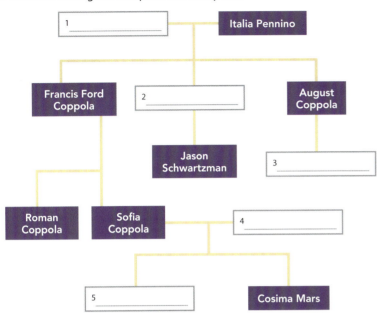

C Complete the table with the words you found in Exercise A.

Female	Male	Female or male
		grandparents

D Add the words in the box to the table in Exercise C.

children   grandfather   grandmother   mother
parents   sister   uncle   wife

E **SPEAK** Work in pairs. Student A – go to the Communication Hub on page 156. Student B – go to the Communication Hub on page 158.

PRONUNCIATION
/ə/ 'schwa'

A Listen and repeat. Notice how we say the underlined sounds.
2.1
/ə/   moth<u>er</u>, broth<u>er</u>, act<u>or</u>

B Say these words with a partner. Underline the /ə/ sound in each word. Then listen, check and repeat.
2.2
cousin   daughter   director   famous   father   husband   parents   sister

GRAMMAR
Possessive adjectives and apostrophes

A Look at the sentences from *Famous families*. Which name matches the word in **bold**? Choose a, b or c.

1 Jason is <u>Sofia's cousin</u>. The actor Nicolas Cage is **her** cousin, too.
   a Jason   b Sofia   c Nicolas

2 Sofia and Thomas live in New York City, and they have two daughters. **Their** <u>daughters' names</u> are Romy Mars and Cosima Mars.
   a Sofia and Thomas   b Sofia   c Thomas

B **WORK IT OUT** Complete the table with the words in the box.

his   its   my   our   your

Subject pronouns	Possessive adjectives
I	1_____
you	2_____
we	3_____
they	their
he	4_____
she	her
it	5_____

C **WORK IT OUT** Look at the underlined words in Exercise A. Then complete the rules.

Possessive apostrophe
1 We add ' / 's to regular singular nouns.
2 We add ' / 's to regular plural nouns.
3 We use the possessive apostrophe to show that something **belongs to** / **doesn't belong to** someone.

D Go to the Grammar Hub on page 124.

SPEAKING

A **PREPARE** Draw your family tree. Include any grandparents, uncles, aunts or cousins.

B **SPEAK** Work with a partner. Take it in turns to tell each other about the people in your family tree.

My grandfather's name is Hiroyuki. He's 98 years old. My grandmother's name is Saya. She's ...

○– Talk about your family

2.2 The same, but different

● Talk about appearance

V— describing appearance G— have/has got P— contracted have

VOCABULARY
Describing appearance

A Work in pairs. Match the people in the pictures (1–2) with the words in the box.

> beard   blonde hair   blue eyes   brown eyes   curly hair
> grey hair   light skin   long hair   short hair   straight hair

B Go to the Vocabulary Hub on page 146.

TWO in a million

This is a picture of Bobby and Riley George on the day they were born. They're twins. They've got curly hair, brown eyes and light skin.

This is Bobby and Riley three years later, and they look really different! Bobby looks like his mother. He's got light skin, blonde hair and blue eyes. Riley looks like his father. He's got dark skin and brown eyes, and short, brown hair. The boys don't look the same, but have they got the same personality? No, they haven't. Bobby is very noisy and Riley is quiet. They really are one in a million!

READING

A Look at picture a in *Two in a million*. Choose three sentences that describe the babies.

1 They are the same age.
2 They look different.
3 They look like each other.
4 They've got the same parents.
5 They've got different parents.

B **READ FOR GIST** Read *Two in a million*. Check your answers to Exercise A. What is the name of the child on the left in picture b?

C **READ FOR DETAIL** Read again. Choose the correct words to complete the sentences.

1 Bobby and Riley's birthdays are on *the same day* / *different days*.
2 Bobby and Riley look *the same* / *different* three years later.
3 Bobby and the twins' mother have got *the same* / *different* skin colour.
4 Riley and Bobby have got *the same* / *different* personalities.

> **look like**
>
> The phrase *look like* means have the same appearance.
> • I/You/We/They + *look like* + noun
>   *I look like my mother. I don't look like my father.*
> • He/She It + *looks like* + noun
>   *My sister doesn't look like me. She looks like our mum.*

D **SPEAK** Work in pairs. Describe someone in your class to your partner. Can they guess who it is?

> A: *He's tall. He's got long, brown hair and brown eyes. He looks a bit like Johnny Depp …*
> B: *Is it Matteo?*

14   PEOPLE

2.2

GRAMMAR
have/has got

A **WORK IT OUT** Look at *Two in a million* again. Complete the sentences with no more than three words from the text.

1 _____ brown hair, brown eyes and dark skin.
2 _____ blonde hair and blue eyes.
3 The boys don't look the same, but have they got the same personality? No, _____.

B **WORK IT OUT** Complete the table with the words from the box.

haven't   've   hasn't

	Positive (+) / Negative (-)		
1	I	_____ / haven't	
2	He/She/It	's / _____	got	blue eyes.
3	You/They/We	have / _____		

C Go to the **Grammar Hub** on **page 124**.

D **PRACTISE** Look at the picture. Complete the conversation about the woman with the correct form of *have/has got*. Use contractions.

A: Who do you look like?
B: My aunt. She's my dad's sister.
A: Has your aunt ¹_____ long hair?
B: No, she ²_____. She ³_____ short, grey hair.
A: ⁴_____ she ⁵_____ glasses?
B: Yes, she ⁶_____.
A: What colour eyes ⁷_____ she got?
B: She ⁸_____ blue eyes. We've also got the same nose.

E **SPEAK** Find out who your partner looks like in their family.

I look like my mother. She's got brown eyes, like me. And we've both got curly hair.

PRONUNCIATION
Contracted *have*

A Listen and repeat the contracted forms of *have* and *has*. Notice the /v/, /z/ and /s/ sounds.
2.3

B Listen choose the correct sound /v/, /z/ or /s/.
2.4
1 he's got   /v/ /z/ /s/
2 it's got   /v/ /z/ /s/
3 I've got   /v/ /z/ /s/
4 she's got   /v/ /z/ /s/
5 they've got   /v/ /z/ /s/
6 you've got   /v/ /z/ /s/

C **SPEAK** Work in pairs. Complete the sentences about people in your class.
1 I've got …
2 You've got …
3 He's/She's got …
4 We've got …
5 They've got …

LISTENING

A Work in pairs. Describe the man in the picture.

B **LISTEN FOR KEY WORDS** Listen to a description of the man in Exercise A. Does it match yours?
2.5

C **SPEAK** Work in pairs. Think of someone in your family. Tell your partner how you and this person are the same, and how you are different.

A: My dad doesn't look like me. He's got grey hair and a beard. I've got brown hair. I've got glasses, but he hasn't.
B: My sister looks the same as me. We're twins!

SPEAKING

Work in pairs. Go to the **Communication Hub** on **page 154**.

◯— Talk about appearance

2.3 Friends — Describe family members and friends

V personality adjectives **P** syllable stress: adjectives **G** using adjectives **S** reading for organisation

VOCABULARY
Personality adjectives

A Complete the descriptions with the adjectives in the box.

friendly   funny   quiet   sad   tidy

1 She's really _____ – she always makes me laugh.
2 My uncle is a _____ person. He doesn't talk much; he just listens.
3 Hakim always puts things away after he uses them – he's very _____.
4 My father's often _____. He doesn't laugh or smile a lot anymore.
5 Reema is a very nice person – she's _____ to everyone.

B Match the adjectives (1–5) with their opposites (a–e).

1 friendly   a messy
2 funny   b unfriendly
3 quiet   c happy
4 sad   d noisy
5 tidy   e serious

PRONUNCIATION
Syllable stress: adjectives

Work with a partner. Say the adjectives, and then add them to the table. Listen and check your answers.
2.6

~~friendly~~   funny   happy   messy   noisy
quiet   sad   serious   tidy   unfriendly

●	●●	●●●	●●●
friendly			

LISTENING

A **LISTEN FOR GIST** Listen to the conversation. Match people (1–3) to the names below.
2.7

Zoe _____   Alice _____   Jody _____

B **LISTEN FOR DETAIL** Look at the questions and tick (✓) the correct person or people. Listen again and check your answers.
2.7

	Speaker	Zoe	Alice	Jody
1 Who's in the same study group?				
2 Who's funny?				
3 Who's tidy?				
4 Who's quiet?				
5 Who's serious?				
6 Who's not tidy?				

C **SPEAK** Work in pairs. Are you like Zoe, Alice or Jody? Give examples.

GRAMMAR
Using adjectives

A **WORK IT OUT** Look at the sentences from the conversation. Underline the adjectives.

1 They're all really friendly.
2 She's a very funny person.
3 She's quite quiet, but I like her.

B Choose the correct words to complete the rules. Use the sentences in Exercise A to help you.

> **Using adjectives**
> 1 We put adjectives *before* / *after* the verb *be*.
> 2 We put adjectives *before* / *after* nouns.

C Go to the **Grammar Hub** on **page 124**.

D **SPEAK** Work with a partner. Tell them about someone you know. Use *really*, *very* or *quite* in your descriptions.

16 PEOPLE

READING

A READ FOR GIST Read Yassir's email. Where is he and who is he talking about?

RE: How're things?
Sent: Friday 10th November 2017, 2.19 pm
To: a.nadar@screen.nett
From: YassirAwad@logbox.com

Hi Ahmed,
I'm having a great time at university! ᵃ___ There are about 20 people in my class, and all of them are friendly. There's a guy in my class called Erdem – he's from Turkey. He's got long hair, a beard and he's really noisy, but he's very funny! He's one of my close friends now. ᵇ___ I met a French guy called Nico at football practice. He's really friendly, but very different from Erdem. He's quite quiet and serious.
ᶜ___ The bad news is about my flatmate. ᵈ___ His name's Erik. He's quiet in the day and noisy in the middle of the night! He's so unfriendly – he never speaks to me. And he's really messy!
ᵉ___ I want to live with a happy, friendly and tidy person!
See you soon,
Yassir

B READ FOR ORGANISATION Read again. Match the sentences (1–5) with the gaps in the email (a–e). Use the information in the box to help you.

> **Reading for organisation**
> To help you understand how a text is organised, think about how one sentence connects to another. Does it add more information? Does it explain something? Does it change topic?

1 I only have one flatmate.
2 There's a lot of work to do, but there are also a lot of fun things to do in my free time.
3 I want to find a new place to live.
4 That's the good news.
5 I always laugh a lot when I'm with Erdem.

SPEAKING HUB

A Imagine you can choose a new flatmate for Yassir. Think about the type of person Yassir wants to live with.

B PLAN Read about these people. Makes notes about who would be a good/bad flatmate for Yassir.

Antonio
Italian

'I'm from Naples, and I love cooking and football. I like listening to music when I study. I've got lots of friends and I like to cook for them.'

Cvetomir
Bulgarian

'I love watching football on TV, but I never play. I never cook at home because I hate cleaning the kitchen. I like to sleep a lot. I'm a good flatmate – I'm very quiet.'

Jonas
Swedish

'I like to study a lot in the day and talk to friends in the evening. My friends say I'm really funny, but I think I can be serious, too. I like to play sport and relax with friends at the weekend.'

C SPEAK Work in groups. Discuss the different people. Who is the best flatmate for Yassir?

○ Describe family members and friends

Café Hub

2.4 Café chaos
F make and respond to requests   **P** stress and intonation

COMPREHENSION

A ▶ Look at the pictures. Then watch the video and tick (✓) the things you see.

a camera ☐

keys ☐

a croissant ☐

a laptop ☐

headphones ☐   an umbrella ☐

a skateboard ☐

a phone ☐

B ▶ Work in pairs. Correct the wrong information in each sentence. Then watch the video again and check.
1 It's the ~~afternoon~~. *It's the morning.*
2 Gaby's cappuccino and croissant is £6.50.
3 Gaby's got a skateboard.
4 Zac is from Detroit.
5 Gaby is Italian.
6 Gaby's mum's name is Maria.
7 Gaby's got a flat.
8 Zac's got a flat.

FUNCTIONAL LANGUAGE
Making and responding to requests

A 2.8 Complete the phrases in the table with the words in the box. Then listen and check.

afraid   ahead   cappuccino   pounds   sit   that

Asking for things
Can/Could I have a ¹_____, please?
Can/Could I ²_____ here?
Saying Yes/No
Sure, no problem.
Go ³_____.
Of course.
No, sorry. I'm ⁴_____ not.
Asking for prices
How much is ⁵_____?
How much are they?
Giving prices
£4.50 / four ⁶_____, fifty.
$2.20 / two dollars, twenty.
€15.75 / fifteen euros, seventy-five.

B Work in pairs. Think of other ways of completing requests 1 and 2 in Exercise A. Practise saying them to each other.
Can I have a pen, please?

C 2.9 How do you say the prices in the box? Practise with a partner, then listen and check.

£5.25 $6.50   €13.30 $8.90   £14.40   €17.70

D Work in pairs. Write down three different prices and say them to your partner. Write what you hear.

MILLY SAM NEENA ZAC GABY

USEFUL PHRASES

A Complete the useful phrases with the words in the box.

| funny | idea | sorry | this | way | wrong |

a. I am so _____.
b. No _____!

c. That's _____!
d. What's _____?

e. I've got a great _____.
f. Let's do _____!

B ▶ 00.58–05:17 Watch the second part of the video again and check your ideas in Exercise A.

PRONUNCIATION
Stress and intonation

A ▶ 00:00–00:58 Watch the first part of the video again and read the conversation. Notice the stress and intonation.

Sam: Morning. What can I get you?
Gaby: Hi! Can I have a cappuccino please?
Sam: Sure. Anything to eat?
Gaby: Could I have a brownie?
Sam: No, sorry. I'm afraid not. There aren't any.
Gaby: OK. Erm. Can I have a croissant then?
Sam: No problem. Is that everything?
Gaby: Yes, thanks. How much is that?
Sam: Four pounds fifty. Take a seat.
Gaby: Thank you.

B ▶ 00:00–00:58 Work in pairs. Watch again and repeat the conversation. Copy the stress and intonation.

C SPEAK Work in pairs. Practise the conversation in Exercise A. Remember to use the correct stress and intonation.

SPEAKING

A PREPARE Work in groups of three. Write your own café conversation.

- Student A is the café owner. Students B and C are customers.
- Use the phrases in Functional Language to help you.
- Include all of the words in the box below.

| afraid ahead sit can you could I |
| course here can we sorry sure |

B DISCUSS Practise your conversation. Perform it for the rest of the class.

A: *Hello! Can I help you?*
B: *Hi! Can I have a coffee, please?*
A: *Sure, no problem.*
B: *And could I have a croissant?*

◯— Make and respond to requests

➤ Turn to **page 161** to learn how to write an email to a friend.

PEOPLE 19

Unit 2 Review

VOCABULARY

A Look at the family tree. Match the beginnings of sentences (1–8) with the ends of sentences (a–h).

1 Anna is Greta's
2 Greta is Bobby's
3 Jack is Greta's
4 Helen is Jack's
5 Anna is Ollie's
6 Greta is Helen's
7 Bobby is Ollie's
8 James is Bobby's

a granddaughter.
b uncle.
c mother.
d grandfather.
e cousin.
f wife.
g sister.
h aunt.

B SPEAK Work in pairs. Tell your partner about your family.

C Complete the descriptions (1–4) with the words in the box.

| beard   curly   fair   fat   glasses   long   tall |

1 Paolo has got _____, straight hair, blue eyes and a big _____.
2 Julia has got _____ skin, brown eyes and blonde, _____ hair.
3 My grandfather is very _____. He's got grey hair and wears _____.
4 My baby brother is very _____.

D Complete sentences (1–6) with the words in the box.

| funny   messy   noisy   quiet   serious   tidy |

1 Laurence is so _____! Why does she shout so much?
2 My brother is so _____. His bedroom is full of dirty clothes and old pizza boxes.
3 Michael is really _____. He always makes me laugh.
4 Your sister never smiles. Why is she so _____ all the time?
5 Erin cleans the kitchen every day. She's a very _____ person.
6 Why is he so _____? I can't hear anything he says!

E Work in pairs. Describe:
- your best friend
- your teacher
- someone you work or study with

GRAMMAR

A Complete the text with pronouns or possessive adjectives.

Hi! ¹_____'m Carrie. I'm Australian and I'm a doctor. ²_____ parents are Mike and Jennifer. ³_____'re actors. I've got one sister. ⁴_____ name is Lula and ⁵_____'s 18. I've got two brothers. ⁶_____ names are Tom and Brad. ⁷_____'re all from Brisbane.

B Correct the sentences by adding 's or s'.

1 Carrie*'s* surname is Pinto.
2 Her sister name is Lula.
3 Her brother names are Tom and Brad.
4 Jennifer children names are Carrie, Lula, Tom and Brad.
5 My brother dog is called Rufus.
6 His parent house is amazing!

C Complete the text with the correct form of *have/has got*.

How many brothers and sisters ¹_____ you ²_____? My family is small. It's just me, my brother, Eric and my mum. I look like my mum. She ³_____ blonde hair and blue eyes. Eric ⁴_____ dark, curly hair, but I ⁵_____ blonde, straight hair. My eyes are blue, like Mum's, but Eric ⁶_____ brown eyes.

D Find and correct one mistake in each sentence.

1 This is a ~~house~~ very big *house*.
2 My sisters are smalls.
3 I'm very quiet not.
4 He's a unfriendly really person.
5 Are you messy very?
6 Erin's quiet quite today.

FUNCTIONAL LANGUAGE

A Reorder the words to make requests and offers.

1 I / please / have / a / Could / sandwich, / ?
   Could I have a sandwich, please?
2 I / open / window / the / Shall / ?
   _____
3 use / Can / please / I / dictionary, / your / ?
   _____
4 help / Would / me / you / like / to / ?
   _____

B Work in pairs. Take turns to read the situations and decide what to say. Make requests and offers.

1 Your friend has got a very big bag.
2 You are cold.
3 You haven't got a pen.
4 You are thirsty.

3 DAYS

> Yesterday's history, tomorrow's a mystery but today is a gift. That's why it's called the present.
> — Alice Morse Earle

People walking through the snow in Tokyo, Japan.

OBJECTIVES

- talk about daily routines
- discuss daily activities
- describe a special day
- make and respond to suggestions
- write a blog post about your day

Work with a partner. Discuss the questions.

1. What's your favourite day of the year?
2. Look at the picture. Where is it?
3. What do you do at the weekend?

DAYS 21

3.1 A typical day — Talk about daily routines

V everyday activities   G present simple positive   P third person -s

LISTENING

Two minutes with Tom Fenn

This week's guest:
Name: Venus Mack
Age: 25
Job: late night radio DJ
Hometown: Los Angeles, USA

A Read the information about a guest on the radio show *Two minutes*. Are the sentences true (T) or false (F)? Correct the false sentences.

1 Venus Mack works for a radio station.   T / F
2 She's in her mid-thirties.   T / F
3 She starts and finishes work in the afternoon.   T / F
4 She's American.   T / F

B LISTEN FOR KEY WORDS Listen to the radio show *Two minutes*. Match the names (1–3) with the nouns (a–c).

1 Bowie   a Venus's producer
2 Reuben   b Venus's dog
3 Joel   c a rock band

C LISTEN FOR DETAIL Listen to the interview again. Choose the correct time to complete the sentences.

1 I have breakfast at *4 pm / 6 pm*.
2 I get to work at *8 pm / 9 pm*.
3 The show starts at *10 am / 10 pm*.
4 I have coffee with friends at *6 am / 9 am*.
5 I go to bed at *2 am / 9 am*.

D SPEAK Work in pairs. Do you agree or disagree with these sentences? Why?

1 Venus's typical day is interesting.
2 Venus works long hours.
3 Venus has a lot of energy.

A: *I agree. I think Venus's typical day is very exciting.*
B: *Why?*
A: *She meets a lot of musicians.*

VOCABULARY
Everyday activities

A Look at the pictures of Tom's morning routine. Complete the phrases with the verbs in the box.

get   get up   ~~have~~   leave   work

1 I _____ at 7.00 am.
2 I _have_ breakfast at 7.30 am.
3 I _____ home at 7.45 am.
4 I _____ to work at 8.30 am.
5 I _____ at a desk all day.

B Go to the Vocabulary Hub on page 147.

C SPEAK Work in pairs. Take turns to ask and answer questions with *What time do you …?* and an everyday activity.

A: *What time do you get up?*
B: *Seven o'clock.*
A: *What time do you have breakfast?*
B: *Seven thirty.*

22   DAYS

3.1

GRAMMAR
Present simple positive

A WORK IT OUT Read the sentences from *Two minutes*. Underline the verbs. Then cross out the incorrect rule in the box.

I get up at four o'clock.
Bowie comes with me.
I go to work by car.
My show starts at 10 pm.

Present simple
1 We use the present simple to talk about everyday habits and routines.
2 We use *be* + the main verb to make the present simple.
3 We add an *-s* (or *-es*) to verbs when the subject is *he, she* or *it*.

B Complete the table with the correct form of the verb *live*.

Present simple		
I/You/We/They	1_____	in a small house.
He/She/It	2_____	

C Go to the **Grammar Hub** on **page 126**.

D SPEAK Work in pairs. Think about someone you know. Tell your partner about their typical day.

A: *My sister gets up at six o'clock.*
B: *My friend Lukas plays video games every night.*

PRONUNCIATION
third person *-s*

A 3.2 There are three different ways of pronouncing the endings of present simple verbs in the third person. Can you hear the difference? Listen and repeat.

1 /s/ She work**s** in an office.
2 /z/ He play**s** video games every night.
3 /ɪz/ He watch**es** the news every morning.

B 3.3 Listen to the sentences. Circle the correct pronunciation of the third person *-s* ending.

1 She leave**s** home at 8 am.   /s/ /z/ /ɪz/
2 He teach**es** French at university.   /s/ /z/ /ɪz/
3 She get**s** home at seven o'clock.   /s/ /z/ /ɪz/
4 He go**es** to bed late at the weekend.   /s/ /z/ /ɪz/
5 She wash**es** her hair twice a week.   /s/ /z/ /ɪz/
6 He look**s** like Johnny Depp!   /s/ /z/ /ɪz/

C 3.3 Listen again and repeat the sentences. Be careful to pronounce the third person *-s* endings correctly.

SPEAKING

A PREPARE Work in pairs. Make a list of five interesting or exciting jobs.

B PLAN Choose one of the jobs in Exercise A. Write sentences to explain a typical day for someone with that job.

- She gets up at six in the morning.
- She goes to the studio at eight o'clock.
- She talks to the actors.

C SPEAK Work in new pairs. Read your sentences and try to guess the job.

A: *She gets up at six o'clock in the morning. She goes to the studio at eight o'clock. She talks to the actors ...*
B: *She's a film director!*
A: *Correct!*

○— Talk about daily routines

3.2 All day, every day

● Discuss daily activities

G adverbs of frequency **P** word stress **V** prepositions of time

READING

A Work in pairs. Look at the photos. Which of the activities do you do every day?

B READ FOR MAIN IDEA Read *Lifestyle online*. Choose the correct option to complete the definition of *essential*.

essential (adj.) = something you *learn* / *need*

C Read the comments on *Lifestyle online*. What four daily essentials do they write about that are not in the *Top 10 daily essentials* list?

D READ FOR DETAIL Read the comments again. Are the sentences true (T) or false (F)? Correct the false sentences.

1 Milos thinks breakfast is essential.   T / F
2 Scotgirl eats breakfast every day.   T / F
3 Topdog44 isn't a football fan.   T / F
4 Lisab needs to exercise every day..   T / F
5 Celine drinks black coffee every night.   T / F

E SPEAK Work with a partner. Make a list of your top ten daily essentials.

GRAMMAR
Adverbs of frequency

A Complete the sentences with adverbs from the text.

1 I _____ eat breakfast, but not every day.
2 I _____ watch football on TV.
3 I'm _____ away from my friends and family.
4 I _____ do exercise, @Lisab!

B WORK IT OUT Read the sentences in Exercise A and complete the rules.

Adverbs of frequency

1 We put adverbs of frequency *before* / *after* main verbs.
2 We put adverbs of frequency *before* / *after* the verb *be*.

Lifestyle *online*

What do you use every day? What couldn't you live without? We asked 100 people for their top 10 daily essentials. Here's what they said …

Top 10 daily essentials

1 the internet   6 a mobile phone
2 a shower or bath   7 a good friend
3 TV   8 a cup of coffee or tea
4 laptop or tablet   9 breakfast
5 a car   10 a pet

Milos
For me, I need a good breakfast and football on TV.

Scotgirl
LOL @Milos! I sometimes eat breakfast, but not every day. For me, it's music. I always listen to music on my way to work.

Topdog44
I never watch football on TV. I think it's really boring. I need my mobile phone. It's an essential – no question.

Fumi
For me, Facebook is essential. I travel a lot for work, so I'm often away from my friends and family. I use Facebook to talk to friends and send pictures of the places I travel to.

Lisab
Hmm … interesting question! For me, it's exercise. I usually do yoga for an hour before work.

Celine
Haha! I rarely do exercise, @Lisab! Coffee is my daily essential. I always start my day with a cup of strong, black coffee. I couldn't live without it.

C Go to the **Grammar Hub** on **page 126**.

D SPEAK Work in pairs. Write five sentences about yourself using adverbs of frequency. Tell your partner.

A: I rarely watch TV.
B: Really? I watch TV every day.

24 DAYS

LISTENING

A PREDICT What is a 'screen-free week'? Discuss your ideas with a partner. Then read the search result and check.

What's on?
Screen-free week
7th November 2017 Most people these days spend at least 15 hours every week online or on their phones. Well, 2nd–8th May, join us and other people around the world in screen-free week – a week when people take a break from screens and the internet. No mobile phone, no internet and no TV. There is life beyond the screen!

B LISTEN FOR GIST Listen to a conversation between Ali and Ian. Does Ali want to do screen-free week? Why/Why not?

C LISTEN FOR DETAIL Listen again. Are the sentences true (T) or false (F)? Correct the false sentences.

1 Ali spends nine hours a week on his phone. T / F
2 He looks at his phone when he wakes up. T / F
3 He uses his phone at work. T / F
4 He plays games online with his friends. T / F
5 He never watches football on TV. T / F

D SPEAK Work in pairs. Answer the questions.

1 How often do you check your phone?
2 Do you think you need a screen-free week? Why/Why not?

PRONUNCIATION
Word stress

A Listen and repeat. Stress the underlined syllables.

••	••	•••	••••
<u>mor</u>ning	on<u>line</u>	<u>in</u>ternet	com<u>pu</u>ter
<u>o</u>pen	be<u>gin</u>	<u>Sa</u>turday	um<u>bre</u>lla

B Add the words in the box to the table in Exercise A. Then listen and check your answers.

before   chocolate   essential   grandmother   laptop
rarely   relax   routine   serious   unfriendly   usually

C Listen again and repeat the words.

VOCABULARY
Prepositions of time

A Look at the phrases from the conversation between Ali and Ian. Then complete the rules with the correct preposition, *in*, *on* or *at*.

1 … *from early **in** the morning to late **at** night.*
2 ***On** Saturday and Sunday, it's non-stop football!*
3 ***At** the weekend, we watch football on TV.*

Prepositions of time
1 We use _____ with a time period (the morning, the afternoon, summer, 1990, etc).
2 We use _____ with the day of the week (Monday, Tuesday, etc) and dates.
3 We use _____ with exact times (6 pm, midday, etc).

B Write the correct preposition of time next to the words.

1 _____ Sunday
2 _____ three o'clock
3 _____ 6th March
4 _____ the evening
5 _____ June
6 _____ my birthday

SPEAKING

A PLAN Work in pairs. Think of ten activities to do in screen-free week.

B PREPARE Make a top ten list. Put the most essential activity at number 1.

C Work in pairs. Discuss your lists from Exercise A. Agree on the top five essentials.

A: I think 'go for a run' is the most essential. I need to do lots of exercise.
B: Really? I'm not sure. What about 'spend time with friends' as number one?

○— Discuss daily activities

DAYS 25

3.3 A special day — Describe a special day

G— present simple negative   P— sentence stress   V— big celebrations   S— listening for detail

READING

A Work in pairs. Look at the pictures in *A birthday to remember* and answer the questions.
1 What can you see in the pictures?
2 Which country are these things from?

B SCAN Read *A birthday to remember* quickly to check your answers to Exercise A.

C READ FOR GIST Read *A birthday to remember* again and answer the questions.
1 Why is Katie in China?
2 Which festival does she write about?
3 Is she enjoying her birthday?

D READ FOR DETAIL Read *A birthday to remember* again. Find and correct five more mistakes in the summary.

> Katie sometimes celebrates her birthday with ~~friends~~ *her mum*. This year, she is on holiday in Asia, and it is the time of the Moon Festival. The festival happens on the same day every September, and it is 150 years old. People wear traditional clothes. They eat mooncakes and watch dancers in modern costumes. They light lanterns to say thank you to their grandparents. Katie loves Moon Festival. She thinks this a good birthday.

Compass Travel

A birthday to remember
6th July | Leave a comment

I don't usually celebrate my birthday. I sometimes go out for a birthday lunch with my mum, but I usually just take it easy. My best friend doesn't understand, but for me, my birthday is no big deal. But this year, my birthday is a little different. I'm on holiday in China at the moment, and my birthday is on the same day as the Moon Festival. It's really cool.

Moon Festival is also called Mid-Autumn Festival, and people in China celebrate it every September or October. It's on a different day every year, but there's always a full moon. The festival is more than 3,000 years old. It's amazing, and really colourful – I love it! The people don't wear traditional clothes, but they eat traditional food, like mooncakes. They are small, round cakes and they're delicious! You can see dancers in colourful costumes perform traditional dances. There are also lots of paper lanterns with bright patterns. People light them to say thank you for children, who make everyone so happy – most of the time! So far, this birthday is one of the best ever!

GRAMMAR
Present simple negative

A WORK IT OUT Look at the sentences from *A birthday to remember* and complete the table with *don't* or *doesn't*.

I **don't** usually celebrate my birthday.
My best friend **doesn't** understand, …
The people **don't** wear traditional clothes, …

Present simple negative		
I/You/We/They	1 _____	eat special food.
He/She/It	2 _____	

B Go to the **Grammar Hub** on **page 126**.

C SPEAK Work in pairs. Write three negative present simple sentences – two true, one false. Then read them to your partner. Guess which sentence is false.

A: *I don't speak French. I don't watch TV. I don't eat meat.*
B: *The second one is false. You always watch TV!*

PRONUNCIATION
Sentence stress

A Listen and repeat. Then underline the stressed words.
3.7
1 I like festivals.   2 I don't like festivals.

B Look at the underlined words in Exercise A. Complete the rules.

Sentence stress in present simple
1 In short present simple positive sentences, we usually stress the *main verb* / *noun*.
2 In short present simple negative sentences, we usually stress the *auxiliary verb (don't/doesn't)* / *main verb*.

1 _____

2 _____

3.3

3 _____ 6 _____ 7 _____

4 _____

5 _____

C
Read the conversations. <u>Underline</u> the stressed words. Then listen and check.
3.8

1 Katia: Do you like mooncakes?
  Bian: Yes, but I don't eat them often.
2 Amelia: Do you like New Year's Eve?
  Lizzie: Err, yes. I like the fireworks.

D SPEAK Work in pairs. Practise the conversations in Exercise C. Be careful to stress the words correctly.

VOCABULARY
Big celebrations

A Match the pictures (1–7) with the words in the box.

| decorations fireworks parade party |
| present special food traditional clothes |

B Complete the questions with the words in the box.

| eat give have put up wear |

1 Do you usually _____ a party on your birthday?
2 When do you _____ decorations?
3 Do you _____ special food on New Year's Day?
4 When do people _____ traditional clothes in your country?
5 When do you _____ presents in your country?

C SPEAK Work in pairs. Answer the questions in Exercise B.

LISTENING

A LISTEN FOR KEY WORDS Listen to a conversation about big celebrations. Which words from Vocabulary Exercise A do they talk about?
3.9

B LISTEN FOR DETAIL Listen to the conversation again and choose the correct options to complete the sentences. Use the information in the box to help you.
3.9

> **Listening for detail**
>
> Sometimes we need to listen for specific information (e.g. what time something opens, etc). Use these ideas to help you listen for detail:
> - Read the questions carefully.
> - Underline key words.
> - Listen carefully for the key words that you underlined.

1 Mexico celebrates Independence Day in *September* / *December*.
2 All of the shops and banks *open* / *close* for the party.
3 In the evening, people go to watch *a big parade* / *the fireworks*.
4 At home, people put up red, white and *green* / *blue* decorations.
5 Carlos *wears* / *doesn't wear* traditional clothes to dance in.

SPEAKING HUB

A PREPARE Think of a special day. It could be:
- a birthday
- a religious day
- a national holiday
- a festival

B PLAN Make notes. Think about:
- the food you eat
- the music you listen to
- the clothes you wear
- the presents you give
- the songs you sing
- the people you see

C DISCUSS Work in groups. Describe your day. Compare your festivals.

> In Japan, families often eat KFC together at Christmas!

> Really? We eat together, but we don't eat fried chicken!

○─ Describe a special day

DAYS 27

Café Hub

3.4 Finding Neena
F – make and respond to suggestions   P – stress and intonation

COMPREHENSION

A ▶ Watch the video and answer the questions.
1. Who lives in the flat? _____
2. Who wants to live in the flat? _____
3. When do they agree to move in? _____
4. How many bathrooms are there? _____
5. What time does Zac start work? _____
6. What time does Neena get up? _____

B Look at the pictures. Which flat (a–c) is the one in the video?

C ▶ 00:29–01:30 Work in pairs. Complete the advert. Then watch part of the video again and check your answers.

D ▶ 02:40–03:25 Put Zac's morning routine in the correct order (1–7). Then watch part of the video again and check your answers.

___ have a shower   ___ finish work
___ start work   ___ brush teeth
___ wake up   ___ have breakfast
___ have a coffee

E **SPEAK** Work in pairs. Compare your morning routine to Zac's.

A: *I wake up at 8 am, not 9. What about you?*
B: *I wake up at 6 am! When do you start work?*

FUNCTIONAL LANGUAGE
Making and responding to suggestions

Complete the phrases with the words in the box. There are two words you do not need.

| about | don't | getting up | let's |
| moving in | not | sounds | sure |

Make suggestions	Say *yes*
What/How ¹_____ this flat?	⁵_____ good/great. Looks good/great! Brilliant! Awesome!
What/How about ²_____ next week?	
Why ³_____ we email her/go now?	**Say *no***
⁴_____ call her.	I'm not ⁶_____.

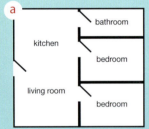   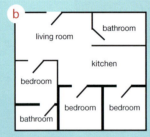   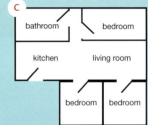

Beautiful flat | £190 pw
Single room(s) | Clapham Common (SW4)

Hi. I'm ¹_____. I need ² _____ lovely new housemates. I live in a ³ _____ bedroom flat on Park ⁴ _____. I'm ⁵ _____. I like ⁶ _____, ⁷ _____ and playing ⁸ _____ games.

Please call
0770 090 ⁹ _____.

MILLY   SAM   NEENA   ZAC   GABY

USEFUL PHRASES

Choose the correct definition of each useful phrase.

1 Any luck?
   a Are you lucky?   b Were you successful?
2 Cool!
   a Great!   b It's cold!
3 Of course.
   a Yes.   b No.
4 Actually, …
   a At the moment,   b In fact, …
5 It's not far.
   a It's near here.   b It isn't near here.
6 Lucky you!
   a I want to do that!   b I don't want to do that!

PRONUNCIATION
Stress and intonation

A ▶ 00:00–02:20 Watch the first part of the video again. Complete the conversations (A-C).

A
Gaby: Hey, ¹_____ this ²_____? It's nice.
Zac: Hmmm … ³_____ sure. It's very small.

B
Gaby: ⁴_____ good. ⁵_____ email ⁶_____?
Zac: No, ⁷_____ call ⁸_____!

C
Zac: Can we see the apartment today?
Neena: Of course. Actually, it's not far. ⁹_____ now?
Zac: ¹⁰_____ great!
Gaby: Brilliant! Let's go!

B ▶ 00:00–02:20 Watch again and repeat the conversations. Copy the stress and intonation.

C SPEAK Work in pairs. Practise the conversations in Exercise A. Remember to use the correct stress and intonation.

SPEAKING

A PREPARE Work in pairs. Complete the suggestions for what to do after school. Use the ideas in brackets.

- What about going to _____ (a place)?
- Let's eat _____ (food).
- Why don't we watch _____ (a film)?
- How about listening to _____ (a band / music)?
- Let's play _____ (a game).

B DISCUSS Go around the class and make suggestions to your classmates. Reply using the Functional language phrases.

A: *How about going to a concert?*
B: *Awesome!*

○— Make and respond to suggestions

➤ Turn to **page 162** to learn how to write a blog post about your day.

3.4

DAYS 29

Unit 3 Review

VOCABULARY

A Complete the sentences with the words in the box.

> get to   get up   have   leave   work

1 I _____ in a large office in King's Cross.
2 I usually _____ toast and coffee for breakfast.
3 I _____ at 6.30 every morning.
4 I try to _____ home before seven o'clock.
5 I _____ work between nine and nine thirty.

B Match the verbs (1–8) with the words (a–h) to make phrases describing everyday activities.

1 have   a to music / to the radio
2 get   b in a house / in a flat / in the USA
3 listen   c a book / a magazine
4 watch   d to work / to bed / for a run
5 live   e up early / home from work
6 read   f for a bank / in Spain
7 work   g breakfast / lunch / a shower
8 go   h a film / TV

C Complete the sentences with the correct prepositions.

1 I usually watch the news _____ the afternoon.
2 I sometimes listen to music _____ night.
3 I sometimes go for a walk _____ the weekend.
4 I have an English class _____ Tuesday.
5 I read the newspaper _____ the morning.
6 I rarely work _____ Fridays.

D Complete the sentences with the words in the box.

> decorations   fireworks   parade   party
> presents   special food   traditional clothes

1 What are you doing on Saturday? Do you want to come to a _____?
2 It's sad, but many people don't wear _____ at the festival anymore.
3 My mum spends three days cooking so we can have _____ on the big day.
4 My family don't put up _____ until the 24th December.
5 We usually open all of the _____ after breakfast.
6 There's a big _____ through the streets with giant balloons, dancers and people wearing costumes.
7 We don't have _____ on New Year's Eve anymore because they scare the dog.

GRAMMAR

A Complete the paragraph with the correct form of the verbs in the box.

> get (x2)   go (x3)   have (x3)   leave   live   work (x2)

Luke Timms [1]_____ six days a week and his days are usually the same. He [2]_____ in a small flat in Milan. He [3]_____ up early every day and [4]_____ a shower. He [5]_____ breakfast and then [6]_____ the flat at around eight. He [7]_____ to work by motorbike. He [8]_____ for a television station in the city centre. He [9]_____ lunch at 2 pm, and then he finishes work at 6.30 pm. He [10]_____ home around 7 pm and [11]_____ for a long run. He usually [12]_____ to bed at around midnight.

B Rewrite the sentences with the adverbs in brackets.

1 I get up at 6 am. (usually)
   _____ *I usually get up at 6 am.* _____
2 I go for a walk in the park. (often)
   _____
3 I watch TV. (sometimes)
   _____
4 I am late for my English class. (never)
   _____
5 I have breakfast at 7 am. (always)
   _____
6 I am late for work. (rarely)
   _____

C Rewrite the sentences to make them negative.

1 We go to work.
   _____ *We don't go to work.* _____
2 People eat special food.
   _____
3 We dance.
   _____
4 People wear special clothes.
   _____
5 People stay at home.
   _____
6 We give presents.
   _____

FUNCTIONAL LANGUAGE

Complete the phrases with the words in the box.

> ~~about~~   how   idea   let's   sounds   why

1 What _____ *about* _____ going out for a meal?
2 _____ good, but I'm not hungry.
3 _____ about watching a film?
4 _____ don't we stay in?
5 That's a great _____!
6 _____ have a nice cup of tea!

30   DAYS

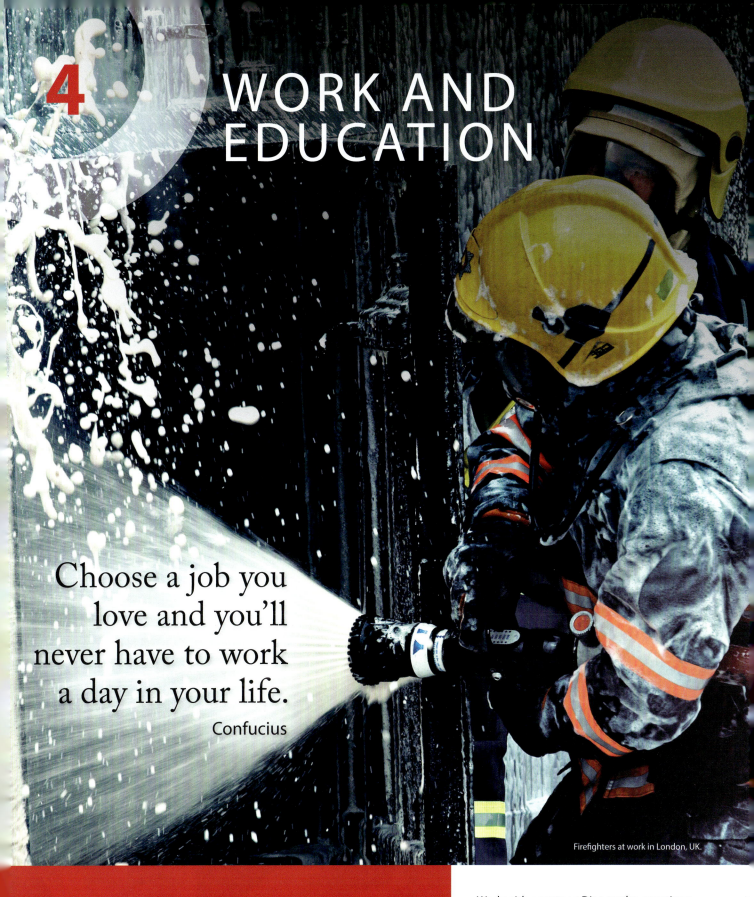

4 WORK AND EDUCATION

> Choose a job you love and you'll never have to work a day in your life.
> Confucius

Firefighters at work in London, UK.

OBJECTIVES

- talk about jobs
- talk about the perfect job
- talk about adult education and career development
- ask for someone and leave a message
- write an email asking for information

Work with a partner. Discuss the questions.

1 Do you like your job?
2 Look at the picture. Do you think this is an easy job? Why/Why not?
3 Would you like to do this job?

WORK AND EDUCATION   31

4.1 What do you do? • Talk about jobs

V — work and jobs   G — present simple *yes/no* questions; short answers   P — linking sounds: *do/does*

VOCABULARY
Work and jobs

A Match the pictures (1–4) with the words in the box.

> doctor   engineer   pilot   teacher

B Go to the Vocabulary Hub on page 147.

C Complete the sentences with the words in the box.

> computer   home   meet   meetings
> office   travel (x2)   wear (x2)

1 I sometimes _____ for my job, but I usually work in an _____. I go to _____ and I meet a lot of different people.

2 I like my job because I _____ new people every day. I _____ a uniform. I don't work in an office – I work in a hospital.

3 I always _____ for my job, but I usually work with the same people. I _____ a uniform and I go to a lot of different places.

4 I usually work from _____. I sometimes go out to meet people. I spend a lot of time on my _____.

D SPEAK Work in pairs. Talk about your job or the job of someone you know. Use the words and phrases in Exercise C to help you.

A: *I'm a designer. I don't work in an office. I work from home.*

B: *My sister is a businessperson. She travels a lot for her work. She always goes to different places.*

READING

A READ FOR GIST Read the interview. Are the sentences true (T) or false (F)? Correct the false sentences.

1 He's a nurse. T / F
2 He works in an office. T / F
3 He sometimes works from home. T / F
4 He loves his job. T / F

B READ FOR DETAIL Read the interview again. Find and correct mistakes in the summary.

> Matheus is an engineer. He works in an office, but he also goes to meetings and he visits hospitals. He doesn't work from home because he never needs to talk to other people. He works for a small company in the USA. He never visits any other countries. He says his job is easy, but he loves it because it's unusual.

C SPEAK Talk to your partner. Do you think Matheus has got an interesting job? Why/Why not?

Working Week – Out for lunch

This week: Matheus Oliveira, 32

Every week, we catch someone on their lunch break and ask them five quick questions about their job.

What's your job?
I'm an engineer, like my brother.

Does your brother work for the same company as you?
No, he doesn't. He works for a big company in the USA.

Do you work in an office?
Yes, I do. I also spend a lot of time out of the office. I go to meetings and I visit factories.

Do you work from home sometimes?
No, I don't. I always need to talk to other people, so I don't stay at home.

Do you travel for work?
Yes, sometimes. I work for a large company in Brazil, but I often go to the USA, China and Japan.

Do you like your job?
Yes, I love it. It's difficult, but it's also interesting and exciting. I'm very lucky.

32   WORK AND EDUCATION

GRAMMAR
Present simple *yes/no* questions; short answers

A Work in pairs. Look at the questions and short answers from the interview. Underline the main verbs in the questions. What is at the beginning of each question?

1 Do you work in an office? Yes, I do.
2 Do you work from home sometimes? No, I don't.
3 Do you travel for work? Yes, sometimes.
4 Does your brother work for the same company as you? No, he doesn't.

B Complete the rules with the words in the box.

do/does (x2)   don't/doesn't   the main verb

Present simple – *yes/no* questions; short answers

- To form questions in the present simple, we use ¹_____ + subject + ²_____.
- In affirmative short answers, we use ³_____.
- In negative short answers, we use ⁴_____.

C Correct the mistakes in the questions and answers.

1 A: Do you go to meetings?   B: Yes, do I.
2 A: Do they work in the same office? B: Yes, they don't.
3 A: Does you work from home?   B: Yes, sometimes.
4 A: Do she have lunch in a café?   B: Yes, she does.
5 A: Do you meet a lot of new people? B: Yes, I meet.

D Use the prompts to write present simple questions.

1 you / work in an office?
   Do you work in an office?
2 you / wear a uniform?
3 you / travel for your job?
4 you / work with people?
5 you / like your job?
6 anyone in your family / have an interesting job?

E Go to the **Grammar Hub** on **page 128**.

F **SPEAK** Ask and answer the questions in Exercise D. Use information about yourself, or imagine you are someone else.

A: *Do you work in an office?*
B: *Yes, I do. It's in the city centre.*
A: *Does anyone in your family have an interesting job?*
B: *Yes, my brother does! He's a police officer.*

PRONUNCIATION
linking sounds: *do/does*

A Listen to the questions and answers. Notice how some sounds link together.
4.1

/dʒʊ/	Do‿you like your job?	Yes, I do.
	Do‿you work from home?	No, I don't.
/dʌziː/	Does‿he travel for his job?	Yes, he does.
/dʌzʃiː/	Does‿she work long hours?	No, she doesn't.

B Listen to the questions again and repeat. Link the sounds together.
4.2

C **SPEAK** Complete the questions with your own ideas, and then ask and answer with a partner. Remember to link sounds together.

1 Do you …   3 Does he …
2 Do you …   4 Does she …

SPEAKING

A **PREPARE** Work in groups. Write ten *yes/no* questions that will help you guess someone's job.

1 *Do you work in an office?*
2 *Do you wear a uniform?*
3 *Do you work with other people?*

B **SPEAK** Follow the steps below to play the game.

Student 1: Choose a job. Don't tell the other students.

Other students: Ask Student 1 the questions. You must guess the job in ten questions (or fewer).

Student 1: Answer the questions. You can only say *Yes, I do.* or *No, I don't.*

A: *Do you work outside?*   A: *Do you work with people?*
B: *No, I don't.*   B: *Yes, I do.*

C **SPEAK** Change roles and repeat.

◯─ Talk about jobs

WORK AND EDUCATION   33

4.2 Good job! — Talk about the perfect job

G— have to / don't have to   P— connected speech: have to   V— time expressions

👍 Good job / 👎 Bad job

Everyone wants to have a good job, but what exactly does a 'good job' mean? Is it the money, the location or the hours? What about the company culture? We speak to two people with very different jobs to find out more.

Jie Chen

I work for a small company, and the office is near my house, so I don't have to take the metro or drive my car. I walk to work every day, and it only takes five minutes!
I really like the office. It's a nice space, and it's very quiet and relaxing. Also, there's an outside space, so we don't have to stay indoors on sunny days – we can work outside!
My salary isn't great, but it's okay. My favourite thing about my job is that I can choose my own hours. I don't have to work nine to five! I usually work from seven in the morning until three in the afternoon. I'm a morning person, so I'm very happy that I can work early, and get home early, too.

Glossary
nine to five (n phrase) the hours of a typical working day in many countries
salary (n) the fixed amount of money that you get for your job
self-employed (adj) working for yourself, not for one company

Mike Carlstrom

I like my job sometimes, but it isn't easy. I'm very busy every day and I have to make a lot of important decisions.
The good thing about my job is the money – I'm very well paid. I haven't got any free time. I have to work long hours. I usually get to the office at 8.30 am, and I often leave at around 9 pm. My office is in the centre of the city, and the drive from my home takes over an hour.
Also, I often have to work at the weekend, so I don't see my family much. I want to work from home and spend more time with my children, so my plan is to become self-employed soon.

READING

A Work in pairs. Rank the things in the box in order of importance for a job (1 = very important, 4 = not important).

___ colleagues/boss   ___ money   ___ hours   ___ location

B READ FOR GIST Read an article about jobs. Which of the things in Exercise A do the two people talk about?

C READ FOR DETAIL Read the article again. Are the sentences true (T) or false (F)? Correct the false sentences.

1 Both Jie and Mike make a lot of money.   T / F
2 Jie and Mike travel to work in different ways.   T / F
3 Jie likes working in the evening.   T / F
4 Jie and Mike work the same hours.   T / F
5 Jie can work outside sometimes.   T / F
6 Both Jie and Mike's jobs are quiet and relaxing.   T / F

D SPEAK Work with a partner. Discuss Jie and Mike's jobs. Talk about:
- the good things about their jobs
- the bad things about their jobs

A: *Mike's got a good salary.*   B: *Yes, but the hours are long.*

GRAMMAR
have to / don't have to

A Complete the sentences with verbs from the article.

1 I don't have to _____ the metro or _____ my car.
2 I don't have to _____ nine to five!
3 I have to _____ a lot of important decisions.
4 I often have to _____ at the weekend.

B Look at the sentences in Exercise A. Choose the correct option to complete the rule.

have to / don't have to
We use *have* or *has to* to talk about rules and things we **need / don't need** to do.

C Go to the **Grammar Hub** on **page 128**.

34 WORK AND EDUCATION

PRONUNCIATION
Connected speech: *have to*

A Listen to the questions. Is there a pause between 'have' and 'to'?
4.3
1 Do you have to work long hours?
2 Do employees have to eat in the company restaurant?

B Listen and repeat the questions.
4.4
1 Do you have to wear a uniform?
2 Does he have to go to a lot of meetings?
3 Do they have to organise a lot of trips?
4 Do you have to ask your boss for holiday?

C SPEAK Write four questions using *have to*. Work with a partner and ask your questions.

A: *Do you have to work at weekends?*
B: *No I don't! I only have to work nine to five, Monday to Friday.*

LISTENING

A LISTEN FOR GIST Listen to the conversation between Hussam and Salah. Which picture is Hussam's work?
4.5

B LISTEN FOR DETAIL Listen again and complete each sentence with one word.
4.5
1 Hussan usually starts _____ at midday.
2 He usually takes it easy in the _____.
3 He sometimes has _____ at 1pm.
4 He can decide when to _____ work.
5 He is self-employed so he works from _____.

C SPEAK Work with a partner. Do you want a job like Hussam's? Why/Why not?

VOCABULARY
Time expressions

A Read the sentences from the conversation. Match the time expressions in **bold** with the times (1–5).

I don't have to work **nine to five**.
I usually start work at **midday**.
I have to start really **early in the morning**.
I don't go to bed until **midnight** or later.
…other days, I eat **late in the afternoon**.

1 12 pm   _midday_
2 4 pm – 6 pm   _____
3 9 am – 5 pm   _____
4 12 am   _____
5 5 am – 9 am   _____

B Complete the sentences with the time expressions from Exercise A.

1 I work better at night. Sometimes I study late in the evenings, until _____ or later.
2 I don't have to work from _____, like my friends in offices. It's great!
3 I have lunch at _____ every day. I start early in the morning, so I'm always hungry by then.
4 I find it difficult to think _____. I just want to go home and relax.
5 I like to go for a run _____ before I go to work.

C SPEAK Work with a partner. Write five questions using the words and phrases from Exercise A. Ask and answer the questions with your partner.

A: *Do you have to work from nine to five?*
B: *No, I can choose my own hours.*

SPEAKING

A PLAN Make a list of five things that make a good job.
1 A big salary!
2 The people you work with.

B SPEAK Work in small groups. Compare your ideas from Exercise A. Together, decide on a top five list.

C PRESENT Read your list to the class. Explain your ideas.

Talk about the perfect job

4.3 Learn something new

● Talk about adult education and career development

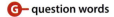 question words    word stress: questions    education collocations    listening for gist

The Open University

It's never too late to learn something new. The Open University is the largest university in the UK, with almost 174,000 students in 2015/2016 alone. It is a distance learning university, and it's for anyone who wants to study and learn a new skill.

FAQs

Who are the courses for?
Open University degree courses are open for anyone. Many people who have jobs or cannot go to a normal university on weekdays choose to study with us. As a distance learning university, it's perfect for anyone who wants to study from home.

How much does it cost?
The cost of full-time study is almost half of other universities in the UK.

What subjects do you teach?
There are nearly 500 courses to choose from.

When do students go to classes?
Students don't 'go' to classes. All of the classes and resources are online, so students can access them when they need to.

Where do students meet their teachers?
They don't. Students usually send homework to their teachers. The teachers reply by email.

How long does an average degree course take?
It takes an average of six years for most students to finish their degrees.

Why do people do distance learning courses?
A lot of people work during the day and study in their free time. The Open University is flexible. You can study anywhere, anytime.

Glossary
course (n) a series of lessons in one subject
degree (n) a qualification you get after you complete a university course
resources (n) things you can use to help you to study
skill (n) the ability to do something well
university (n) a place where adults study

READING

A Work with a partner. Discuss the questions.
1 Why do people with a job study in their free time?
2 What kinds of things do they study?

B **READ FOR GIST** Read the webpage about the Open University. How is it different from a typical university?

C **READ FOR DETAIL** Read the webpage again. Work in pairs. What do these numbers refer to?
1 174,000   2 500   3 6

D Read the webpage again. Are the sentences true (T) or false (F)? Correct the false sentences.
1 The Open University is the largest university in Europe.   T / F
2 It's only for British people.   T / F
3 You study when you want to.   T / F
4 Students don't usually meet their teachers.   T / F
5 A lot of people study during the day.   T / F

GRAMMAR
Question words

A Look at the questions on the webpage. Complete the rules with the question words in the box.

| How long   How much   What   When   Where   Who   ~~Why~~ |

Question words
1 _Why_ to ask for a reason.
2 _____ to ask a question about a thing.
3 _____ to ask a question about a place.
4 _____ to ask a question about a person.
5 _____ to ask a question about quantity.
6 _____ to ask about a length of time.
7 _____ to ask a question about a time.

B Go to the **Grammar Hub** on **page 128**.

C Complete the questions with words from Exercise A.
1 _____ subjects are popular in your country?
2 _____ are they so popular?
3 _____ can you get information about courses?
4 _____ does it cost to go to university?
5 _____ do people usually start and finish classes?
6 _____ do people usually study for (e.g. three years, four years, etc)?
7 _____ is your favourite teacher? Why?

D **SPEAK** Ask and answer the questions in Exercise C.

36 WORK AND EDUCATION

PRONUNCIATION
Word stress: questions

 Listen and repeat the questions. <u>Underline</u> the stressed words.

1 Where do you work?
2 Why do you study history?
3 When do you start work?
4 What do you do?
5 How much does your course cost?

LISTENING

A LISTEN FOR GIST Listen to a conversation. Choose the correct summary (1–3).

> **Listening for gist**
>
> Gist is the main idea. When you listen for gist, you don't need to understand every word. Listen for key words, which help you to understand the main idea(s) and summarise what you heard.

1 Lily is a teacher. She wants to teach art history to Tom.
2 Lily works in an office. She wants to teach art history like Tom.
3 Lily wants to study art history at university so she can work in an office.

 B LISTEN FOR DETAIL Listen again. Match the beginnings of sentences (1–5) with the ends of sentences (a–e).

1 I recommend distance   a by email.
2 We offer over   b materials.
3 You send your homework to us c learning.
4 You study when   d 800 courses.
5 You pay for access to our online   e you want.

C SPEAK Work in groups. Discuss the questions.

1 How long do you have to study to become a teacher in your country?
2 Who pays for it?

VOCABULARY
Education collocations

A Choose the correct verbs to complete the sentences.

1 I want to *do / get* a course in my free time.
2 I don't want to *study / train* a subject I don't like!
3 I want to *train / do* to be a teacher.
4 I want to *go / study* to university.
5 I have to *take / get* a lot of exams.
6 Then, after two more years, I can *study / get* a degree.
7 My company says I have to *take / get* a qualification.

B <u>Underline</u> the verb–noun collocations in Exercise A.

SPEAKING HUB

A PLAN Work in small groups. Imagine you are planning a new course for adults who want to retrain.
- Think about the types of jobs that adults retrain for in your country.
- Choose the type of course (for example, English, science, business).

B PREPARE Plan the course. Decide on your answers to these questions:
- When will the course happen? (weekdays, weekends, any time)
- Where? (in a college, at a university, online)
- How long will it take?
- How much will it cost?
- What exams do students have to take?
- What qualifications do they get?

C DISCUSS Imagine you are at a careers fair.
- Present your course to the rest of the class.
- Be prepared to answer questions.
- Watch the other groups' presentations. Ask them questions about their courses.

D THINK ABOUT IT Have a class vote. Find out how many people are interested in each course.

○— Talk about adult education and career development

Café Hub

4.4 Busy day

F – ask for someone and leave a message
P – stress and intonation

COMPREHENSION

A ▶ Watch the video. Are the sentences true (T) or false (F)? Correct the false sentences.

1 Neena works in an office. T / F
2 Richard Sharp is busy. T / F
3 Neena's surname is Patel. T / F
4 She has to finish the Smith account today. T / F
5 She meets her mum for dinner. T / F
6 She usually finishes work at 10 pm. T / F
7 Neena wants a new job. T / F
8 She tells her mum about her new housemates. T / F

B ▶ Number the events in the order they happen. Then watch the video again and check.

Neena leaves a message for Richard Sharp.

Neena gets more work.

Neena gets started.

Lunchtime?

Neena speaks to her mum.

Finished?

FUNCTIONAL LANGUAGE
Asking for someone and leaving a message

A ▶ 00:00–01:37 Complete Neena's conversation with the receptionist. Then watch the first part of the video again and check.

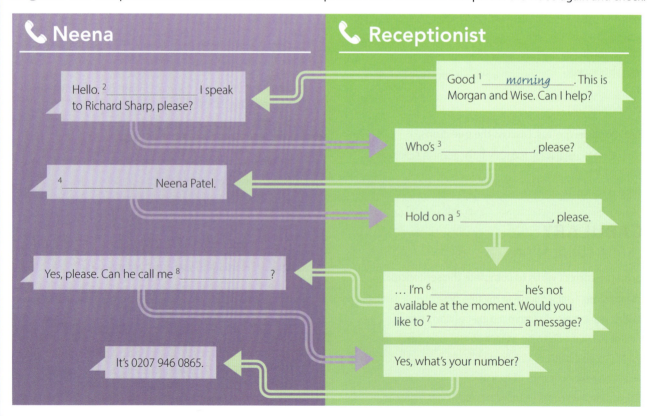

Neena

Hello. ² _____ I speak to Richard Sharp, please?

⁴ _____ Neena Patel.

Yes, please. Can he call me ⁸ _____?

It's 0207 946 0865.

Receptionist

Good ¹ _morning_. This is Morgan and Wise. Can I help?

Who's ³ _____, please?

Hold on a ⁵ _____, please.

… I'm ⁶ _____ he's not available at the moment. Would you like to ⁷ _____ a message?

Yes, what's your number?

B Work in pairs. Practise the conversation using your own name. Copy the stress and intonation.

WORK AND EDUCATION

MILLY   SAM   NEENA   ZAC   GABY

USEFUL PHRASES

Match the phrases (1–5) with their uses (a–e).

1 Hi, [mum]. It's me.
2 Right then,
3 Oh, dear.
4 Look,
5 Anyway,

a To change the subject.
b To react to bad news.
c To start a voicemail to someone you know.
d To make someone listen/understand.
e To begin a big or difficult job.

PRONUNCIATION
Stress and intonation

A ▶ 00:59–01:27 Watch part of Neena's conversation with the receptionist again. Notice the stress and intonation.

Neena:	Yes, please. Can he call me back?
Receptionist:	Yes, what's your number?
Neena:	It's 0207 946 0865.
Receptionist:	So, that's 0207 946 0865.
Neena:	Yes, that's right.

B ▶ 00:59–01:27 Watch again and repeat the conversation. Copy the stress and intonation.

Saying '0'
In British English, we usually say 'oh'.
In American English, we usually say 'zero'.

C Work in pairs. Practise the conversation in Exercise A, but change the phone number. Remember to use the correct stress and intonation.

SPEAKING

A PLAN Work in pairs. Write a telephone conversation between yourself and a receptionist. Include these stages:

• You want to speak to a famous person.
• The famous person isn't available.
• You leave your name and number.

B PRACTISE Practise your conversation. Be careful with your stress and intonation.

C PRESENT Perform your conversation for the class.

A: *Hello. Could I speak to Adele, please?*
B: *Who's speaking, please?*

○— Ask for someone and leave a message

➤ Turn to **page 163** to learn how to write an email asking for information.

WORK AND EDUCATION 39

Unit 4 Review

VOCABULARY

A Complete the definitions with the jobs in the box.

> dentist   designer   doctor   hairdresser
> journalist   mechanic   pilot   shop assistant

1 _____ (n) a person that helps sick people

2 _____ (n) a person that cuts people's hair

3 _____ (n) a person that fixes cars

4 _____ (n) a person that flies planes

5 _____ (n) a person that fixes your teeth

6 _____ (n) a person that works in a shop

7 _____ (n) a person that decides how something looks or works

8 _____ (n) a person that reports the news

B Choose the correct words to complete the sentences.

1 In my country, teachers earn a good *money* / *salary*.

2 My sister works *full time* / *part time*. She's in the office three days a week.

3 I work for an electronics *company* / *boss*.

4 My father's an actor. He's *salary* / *self-employed*.

5 There are 200 *colleagues* / *employees* in the company.

6 My brother is a nurse. He works *long hours* / *nine to five* at night.

C Complete the sentences with the time expressions in the box.

> early in the morning   late in the afternoon
> midday   midnight   nine to five

1 The restaurant closes at 11 pm, so I usually don't get home until after _____.

2 I have a normal office job. I work from _____.

3 My wife starts work at 6 am, so she has to get up really _____.

4 I have a meeting at _____. Maybe we could go for lunch after that?

5 I work all night, so I sleep for most of the day. I usually don't get up until _____.

D Complete the text with the words in the box.

> course   degree   exam   study   train   university

At the moment, I'm in my last year of school, but after that I want to go to [1]_____. I want to [2]_____ medicine, then [3]_____ to be a doctor. I need to take an [4]_____ at the end of this year before I can go to university and start my [5]_____. It takes five years to do the [6]_____, and it's a lot of work – but it's my dream!

E **SPEAK** Work in pairs. Discuss the questions.

1 Do you have a degree? Do you want one?

2 Does anyone in your family go to university? Where? What do they study?

3 What would you like to take a course in?

4 How do you feel before an exam?

GRAMMAR

A Use the prompts to write *yes/no* questions then write short answers that are true for you.

1 you / work / outside?

    Do you work outside? Yes, I do.

2 your colleagues / work / full time?

    _____

3 your company / make computers?

    _____

4 your boss / earn / a good salary?

    _____

5 you / like / your job?

    _____

B Complete the text with the correct form of *have to* and the verbs in brackets.

My sister's a police officer in our hometown. She [1]_____ (*work*) long hours, sometimes 10 or 12 hours a day, and she often [2]_____ (*get up*) early, at 4 am. She [3]_____ (*wear*) a blue uniform when she works outside, but when she's in the office, she [4]_____ (*wear*) special clothes – she can wear her normal clothes. She and her colleagues often [5]_____ (*help*) people in dangerous situations.

C Write questions to match the answers.

1 A: _____

   B: I live in a small flat in the city centre.

2 A: _____

   B: My teacher is Ms Magnabosco.

3 A: _____

   B: I do my homework at the weekend.

4 A: _____

   B: My English course is two years.

FUNCTIONAL LANGUAGE

Complete the conversation with the words in the box.

> call   hang   here   message   number   speak   that's

A: Hello?

B: Hi, it's Joe. Can I [1]_____ to Maria, please?

A: She's not [2]_____ at the moment.

B: Oh, right. Can I leave a [3]_____?

A: [4]_____ on a minute. I haven't got a pen … OK, I'm ready.

B: Can she [5]_____ me back? My [6]_____ is 0768 939925.

A: OK, so [7]_____ 0768 939925.

B: That's right. Thanks!

40   WORK AND EDUCATION

5 PLACES

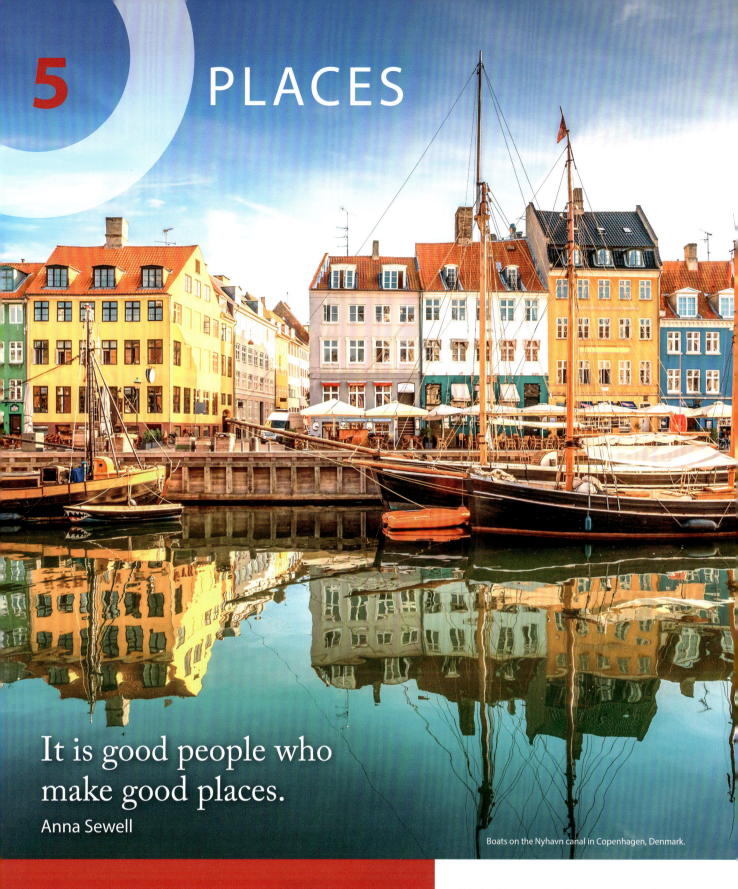

It is good people who make good places.
Anna Sewell

Boats on the Nyhavn canal in Copenhagen, Denmark.

OBJECTIVES

- describe a home
- describe a neighbourhood
- describe an interesting building
- ask for and give directions
- write a description of a place

Work with a partner. Discuss the questions.

1 Where do you live?
2 Look at the picture. Would you like to live there? Why/Why not?
3 What's your favourite city?

PLACES 41

5.1 There's no place like home

● Describe a home

V— rooms and furniture; prepositions of place   P— /b/, /d/ and /g/   G— there is/are

VOCABULARY
Rooms and furniture

A Work in pairs and discuss the questions.
1 Do you live in a house or flat?
2 Who do you live with?
3 How many rooms are there?
4 Where do you spend most of your time?

B Go to the Vocabulary Hub on page 148.

C SPEAK Work in pairs. Student A – imagine you are in a room in your house or flat. Describe what you can see. Student B – guess which room your partner is talking about.

A: *I can see a TV and a lamp.*
B: *You're in the living room!*
A: *No, I'm in the bedroom!*

PRONUNCIATION
/b/, /d/ and /g/

A The words below all begin with /b/, /d/ or /g/ sounds. Listen and repeat.
5.1

/b/	/d/	/g/
bedroom	dining	garden
bathroom	don't	go
brother	day	grow

B Listen and write the words in the correct place in Exercise A.
5.2

C Listen, check and repeat.
5.3

LISTENING

A Work in pairs. Look at the pictures. Where would you prefer to stay on holiday? Why?

B Read the advert. What is it for?

Houseswap

Laguna Beach, California, USA
Caravan on private beach near Los Angeles. Fantastic home right on the Pacific Ocean. Sleeps four. Close to Disneyland.

My dream swap: Italy, Greece, France, UK
Contact Luke Westman on +1 (213) 509 6995

C LISTEN FOR GIST Listen to Sadie talking to Luke about his house. Which sentence (1–3) best describes their conversation?
5.4

1 Sadie doesn't like the house.
2 Sadie and Luke agree to swap houses.
3 Sadie doesn't understand the house swap rules.

D LISTEN FOR KEY WORDS Listen again. Choose the correct words to complete the sentences.
5.4

1 Sadie is from the south of *France / England*.
2 Luke's caravan has got *two / three* beds.
3 Luke's caravan *has / hasn't* got a swimming pool.
4 Luke's caravan *has got four / hasn't got any* chairs.
5 Sadie *has / hasn't got* a house.

E SPEAK Work in pairs. What do you like about Luke's home? What don't you like?

city flat

yurt

42 PLACES

GRAMMAR
there is/are

A WORK IT OUT Read three parts of Luke and Sadie's conversation. Complete the table using the conversation as an example.

1
Sadie: Er … yes. So, are there any beds in your house?
Luke: Beds? Yes, there are. There are two beds. There's a bed in the bedroom and another bed opposite the kitchen.

2
Sadie: I see. Is there a swimming pool?
Luke: … No, there isn't a swimming pool.

3
Sadie: OK … Well, are there any chairs in the dining room?
Luke: No, there aren't any chairs.

there is/are	Singular	Plural
Positive +	There¹ ___'s___ a dining room.	There² _____ two bathrooms.
Negative -	There³ _____ a TV.	There⁴ _____ any plants.
Questions ?	⁵ _____ a washing machine?	⁶ _____ any chairs?

some and *any*

We use *some* in positive sentences with plural nouns.
We use *any* in questions and negative sentences with plural nouns.

A: Are there any armchairs?
B: No, there aren't any armchairs, but there are some chairs.

B Go to the **Grammar Hub** on **page 130**.

C SPEAK Work in pairs. Ask your partner about their home using some of the words in the box.

| armchair bath coffee machine cupboard |
| fridge lamp plant shower sink sofa |
| table TV washing machine window |

A: *Are there any lamps in your living room?*
B: *No, there aren't. But there is a lamp in the bedroom. Is there a washing machine in your kitchen?*
A: *Yes, there is.*

beach house

VOCABULARY
Prepositions of place

Look at the pictures of Luke's caravan. Match sentences (1–5) to objects (a–e).

1 They're **in** the small cupboard **near** the coffee machine.
2 They're **behind** the lamp.
3 It's **under** the window, **between** the plant and the wall.
4 They're **on** the small table, **opposite** the sofa.
5 It's **next to** the kitchen sink.

a coffee machine   d keys
b bed   e TV and DVD player
c books

SPEAKING

A Imagine you have a holiday home. Where is it?

B PLAN Write notes about your holiday home. Think about these questions:
- What type of home is it?
- How many rooms are there?
- Does it have a big or small kitchen?
- Is there a garden or swimming pool?

C PREPARE Write an advert for a house swap.

D SPEAK Work in groups. Read each other's adverts. Ask questions and decide who you want to swap with.

Describe a home

5.2 My neighbourhood — Describe a neighbourhood

 places in a town or city can  weak forms: can/can't

VOCABULARY
Places in a town or city

A **SPEAK** Work in pairs. Which of the sentences (1–3) best describes you?
1 I like quiet areas away from the centre of the city.
2 I like busy areas in the city, with lots of people and shops.
3 I don't like the city. I like small towns and the countryside.

B Work in pairs. Look at the pictures. Which of the places in the box can you see?

> café cinema gym hospital library market
> museum park shops supermarket theatre

C Go to the Vocabulary Hub on page 148.

D **SPEAK** Work in pairs. Which of the places in Exercise B or in the Vocabulary are there in your neighbourhood? Which would you like to have?

In my neighbourhood, there's a supermarket, but there aren't any small shops.

READING

A **READ FOR GIST** Read the comments in the *Chicago Expat Forum*. Who is Grace and what is her problem?

B **READ FOR SPECIFIC INFORMATION** Read the comments again and answer the questions.
1 Where is Grace from?
2 Where is Grace's new job?
3 Which two places can she go to in Jackson Park?
4 What does Grace like doing?
5 Where is the gym?
6 How far is Hyde Park from the centre of Chicago?

C **SPEAK** Work in pairs. Do you think Hyde Park is a good place for Grace to live? Why/Why not?

Chicago Expats

amazinggrace26: Hi, people of Chicago! My name's Grace. I'm 26 and I'm a nurse in the Philippines. I have a new job at the University Hospital in Hyde Park, and I'm a bit nervous because this is my first time abroad. Can you tell me something about the neighbourhood? What is there to do in Hyde Park? I like warm weather, and my hobbies are reading and keeping fit.
Yesterday, 08:39   Reply | Like

Marco: Hi Grace. I work at the University Hospital, too. There are a lot of things you can do in Hyde Park. There are some good restaurants and cafés, and Jackson Park nearby is really nice. Can you play tennis? There are some very good tennis courts in Jackson Park. There's even a science museum there, too!
Yesterday, 12:21   Reply | Like

amazinggrace26: Thanks, Marco. It sounds great. I can't play tennis, but I'd like to learn! And the museum sounds fantastic! Is there a gym at the hospital? I like to swim and keep fit.
Yesterday, 15:05   Reply | Like

Marco: There isn't a gym at the hospital, but there is one very close to it. And it's cheap for people who work at the hospital 😊
Yesterday, 17:12   Reply | Like

helen264: Hi, Grace. Hyde Park is nice, but for me, it can be boring. I prefer the city centre – it's only 20 minutes away. You can go to the theatre, shops and cinemas. Sorry, but I can't promise you good weather! Chicago is often cold!
Today, 09:45   Reply | Like

amazinggrace26: Thanks for your advice, @Helen264. I feel really excited about Chicago now!

Glossary
expat (n) someone who lives in a country that is not their own

44 PLACES

GRAMMAR
can

A WORK IT OUT Read the sentences from the *Chicago Expat Forum*. Then choose the correct words to complete the rules.

Can you play tennis?   … it can be boring.
You can go to the theatre …   I can't play tennis …

can
1. We use *can* to talk about **ability and possibility / the past**.
2. In positive and negative sentences, *can* comes **before / after** the main verb.
3. We use the infinitive **with / without to** after *can*.
4. We **use / don't use** questions that start with *Do …?*
5. We **add / don't add** -s in the third person.

B Go to the Grammar Hub on page 130.

C SPEAK Work in pairs. Ask each other questions starting with *Can you …?* Use the ideas below to help you.
- arrive at work when you want
- go to the cinema in your neighbourhood
- play a musical instrument
- play tennis
- speak another language
- swim
- work from home

A: *Can you arrive at work when you want?*
B: *I don't work, but I can usually arrive at university when I want. Can you play football?*

PRONUNCIATION
Weak forms: *can/can't*

A Listen and read. What do you notice about the pronunciation of *can* and *can't*?
5.5
1. Can you speak another language?
2. Yes, I can. I can speak Italian fluently.
3. No, I can't. I'm not very good at languages.
4. I can speak a bit of French, but I can't speak it very well.

B Listen again and repeat the sentences. Copy the pronunciation of *can* and *can't*.
5.5

SPEAKING

A PREPARE Imagine you want to move to a new neighbourhood. Work with a partner to rank questions (a–g) from 1 (very important) to 8 (not important).

a What are the people like?   ___
b Are there any good schools?   ___
c What's the weather like?   ___
d How far is it from the airport? ___
e What's in the city centre?   ___
f Are there any good shops?   ___
g Is there a train station?   ___

A: *It's important for me to be close to my family and friends.*
B: *Yes, that's a good point. And public transport is important to me.*

B ORGANISE What can you do in your neighbourhood? Make notes.

C SPEAK Work in pairs. Imagine your partner is interested in moving to your neighbourhood. Describe it to them, explaining what is good and bad about the area.

There are a lot of shops, but there aren't any parks.

D SPEAK Ask questions about your partner's neighbourhood. Decide if you want to move there.

○— **Describe a neighbourhood**

PLACES 45

5.3 Amazing buildings — Describe an interesting building

G imperatives   **V** adjectives to describe the appearance of things   **P** word stress: adjectives
S reading for specific information

READING

A Look at the famous buildings (1–5) in *The world's most interesting buildings*. What do you know about them? Do you know where they are?

B **READ FOR GIST** Read *The world's most interesting buildings*. Match pictures (1–5) with paragraphs (a–d). There is one picture you do not need.

C Read the article again. In which building(s) can you do these things? Use the information in the box to help you.

> **Reading for specific information**
> - Read the text quickly and look for keywords that help you find the information you're looking for.
> - For example, if you want to know about prices or times, look for numbers. Then read around them to find the information.

1 have lunch _____
2 see art _____
3 swim _____
4 work _____
5 live _____

D **SPEAK** Work in pairs. Which building is your favourite? Which building don't you like? Why?

1

The world's *most interesting buildings*

What happens when you mix buildings and art? Read on and find out! This week's topic in *Architecture Online* is the world's most **interesting** and original buildings. These are our favourite buildings. Tell us which ones you like.

a This **strange** building isn't falling down! It's the Dancing House, in Prague, Czech Republic. It's **funny**! There are offices in the building, and there's a restaurant on the top floor. Look at how many windows there are! Some people don't like the Dancing House because it's next to a lot of old buildings in a historic part of the city on a busy road. They think it's **terrible**. _____

b These yellow and white buildings that look like trees are Piet Blom's Cube Houses in Rotterdam, the Netherlands. They are **tall** and **beautiful**. The living rooms are downstairs and the bedrooms are on the top floor. Some houses have a garden on the roof. _____

c This **amazing** house looks very **old**, but it isn't. In fact, it's only 40 years old. It's *Casa do Penedo*, or 'Stone House' in Portugal. The **small** house sits between four **big** rocks. There's a swimming pool in one of the rocks. You can visit the house because it's a local history museum. _____

d This is the Niterói Contemporary Art Museum in Rio de Janeiro, Brazil. It's an art gallery and a museum. The building is next to a beach and has views of Rio and the Sugarloaf Mountain. The museum is very popular with tourists. We think this **modern** building is **cool**. _____

2

3

46 PLACES

GRAMMAR
Imperatives

A WORK IT OUT Look at the sentences from *The world's most interesting buildings*. Then choose the correct words to complete the rules.

Read on and **find** out!

Tell us which ones you like.

> **Imperatives**
> 1 We use imperatives when we want to *tell someone to do something / talk about the future*.
> 2 We use the infinitive *with to / without to* to make imperatives.
> 3 We *can / can't* use *please* with imperatives.

B Find and underline one more imperative in *The world's most interesting buildings*.

C Go to the Grammar Hub on page 130.

D SPEAK Work in pairs. Use the verbs in the box to make imperative sentences. Remember to say *please*.

give lend sit down spell stand up tell write

Stand up, please.

VOCABULARY
Adjectives to describe the appearance of things

A Look at the adjectives in **bold** in *The world's most interesting buildings*. Which are positive? Which are negative? Which are neutral?

Positive: _____

Negative: _____

Neutral: _____

B Match adjectives (1–5) with their opposites (a–e).

1 beautiful   a boring
2 interesting   b old
3 amazing   c small
4 big   d terrible
5 modern   e ugly

C SPEAK Work in pairs. Describe an interesting building in your neighbourhood using adjectives from Exercise B.

There's a new shopping centre in the middle of town. It's a big, modern building with lots of windows.

PRONUNCIATION
Word stress: adjectives

A Listen and repeat. Copy the word stress.
5.6

●●	●●●
boring	beautiful

B Complete the table in Exercise A with the words in the box. Then listen and check.
5.7

~~beautiful~~ ~~boring~~ building funny gallery
interesting modern popular terrible ugly

C Listen again and repeat the words. Copy the word stress.
5.7

SPEAKING HUB

A SPEAK Work in pairs. Go to the Communication Hub on page 154.

B DISCUSS Work in groups. Discuss the questions.
1 Which of the buildings in the Communication Hub is your favourite? Why?
2 What's your favourite building in your country? Why do you like it?
3 Do you think it's important for buildings to look interesting? Why/Why not?

C Have a class vote on the most interesting building.

○— Describe an interesting building

4

5

PLACES 47

Café Hub

5.4 Moving in
F – ask for and give directions
P – stress and intonation

COMPREHENSION

A ▶ Watch the video without sound. Tick (✓) the items you see.

- [ ] café
- [ ] chair
- [ ] cinema
- [ ] fridge
- [ ] gym
- [ ] house
- [ ] lamp
- [ ] library
- [ ] park
- [ ] plant
- [ ] sofa
- [ ] supermarket
- [ ] table
- [ ] theatre

B **SPEAK** Work in pairs. Ask questions to check your answers to Exercise A.

A: *Is there a gym?*
B: *No, there isn't. Is there a café?*
A: *I'm not sure …*

C ▶ Watch the video with sound and choose the correct option to complete the sentences.

1. Gaby *gets / doesn't get* cash.
2. Gaby *loses / doesn't lose* her phone.
3. Gaby *has to / doesn't have to* ask for directions twice.
4. Gaby *can / can't* find her door key.
5. Gaby *spends / doesn't spend* the evening with Neena.

FUNCTIONAL LANGUAGE
Asking for and giving directions

A Label pictures (1–4) with the directions in the box.

Go straight on   Turn right   Turn right at the café   Turn left

1   2   3   4

_____   _____   _____   _____

B Match the directions in the box to images (1–4).

Asking for directions	Excuse me, is there a cash machine near here? Excuse me, can you tell me the way to Park Road?
Giving directions	___ Go straight on to the end of the road. ___ Go past the shops. ___ Take the third turning on the left. ___ The cash machine is next to the supermarket.

C **SPEAK** Work in pairs. Take turns giving directions from your school to:

- a cash machine
- a train station
- a coffee shop

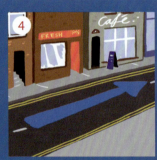

48 PLACES

MILLY   SAM   NEENA   ZAC   GABY

PRONUNCIATION
Stress and intonation

A ▶ 00:00–00:47 Watch the first part of the video again. Listen to the conversation between Gaby and the passer-by. Notice the stress and intonation.

Gaby:	Ex<u>cuse</u> <u>me</u>, is there a <u>cash</u> ma<u>chine</u> near here?
Passer-by:	<u>Sure</u>. Go <u>straight</u> <u>on</u> to the <u>end</u> of the <u>road</u>. Turn <u>right</u> at the <u>café</u>. And the <u>cash</u> ma<u>chine</u> is next to the <u>su</u>permarket.

B ▶ 00:00–00:47 Watch again and repeat the conversation. Copy the stress and intonation.

C **SPEAK** Work in pairs. Practise the conversation in Exercise A. Remember to use the correct stress and intonation.

SPEAKING

DISCUSS Work in pairs. Ask for and give directions using the map. Use some of the Functional language and the prepositions in the box to help you.

| behind   between   near   next to   on |

A: *Excuse me. Is there a school near here?*
B: *Sure, take the second turning on the left.*

○— **Ask for and give directions**

▶ Turn to **page 164** to learn how to write a description of a place.

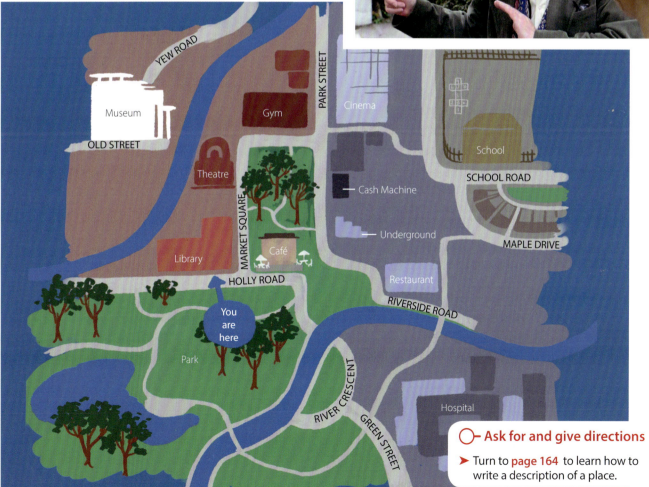

PLACES 49

Unit 5 Review

GRAMMAR

A Match the beginnings of sentences (1–5) with the ends of sentences (a–e).

1 There's
2 There aren't
3 Are there
4 Is there
5 There are

a a table in the kitchen?
b some cupboards in the bathroom.
c a shower in the bathroom.
d any lamps in the sitting room?
e any chairs in the dining room.

B Complete the conversation with the correct form of *can*.

Simon: ¹___Can___ you ride a motorbike?
Patrick: No, I ²_____, but I ³_____ drive a car. Do you want a lift?
Simon: ⁴_____ we walk to the park from here?
Patrick: Well, we ⁵_____, but it takes a long time.

C Choose the correct words to complete the sentences.

1 *Tell / To tell* me more about the Colosseum in Rome.
2 *Look / Looking* at the tourists.
3 *Please give / Give please* me more information.
4 *Ask / To Ask* at reception for more information.
5 *Write / Wrote* about your favourite building.

VOCABULARY

A Complete the furniture and rooms with *a, e, i, o* or *u*.

1 We have a sh_o_w_e_r, but we don't have a b_a_th in our b_a_thr_o__o_m.
2 We have a modern c____k____r and fr___dg___ in our k___tch___n.
3 There's a TV, a big c___pb_____rd, a s___f___ and two ___rmch_____rs in our sitting room.
4 There's a l___mp on the t___bl___ by my bed in my b___dr_____m.

B Look at the picture. Choose the correct prepositions to complete the sentences.

1 The coffee machine is **between / next to** the cooker and the sink.
2 The house keys are hanging **on / in** the wall.
3 The dishwasher is **next to / behind** the cooker.
4 The note is **above / under** the window.

C Complete the sentences with the places in the box.

airport   gym   ~~hospital~~   library   market

1 You see a doctor at the ___hospital___.
2 You take a plane at the _____.
3 You borrow a book from the _____.
4 You buy fresh food at a _____.
5 You do exercise at the _____.

D Complete the text with the correct adjectives.

My favourite building is Habitat 67, in Montréal, Quebec. It's ¹a_m_a_z_i_ng – it's ²b___g and looks quite ³m_____n, even though it's 50 years old. It isn't one building, it's about 150 ⁴s_____l houses on top of each other. Some people think it looks ⁵s_____e, but I think it's ⁶b_____l. You can see the sky through it, which is ⁷c_____l.

FUNCTIONAL LANGUAGE

A Complete the conversation with the words in the box.

down   ~~excuse~~   here   how   on   tell   turn   turning

A: ¹___Excuse___ me.
B: Yes?
A: Can you ²_____ me the way to New Street?
B: Sorry?
A: Is New Street near ³_____?
B: Pardon?
A: ⁴_____ do I get to New Street?
B: Oh, yes. Go ⁵_____ College Road. ⁶_____ right into the High Street and Moon Street is ⁷_____ your right.
A: Moon Street? I want New Street.
B: New Street? No, no. New Street is near here. Take the second ⁸_____ on the right.
A: Oh, thanks.

B **SPEAK** Work in pairs. Give each other directions from your school to:

- a book shop
- a train station
- a museum

50 PLACES

6 THAT'S ENTERTAINMENT

> If music be the food of love, play on.
> William Shakespeare

An actor on stage in the Théâtre du Châtelet in Paris, France.

OBJECTIVES

- talk about likes and dislikes
- talk about entertainment in the present and the past
- talk about your life
- ask for and give opinions
- review an event

Work with a partner. Discuss the questions.

1 What's your favourite kind of music?
2 Look at the picture. What's he doing?
3 How often do you go to the cinema?

THAT'S ENTERTAINMENT 51

6.1 Let's go out ● Talk about likes and dislikes

V — entertainment   P — word stress: noun patterns   G — likes and dislikes

VOCABULARY
Entertainment

A Match pictures (1–6) with the places and events (a–f).

a a comedy show ___ d a concert ___
b an exhibition ___ e a festival ___
c a cinema ___ f a theatre ___

B SPEAK Work with a partner. How often do you go to the places and events in Exercise A?

PRONUNCIATION
Word stress: noun patterns

A Listen and repeat the words. Copy the word stress.
6.1

cinema   comedy   concert   exhibition
festival   internet   magazine

B Complete the table with the words from Exercise A. Then listen, check and repeat.
6.2

●●	●●●	●●●	●●●●

READING

A Read the *City Guide*. Tick (✓) the information you can get from it.

☐ the date of an event
☐ how much an event costs
☐ what time the events start/finish
☐ how often the event happens
☐ how to get to an event
☐ where an event is
☐ the writer's opinion of an event
☐ things to do in October

📍 City Guide

What's on?

Today | **This week** | This weekend

Things to do this week (10th – 16th August)
No plans this week? Well, not any more. We're here to help! From films to festivals, here's your guide to the next seven days. Let's go out!

Star Wars ★★★★★
Watch the first three *Star Wars* films, a different film each evening over three nights. Saturday is a special family day when you can wear costumes.
Langley Open-Air Cinema, 6 pm, from Thursday 13th August

Cow ★★★
Californian rock band, Cow, often play in strange locations. This Friday, their concert is in an old swimming pool. Enjoy some old favourites and songs from their new album.
The Old Baths, 9 pm, Friday 14th August

Comedy Underground ★★★★
For one night, comedians Lily O'Connor and Josh Peet take their new show underground. That's right – two hours of free comedy as you travel on the tube!
City Line, 8 pm – 10 pm, Thursday 13th August

Kwame Abraham ★★★★★
This exhibition of Kwame Abraham's photographs shows people from his country, Ghana, during the 1960s. His images tell amazing stories.
The Hayforth Gallery, 10 am – 9.30 pm, Wednesday 12th August – Sunday 6th September

Glossary
comedian (n) someone who tells jokes and stories to make people laugh
free (adj) something that doesn't cost anything
costume (n) clothes that performers wear in a play, film, etc
open-air (adj) happening outside
location (n) where something is or where something happens
silent (adj) not making any noise

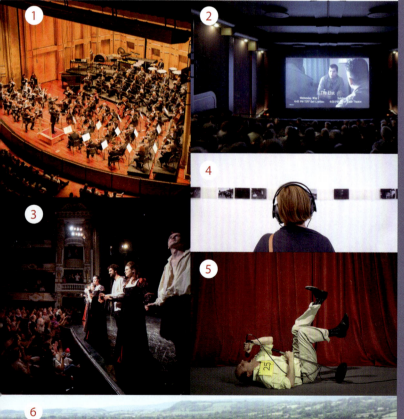

52 THAT'S ENTERTAINMENT

B READ FOR SPECIFIC INFORMATION Read the guide again. Complete the sentences with no more than three words from the text.

1 The Kwame Abraham exhibition finishes on _____.
2 The music festival lasts for _____ days.
3 The Star Wars event starts at _____ on Thursday 13th August.
4 Cow's performance is in a _____ in The Old Baths.
5 James Cave is _____ in the performance of *Romeo and Juliet*.

Silent disco ★★★★
The silent disco craze continues! Put on your headphones, choose any kind of music and dance to your favourite tunes.
Nanette's, 10 pm – 5 am, Saturday 15th August

Lost in the Forest Festival ★★★★
A three-day music festival with great food and dancing under the tall, green trees of Coney Forest.
Coney Forest, Friday 14th – Sunday 16th August

Shakespeare in the park ★★★
Tonight's play is *Romeo and Juliet*, Shakespeare's famous love story. With James Cave as Romeo and Ameera Hussain as Juliet. Bring warm clothes and a picnic.
Linkside Park, 6 pm, Tuesday 11th August

C How do you know which events the *What's on?* guide recommends? Which events have four- (★★★★) or five-star (★★★★★) ratings?

D SPEAK Work in pairs. How do you find events?

online   apps   newspaper   magazine
friends   family   social media

I find events on an app on my phone. I go to pop-up events all the time.

GRAMMAR
Likes and dislikes

A 🔊 6.3 Listen to Dan and Lucy planning a night out. Which events in the *What's on?* guide do they talk about? What do they decide to do?

B 🔊 6.3 Complete the sentences from the conversation with the words in the box. Then listen again and check your answers.

don't like (x2)   hate   like   love

1 Dan: I _____ staying in on Friday night. Let's go out.
2 Dan: It's that rock band from California, Cow. I _____ their music.
3 Lucy: Sorry, I don't really like them. I _____ rock music.
4 Lucy: I _____ sitting outside. It's too cold.
5 Dan: You _____ photography, don't you?

C WORK IT OUT Look at the sentences in Exercise B. Complete the rules with *noun* or *verb*.

Likes and dislikes
1 We use *like, love, don't like* and *hate* + _____
2 We use *like, love, don't like* and *hate* + _____ + -ing.

D Go to the **Grammar Hub** on **page 132**.

E SPEAK Work in small groups. Discuss the questions.
1 What do you like doing in your free time?
2 What kind of events do you love? Which do you hate? Why?
3 What do you like doing on your birthday?
4 Do you like going to outdoor events (e.g. festivals, open-air cinemas, etc)? Why/Why not?

SPEAKING

A PREPARE Work in pairs and discuss what you *like, love, don't like* and *hate* in the *What's on?* guide.

B SPEAK Go to the **Communication Hub** on **page 154**.

○− Talk about likes and dislikes

THAT'S ENTERTAINMENT   53

6.2 It was fun
● Talk about entertainment in the present and the past

G was/were   P  weak forms: was/were   V — past time expressions

1 _____   2 _____
3 _____   4 _____

LISTENING

A Work in pairs. Label the pictures (1–4) with the time periods in the box.

1930s   1950s   1980s   2000s

B LISTEN FOR KEY WORDS Listen to Carrie and her grandad talking about TV. Tick (✓) the things that they talk about.

- TV channels ☐
- movie night ☐
- TV on demand ☐
- laptops and tablets ☐
- TV dinners ☐
- an old TV show ☐

6.4

C LISTEN FOR DETAIL Listen to the conversation again. Are the sentences true (T) or false (F)? Correct the false sentences.

1 Carrie can't watch the nature programme. T / F
2 Carrie watches her favourite TV programme on demand. T / F
3 Carrie's grandad's favourite TV programme was on once a week. T / F
4 When Carrie's grandad was young, there were a lot of TV channels. T / F
5 TVs weren't expensive in the 1950s. T / F
6 Carrie's grandad thinks families today don't do things together. T / F

D SPEAK Work in pairs. Answer the questions.

1 What are your favourite TV programmes?
2 Do you watch them with friends and family or alone?
3 How often do you watch programmes on demand?

GRAMMAR
was/were

A Read the sentences from the conversation between Carrie and her grandad. Underline the verbs.

1 They were expensive.
2 There weren't many TV channels.
3 Was that nice, Grandad?
4 I wasn't lonely.
5 It was fun.

B WORK IT OUT Look at Exercise A. Complete the rules with was, wasn't, were or weren't.

was/were	
1	_____ is the past form of *is*.
	_____ is the past form of *are*.
2	_____ is the past form of *isn't*.
	_____ is the past form of *aren't*.
3	We make yes/no questions with _____ or _____ + subject.

C Go to the Grammar Hub on page 132.

D SPEAK Ask *Where were you …?* using the times below.

- at 11 pm last night
- at 6 pm on Friday
- at 8 am this morning
- at 10 am on Saturday morning
- at 2 pm yesterday

Where were you at 11 pm last night?

54   THAT'S ENTERTAINMENT

PRONUNCIATION
Weak forms: was/were

 A Listen and read. What do you notice about the pronunciation of was and were?

1 When I was young, my favourite TV programme was on once a week.
2 How many TV channels were there?
3 Yes, they were.
4 Was that nice, Grandad?
5 Yes, it was. I wasn't lonely. People did things together. It was fun.

 B Underline the weak forms of was and were in Exercise A. Then listen again and check.

C Work in pairs. Practise saying the sentences in Exercise A. Remember to use the correct forms of was and were.

VOCABULARY
Past time expressions

A Work in pairs to complete the *Big screen, small screen* quiz.

B Use the words in the box to make a table of past time expressions. Some words can go in more than one place.

| 10 minutes | 1952 | Friday | June | month |
| six weeks | two years | weekend | winter | year |

in	ago	last

C Complete the sentences with *in*, *ago*, *last* or *yesterday*.

1 I was in Mexico _____ year.
2 Our exams were exactly one year _____.
3 I wasn't at home _____ July. I was on holiday.
4 I was a student two months _____. Now I've got a job!
5 My parents were students _____ 1982.
6 I was at home with my family _____.

D SPEAK Work in pairs. Ask and answer questions beginning with *Where were you …?* Use the table in Exercise B to help you.

A: *Where were you last month?*
B: *I was in Istanbul last month. Where were you at this time yesterday?*
A: *I was in this class!*

SPEAKING

A PREPARE Write five questions about entertainment now and in the past. Use time expressions in your questions.

What's your favourite TV programme?
What was your favourite film ten years ago?

B SPEAK Work in pairs. Ask and answer the questions in Exercise A.

five/ten/twenty years ago   in the 80s/90s   last year

A: *What were your favourite TV programmes ten years ago?*
B: *My favourite TV programme 10 years ago was …*

BIG SCREEN, SMALL SCREEN

1 When was the first film?
   a in the 1850s
   b in the 1880s
   c in the 1900s

2 When was the first film with sound?
   a in the 1910s
   b in the 1920s
   c in the 1930s

3 When was the first TV introduced?
   a 90 years ago
   b 70 years ago
   c 50 years ago

4 When was the first on demand TV service introduced?
   a last year
   b this century
   c last century

○— Talk about entertainment in the present and the past

6.3 Life stories — Talk about your life

 past simple regular and irregular verbs   past simple regular endings V – life events S – scanning for names

Entertainer Magazine
Inspiring stories

Carlos Acosta
by Helena Nowak

Carlos Acosta was born into a large, poor family in Havana, Cuba, in 1973. When he was nine years old, his father, Pedros Acosta, **sent** him to dance school. At first, he hated it – he just wanted to play football with his friends. But he worked hard and, eventually, **became** a talented dancer. He **studied** at the National Ballet School of Cuba and graduated with a gold medal.

Between 1989 and 1991, he performed around the world. He was the principal dancer at the Houston Ballet from 1993 to 1998, and then he **started** a new job at London's Royal Ballet. He met his wife Charlotte Holland in 2004. They **got** married eight years later. They had a child – a daughter, named Aila.

He **went** back to Cuba in 2011 to start a foundation to help young dancers. Acosta is also an actor. He appeared in the films *New York, I Love You* (2008) and *Our Kind of Traitor* (2016).

Glossary
inspiring (adj) making you feel excited about something

Venus Williams
by Nao Yamauchi

Venus Williams was born in Lynwood, near Compton in Los Angeles, in 1980. There was a lot of crime in the local area and her father, Richard Williams, thought tennis was a chance for Venus and her younger sister Serena to be rich and successful.

The Williams sisters **played** tennis on old courts. They **practised** with tennis balls from nearby country clubs. Their father was their coach, and their mother, Oracene Price, **gave** them school lessons at home. When she was ten, Venus **moved** to Florida where she went to Rick Macci's tennis academy. Before she was a teenager, she won 63 matches without losing one.

In February 2002, Venus Williams became the first African American to be the world's number one tennis player. In July of the same year, Venus played Serena in the Wimbledon final, and Serena won and became world number one. These sisters, from a poor neighbourhood in Los Angeles, are now recognised as two of the greatest female tennis players in the world.

READING

A Work in pairs. Look at the pictures in the article. What do you know about these people?

B READ FOR GIST Work in pairs. Student A – read about Carlos Acosta. Student B – read about Venus Williams. Tell your partner about your person.

C READ FOR DETAIL Read the article again and complete the sentences with names from the text. Use the information in the box to help you.

Scanning for names
• When scanning for names of people or places, look out for CAPITAL LETTERS.
• When scanning for names of films, albums and books, look out for *italics*.

1 _____ wanted Venus and Serena to learn tennis.
2 Carlos got married to _____.
3 In 2008, Carlos was in a film called _____.
4 Venus moved to _____ in 1990.
5 _____ sent Carlos to dance school for the first time.
6 _____ became world number one in July 2002.
7 Carlos got a gold medal from _____.
8 _____ helped Venus with school lessons at home.

D SPEAK Work in pairs. Which person inspires you? Why?

A: *I like Carlos Acosta because he helps young dancers.*
B: *I think Venus is more inspiring. She was the first African American to be the world's number one tennis player.*

THAT'S ENTERTAINMENT

6.3

GRAMMAR
Past simple regular and irregular verbs

A **WORK IT OUT** Read *Inspiring stories* again. Complete the table with past verbs from the article.

Past simple regular and irregular verbs			
Regular		**Irregular**	
move	_____	become	_____
play	_____	get	_____
practise	_____	go	_____
start	_____	give	_____
study	_____	send	_____

B Look at the rules about past simple regular verbs. Tick (✓) the rules that are true.

Past simple regular verbs	
1	☐ We add -*ed* to most verbs.
2	☐ We add -*d* to verbs ending in -*e*.
3	☐ We add -*s* to the third person.
4	☐ With verbs ending in -*y*, we cut the -*y* and add -*ied*.

C See the **Irregular verbs** list on **page 121**.

D Go to the **Grammar Hub** on **page 132**.

E **SPEAK** Work in pairs. Tell your partner three things you did last year.

A: *I went to Greece, I bought a new laptop and I passed my English exam! What about you?*

B: *Well done! I joined a gym, I met my best friend and I started university.*

PRONUNCIATION
Past simple regular endings

🔊 **A** There are three different ways of pronouncing the
6.6   endings of past simple regular verbs. Can you hear the difference? Listen and repeat.

/d/	/t/	/ɪd/
di**ed**	li**ked**	wait**ed**

🔊 **B** Listen and add the verbs in the box to the table in
6.7   Exercise A.

> asked   decided   moved   stopped
> studied   wanted   worked

🔊 **C** Listen again and repeat the verbs.
6.7

VOCABULARY
Life events

A Complete the phrases with the infinitives in the box. Use the words in bold in *Inspiring stories* to help you.

> be   become   get   go   have   move   start   study

1 _____ married
2 _____ a dancer/musician/singer
3 _____ to school/university
4 _____ work
5 _____ art / a language
6 _____ born
7 _____ children
8 _____ house / to a different city

B **SPEAK** Put the life events in Exercise A in the order that you think they happen. Then work in pairs. Are your life events in the same order? Can you think of any other life events?

A: *What about learning to drive? That's a big life event for most people.*

B: *That's true. I learnt to drive when I was 17. It really changed my life!*

⭕ SPEAKING HUB

A **PREPARE** You are going to write about your life. Think about how to complete the sentences.

- I was born in …
- I went …
- I studied …
- I started …
- I moved …

- I got married to …
- I had …
- I lived in …
- I worked in …

B **PLAN** Choose the five most important events in your life. Write each one on a separate piece of paper and then fold it in half.

C **ORGANISE** Work in groups. Put all of your sentences in the middle. Take turns reading sentences aloud and guessing who wrote them. Award one point for every correct guess.

> I graduated from Bologna University.

> It's Francesca's sentence!

D **DISCUSS** Work in groups. Try to remember the events of other people's lives.

> Sayeed studied English in Australia.

> Yes, and Ana got married last month!

⭕— **Talk about your life**

THAT'S ENTERTAINMENT   57

Café Hub

6.4 Love hate
F – ask for and give opinions   P – stress and intonation

COMPREHENSION

A ▶ 00:00–00:56 **SPEAK** Work in pairs. Watch the first part of the video. What is Zac's big news?

B ▶ 00:56–03:57 Watch the second part of the video and complete the table. Draw ☺ if the housemates like the song or ☹ if they don't like it.

Song	Zac	Gaby	Neena	Me
The river				
Move				
Chimes				
Check it out				

C **SPEAK** What do you think of the songs? Complete the *Me* column of the table with ☺ or ☹.

FUNCTIONAL LANGUAGE
Asking for and giving opinions

A Complete the table with the phrases in the box.

> I hate it.   I like it.   I love it!   I really hate it.
> It's good.   I think it's awful.   I'm not sure.
> It's awesome!   It's great!   It isn't great.

Asking for opinions	What do you think of it/this?
	How about you?
Giving opinions	☺☺☺ _____
	☺☺ _____
	☺ _____
	☹ _____
	☹☹ _____
	☹☹☹ _____

B Rank the adjectives below from ☺☺☺ (very positive) to ☹☹☹ (very negative). Then, compare your answers with a partner.

1 great   ☺☺
2 amazing   _____
3 bad   _____
4 awful   _____
5 happy   _____
6 sad   _____
7 terrible _____
8 good   _____

58 THAT'S ENTERTAINMENT

6.4

MILLY **SAM** **NEENA** **ZAC** **GABY**

USEFUL PHRASES

A Match the beginnings (1–7) and the endings (a–g) of the useful phrases.

1	That's	a	sorry.	___
2	OK	b	one then.	___
3	I'm	c	it?	___
4	It makes me	d	go!	___
5	OK. Not that	e	Let's add it to the playlist.	___
6	My	f	then.	___
7	Finally!	g	feel sad.	___

B ▶ Watch the video again. Check your answers to Exercise A. Who says it? Write G (Gaby), N (Neena) or Z (Zac) next to each useful phrase.

PRONUNCIATION
Stress and intonation

A Listen and repeat. Copy the stress and intonation.
6.8

B Work in pairs. Student A – name a song, a singer or a band. Student B – give your opinion. Take turns.

A: Ed Sheeran.
B: He's OK. How about Haim?
A: I love them!

SPEAKING

A **PREPARE** Imagine you are going on a road trip. Make a list of your five favourite songs.

B **SPEAK** Work in small groups. Agree on a playlist of ten songs for your road trip. Use phrases from the Functional language section to help you.

C **PRESENT** Work in pairs. Compare your playlist. Do you like the same music?

◯− Ask for and give opinions
▶ Turn to page 165 to learn how to write a review of an event

THAT'S ENTERTAINMENT 59

Unit 6 Review

GRAMMAR

A Write sentences about what Kyle likes and dislikes.

love   like   don't like   hate

1 play football ❤   _Kyle loves playing football._
2 dance ☹ _____
3 go clothes shopping ☹ _____
4 Wes Anderson films ☺ _____
5 watch basketball ☺ _____
6 listen to jazz music ☹ _____
7 play video games ❤ _____
8 Japanese food ☹ _____

B Complete the conversation with *was*, *were*, *wasn't* or *weren't*.

A: [1] ____*Were*____ you at home last night?

B: No, I [2] _____. I [3] _____ at a comedy show.

A: Where [4] _____ your flatmates?

B: They [5] _____ out, too.

A: [6] _____ they at the concert?

B: No, they [7] _____.

C Complete the text with the past simple form of the verbs in brackets.

In 2016, Elvis Presley [1] _____*was*_____ (be) on the Forbes list of highest-paid dead entertainers. He [2] _____ (earn) $27 million! Other musicians on the list [3] _____ (include) Prince and David Bowie, who both [4] _____ (die) in 2016. David Bowie [5] _____ (make) his last album *Blackstar* in 2016. He [6] _____ (get) $10.5 million. Prince [7] _____ (sell) more than 2.5 million albums last year.

VOCABULARY

A Complete the conversation with the words in the box.

concert   exhibition   festival   film   play

Luis: Do you like Picasso? There's an [1] _____ of his paintings.

Manu: I don't like looking at paintings.

Luis: OK. Well, how about going to see a [2] _____ at the cinema?

Manu: Hmm. I'm not sure.

Luis: There's a [3] _____ at the theatre.

Manu: That's boring. I want to listen to some music. There's a rock [4] _____ on tonight.

Luis: But I hate rock music.

Manu: Oh, right. There's a jazz music [5] _____ this weekend. It's in the park. It starts at 2 pm.

B Complete the sentences with *in*, *last*, *ago* and *yesterday*.

1 I went to my first concert ____*in*____ 2010.
2 We saw that band two weeks _____.
3 The exhibition opened _____.
4 I met my best friend _____ year.
5 The first 3D films were _____ the 1920s.
6 I went to the cinema _____ afternoon.

C Complete the sentences with the verbs in the box.

became   got   had   moved started   studied   was   went

1 My grandmother _____ born in 1959.
2 I _____ an English teacher in 2015.
3 My parents _____ married on a beach in Hawaii.
4 My brother _____ to Oxford University to study law.
5 Sarah _____ a baby a few months ago.
6 My sister _____ house last summer.
7 Beth _____ her new job two days ago.
8 I _____ history at university.

D SPEAK Work in pairs. Tell your partner about five important events in your life.

A: *A really important event in my life was getting married. I got married in 2016. It was sunny. I was very happy. What about you?*

B: *That sounds amazing! An important event in my life was starting university. I met lots of interesting people on my first day.*

FUNCTIONAL LANGUAGE

A Choose the correct words to complete the sentences.

1 What do you *think* / *know* about the singer Katy Perry? I think she's great.
2 Listen to this! I *think* / *sure* Foals are great.
3 How *about* / *think* you?
4 I'm not *sure* / *know* about that.
5 I *love* / *loving* them!
6 I really *awful* / *hate* them!
7 This exhibition is boring. It isn't *great* / *sure*.

B SPEAK Work in pairs. Take turns to ask and answer about these things. Use the sentences in Exercise A to help you.

- a band you like / don't like
- a famous singer
- a famous film
- a film you like

A: *I love the new Jennifer Lawrence film.*

B: *Me too! She's a great actress.*

60   THAT'S ENTERTAINMENT

7 TRAVEL AND TRANSPORT

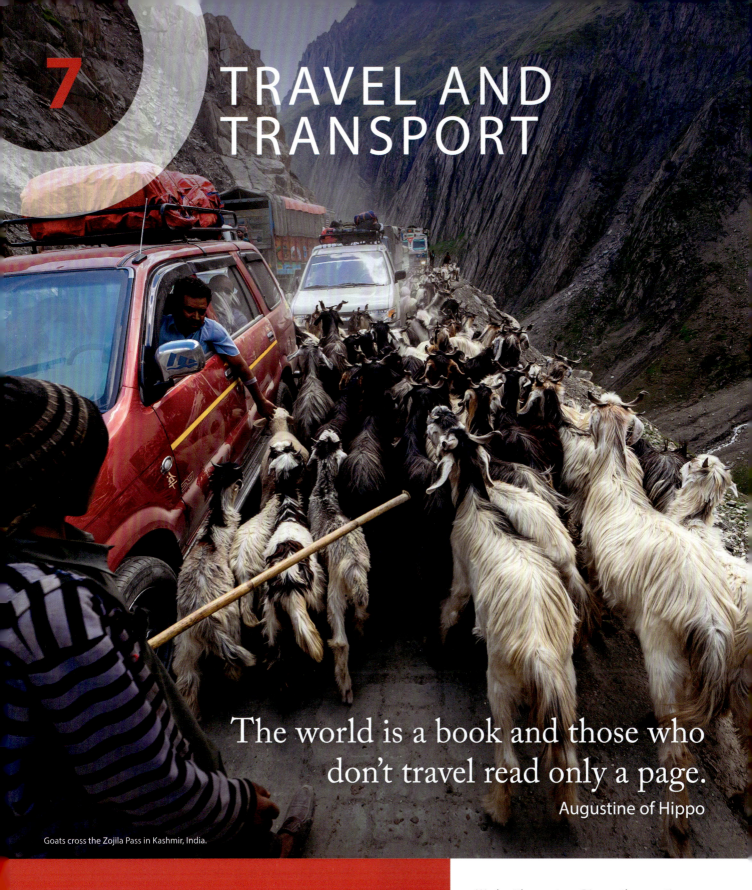

The world is a book and those who don't travel read only a page.

Augustine of Hippo

Goats cross the Zojila Pass in Kashmir, India.

OBJECTIVES

- talk about transport in a city
- talk about a journey
- talk about a holiday
- check in and out of a hotel
- write a short article about a travel experience

Work with a partner. Discuss the questions.

1 Where did you go on holiday last year?
2 Look at the picture. Would you like to drive here? Why/Why not?
3 Which countries would you like to visit?

TRAVEL AND TRANSPORT 61

7.1 Getting around — Talk about transport in a city

V transport   **P** /eɪ/ and /əʊ/   **G** could

VOCABULARY
Transport

A Look at the pictures in *Where in the world are they?* What types of transport can you see? What other types of transport can you think of?

B Go to the **Vocabulary Hub** on **page 149**.

C SPEAK Work in pairs. Think about a time you were in a different country or city. Answer the questions.
1 What types of transport did you use?
2 Were they difficult to use? Why?
3 Were they cheap or expensive?

When I was in Vietnam last year, I took a motorbike taxi. It was cheap and easy to organise.

PRONUNCIATION
/eɪ/ and /əʊ/

A Listen and repeat the transport words in the box.
7.1
| boat   coach   motorbike   plane   train |

B Listen to the vowel sound /əʊ/ in boat. Then underline
7.2 the words in the box in Exercise A that have the same vowel sound. What letters can make the /əʊ/ sound?

C Listen to the vowel sound /eɪ/ in plane. Then circle the
7.3 words in the box in Exercise A that have the same vowel sound. What letters can make the /eɪ/ sound?

D SPEAK Work in pairs. Practise saying the transport words. Listen and check your partner's pronunciation. Be careful to pronounce the words correctly.

READING

A READ FOR GIST Read *Where in the world are they?* What is it about?
1 buildings   2 countries   3 transport

B SPEAK Work in pairs. Complete the quiz.

C SCAN Read *Six quick facts*. Match facts (a–f) with pictures (1–6) in the quiz.

D READ FOR DETAIL Read *Six quick facts* again. Answer the questions.
1 How old are the buses in Mumbai?
   _____
2 How many San Francisco trams are there today?
   _____
3 How many underground stations are there in Moscow?
   _____
4 What two types of transport can you take from Amsterdam station? _____
5 Where does the Star Ferry go between?
   _____
6 What are three popular types of transport in Hanoi?
   _____

E SPEAK Work in pairs. Think about the cities in the quiz. Which do you think are difficult to travel around? Why?

A: *I think it's easy to travel around Hong Kong. It's quite a small place. What do you think?*
B: *Yes, I agree.*

Where in the world are they?

Do you know what colour the taxis are in New York? And which Italian city has no cars? If you answered *yellow* and *Venice*, do our quiz!

Look at the pictures 1–6. Where are they? Choose a, b, or c.

1 a Mumbai   b Hong Kong   c London
2 a Lisbon   b San Francisco c Mexico City
3 a Hanoi   b Bangkok   c Manila
4 a Budapest   b Moscow   c Kiev
5 a Shanghai   b Sydney   c Hong Kong
6 a Berlin   b Amsterdam   c Rio de Janeiro

Answers: 1 a, 2 b, 3 a, 4 b, 5 c, 6 b

62 TRAVEL AND TRANSPORT

7.1

GRAMMAR
could

A WORK IT OUT Scan *Six quick facts* again. <u>Underline</u> sentences with *could* or *couldn't*.

B Look at the sentences you underlined in Exercise A and complete the rules.

could
1 We use *could* to talk about abilities in the *past / present*.
2 We use *could* **before** / *after* the main verb.
3 We use the infinitive **with** / *without to* after *could*.
4 The *negative / future* form of *could* is *couldn't*.

C Go to the Grammar Hub on page 134.

D SPEAK Work in pairs. Tell your partner some things you *could* and *couldn't* do or see five or ten years ago.

A: Five years ago, I couldn't drive a car.
B: Ten years ago, you could see a lot of bicycles in my town.

SPEAKING

A PREPARE Think about the transport in a city you know well.

B Write some questions to ask your partner about the transport in their city. Use the ideas below to help you.
1 what / colour / buses? *What colour are the buses?*
2 is / river? _____
3 is / ferry? _____
4 where / ferry / go / between? _____
5 how many / train stations? _____
6 are / many / traffic jams? _____
7 bicycles / popular? _____

C SPEAK Work in pairs. Ask questions and guess your partner's city. Then answer questions about your city.

A: What colour are the taxis?
B: They're yellow.
A: Is there a ferry?
B: Yes, there is.
A: Where does the ferry go between?
B: The main ferry goes between Queens and Manhattan.

Six quick facts

a ___ Scooters and motorbikes are the most common type of transport in Hanoi, Vietnam. There are also lots of bicycles. Twenty years ago, you couldn't see so many scooters and motorbikes on Hanoi's streets, but you could see a lot of bicycles.

b ___ Every day, 250,000 people go through Amsterdam Central Station. It's the city's main train and bus station.

c ___ The famous Star Ferry in Hong Kong carries over 70,000 passengers a day between Hong Kong Island and Kowloon. That's 26 million passengers a year!

d ___ No, this isn't London – it's Mumbai! These Indian buses are 80 years old. The design and colour is the same as London buses.

e ___ Take a tram in San Francisco for a traditional experience. But there aren't many these days. One hundred years ago, you could see hundreds of trams in San Francisco. Today, there are only about 40.

f ___ Opened in 1935, there are now 206 underground stations in Moscow. Many of the stations are very beautiful. Each one is like an art gallery.

Talk about transport in a city

7.2 A love of adventure — Talk about a journey

 past simple negative  travel phrases 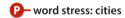 word stress: cities

READING

A Work in pairs. Look at the routes around the world. Which route would you take? Why?

B READ FOR GIST Read *The Nellie Bly route*. Which route in Exercise A matches the one Nellie Bly took?

TRADITIONAL TRAVEL ADVENTURES

We travel the traditional way: by boat, train and bus.
Route 1: London, Reykjavík, St Petersburg, Tokyo, Sydney, Cape Town, Rio de Janeiro
Route 2: New York, London, Paris, Brindisi, Port Said, Singapore, Hong Kong, Tokyo, San Francisco
Route 3: Miami, Cancún, Lima, Melbourne, Nairobi, Munich

SPECIAL OFFER! This week, choose our Nellie Bly Adventure and get 30 per cent off your holiday.

THE NELLIE BLY ROUTE

In 1872, Jules Verne wrote about Phileas Fogg, an adventurer who travelled around the world in 80 days. But Fogg wasn't a real person, and nobody knew if this was actually possible.

In 1889, Nellie Bly, a 25-year-old American journalist, followed Phileas Fogg's route around the world. She went alone. She didn't take much luggage. She just took a large coat and a small suitcase. Her newspaper, the *New York World*, paid for her trip and told her story.

But a magazine, *Cosmopolitan*, sent their journalist, Elizabeth Bisland, to race against Nellie. Bisland left New York on the same day, but Nellie didn't know about it!

Car and plane travel didn't exist at the time, so Nellie travelled by bus, train and ship. She had many adventures, just like Phileas Fogg, and she sent her stories back home from every place.

Nellie crossed the Atlantic to London by ship. From there she travelled by train and ferry to northern France, where she met Jules Verne. She then continued by train to Brindisi, in Italy, where she took a ship to Egypt. She visited Port Said, in Egypt, where she rode on a donkey. Her ship then went to Singapore (where she bought a monkey), Hong Kong and Tokyo. Finally, the ship crossed the Pacific Ocean to San Francisco, where she took the train to New York. This took four days. She arrived in New York 72 days after her journey began. It was a new world record! Her story was in the newspapers.

And Elizabeth Bisland? She didn't join the celebrations. She missed her boat and returned to New York four days later.

Glossary

adventurer (n) someone who goes to exciting, unusual and sometimes dangerous places
route (n) a way that buses, trains, ships or planes travel regularly

TRAVEL AND TRANSPORT

7.2

C READ FOR DETAIL Read the article again. Number the pictures in the order they are written about.

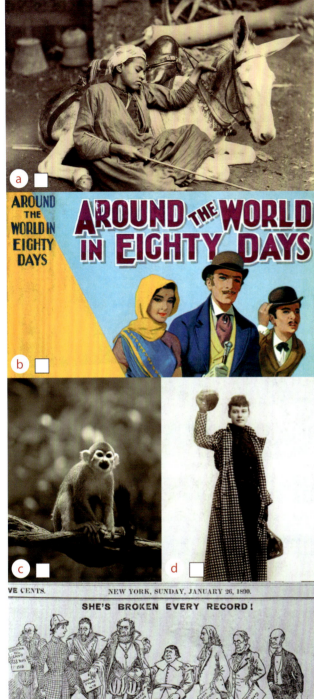

D READ FOR SPECIFIC INFORMATION Read the article again. Write down how Nellie travelled at each stage.

1 New York to London by _____ *ship*
2 London to France by _____
3 Tokyo to San Francisco by _____
4 San Francisco to New York by _____

E SPEAK Work in pairs. Answer the questions.

1 Do you know any of the places Nellie visited?
2 Do you know about any other famous journeys?

GRAMMAR
Past simple negative

A WORK IT OUT Complete the sentences with words from the text.

1 She _____ much luggage.
2 Nellie _____ about it.
3 Car and plane travel _____ at the time.
4 She _____ the celebrations.

B Read the sentences in Exercise A. Choose the correct options to complete the rule.

Past simple negative
To make the past simple negative we use *did / didn't* + infinitive *with to / without to*.

C Go to the **Grammar Hub** on **page 134**.

D SPEAK Work in pairs. Which forms of transport did you use last year? Which didn't you use?

VOCABULARY
Travel phrases

A Complete the definitions with the words in the box.

arrive   leave   miss   return   take

1 _____ (v) to be too late for a train, bus, etc
2 _____ (v) to use a particular type of transport
3 _____ (v) to go somewhere and come back
4 _____ (v) to go away from a place
5 _____ (v) to get to a place

B Go to the **Vocabulary Hub** on **page 149**.

PRONUNCIATION
Word stress: cities

A Listen and repeat the cities. Copy the word stress.
7.4

B Work in pairs. Add the cities in the box to the table. Then listen, check and repeat.
7.5

~~Ankara~~   Berlin   ~~Cairo~~   Dubai   London   Miami
Nairobi   Paris   Reykjavík   Singapore   Tokyo

●●	●●	●●●	●●●	●●●
Cairo			Ankara	

SPEAKING

SPEAK Work in pairs. Go to the **Communication Hub** on **page 155**.

◯ Talk about a journey

TRAVEL AND TRANSPORT 65

7.3 A trip to remember

Talk about a holiday

G— past simple questions P— connected speech V— verb phrases S— guessing the meaning of unknown words

LISTENING

A Work in pairs. Look at the pictures. What country do you think it is? Why?

B LISTEN FOR GIST Listen to Emma talking to a colleague about a trip. What was unusual about it?

C LISTEN FOR DETAIL Listen to the conversation again. Tick (✓) the things Emma did.

1 She decided to go to China. ☐
2 She went to Beijing. ☐
3 She saw pandas. ☐
4 She went sightseeing. ☐
5 She stayed with friends. ☐
6 She visited the Great Wall. ☐

D Listen to part of the conversation from Exercise B. Choose the correct meaning of the words. Use the information in the box to help you.

> **Guessing the meaning of unknown words**
> - When you don't know a word, listen for other words that you do know to help you understand.
> - Think about: *What is the main idea? What is before and after the word that I don't understand?*

1 budget
   a the amount of money a person has
   b the amount of time a person has
2 destination
   a the place where someone is going
   b the place where someone is
3 surprise
   a something that we don't know about
   b something that we do know about

E SPEAK Work in pairs. Would you like to go on a mystery holiday? Why/Why not?

GRAMMAR
Past simple questions

A WORK IT OUT Look at the past simple questions from the conversation. Then choose the correct words to complete the rules.

Where did you go?
Did you visit the Great Wall?
Did you know the holiday was in China?

> **Past simple questions**
> 1 To make *Yes/No* questions in the past simple we use *do / did* + subject + infinitive **with to / without to**.
> 2 To make *Wh-* questions in the past simple we use question word + *do / did* + subject + infinitive **with to / without to**.

B Go to the **Grammar Hub** on **page 134**.

C PRACTISE Reorder the words to write past simple questions.

1 to / Emma / China / did / fly / ?
   _____*Did Emma fly to China?*_____
2 a lot of / visit / she / cities / did / ?
   _____
3 she / on / boat / a / sleep / did / ?
   _____
4 do / she / did / Beijing / what / in / ?
   _____
5 go on / mystery / holiday / a / did / she / why / ?
   _____

D SPEAK Work in pairs. Ask and answer the questions in Exercise C.

66 TRAVEL AND TRANSPORT

PRONUNCIATION
Connected speech

A Listen to the sentences. What do you notice about them?
1 Where did you go?   2 Did she stay in a hotel?
3 She went to a temple.

B Listen and repeat the sentences. Mark the links between the words.
1 Did Emma see a panda?
2 Did she stay with a family?
3 She visited a lot of cities.
4 Did she have a good time?

VOCABULARY
Verb phrases

A SPEAK Work in pairs. What do you think makes a great holiday?

B READ Read the three travel stories. Answer the questions.
1 What did TravelBob do every day in Ibiza?
2 What happened to Kate956 one evening in New York?
3 Where did LisaChorley lose her camera?

Kate956
7 January, 1.36

Last year, my husband and I went to New York. We **visited museums** and we **went shopping**. But New York is really big, and one night we **got lost**. After an hour, we were tired, so we stopped at a nice, small restaurant. We **ate some delicious food**, and then got a taxi back to our hotel!

LisaChorley
7 January, 1.41

Three years ago, I went to Thailand. I travelled around for two months, and I **met some really nice people**. In Bangkok, I went sightseeing and **took a lot of pictures**. But I **lost my camera**! I was really sad, but two days later a man brought it back. He saw a picture of me and my hotel!

C READ Read the comments again. Use the words in the box to create verb phrases.

| eat | get | go | have | lose |
| meet | read | swim | take | visit |

1 _____ in the sea
2 _____ shopping
3 _____ museums
4 _____ pictures
5 _____ people
6 _____ a book
7 _____ lost
8 _____ food
9 _____ a good time
10 _____ your camera

D SPEAK Work in pairs. Go to the **Communication Hub** on **page 155**.

SPEAKING HUB

A PREPARE Think of a holiday you went on where something unusual or funny happened. Make notes about the holiday using the ideas below.

- accommodation
- people
- place
- the ending
- the problem or a funny situation
- transport

B DISCUSS Work in pairs. Ask and answer questions about your holidays using the prompts.
1 Where / go?   3 Where / stay?
2 How / travel / there?   4 What / happen?

(Where did you go?)

(I went to Moscow.)

C DISCUSS Work in groups. Tell your group about your partner's holiday. Have a group vote on the most unusual or funny holiday.

TravelBob
7 January, 1.25

One spring, I went to Ibiza with my family. The hotel was really nice, and we **swam in the sea** every day. But on the last day of our holiday, we lost our passports and we couldn't fly home! We stayed for ten more days. We didn't have any money, but we **read a lot of books**! We **had a great time**.

Talk about a holiday

Café Hub

7.4 New York
- check in and out of a hotel
- intonation in questions

COMPREHENSION

A ▶ 00:00–00:42 Work in pairs. Watch the first part of the video. Answer the questions.

1. Where did Sam and Zac meet?
2. What did Zac hate?
3. Why do you think he hated it?

B ▶ 00:42–04:38 Watch the second part of the video. Look at the hotel manager's checklist. Tick (✓) the things Zac does. Cross (✗) the things Zac doesn't do.

NEW HOTEL RECEPTIONIST

1. Greet guests correctly. ☐
2. Check guests' identity. ☐
3. Give correct information: breakfast time/price. ☐
4. Offer to help with bags. ☐
5. Check guests' room number and print out the bill. ☐

USEFUL PHRASES

A ▶ Complete the useful phrases with the words in the box. Then watch the video again and check your answers.

| can | it | look | mean | new | nice | things | what |

1. Hey guys. How are _____?
2. Hi! How's _____ going?
3. I _____, good afternoon, sir!
4. I'm so sorry, sir. He's _____.
5. So, _____ happened next?
6. OK, _____ – it's fine!
7. You _____ call me Sam.
8. Have a _____ day!

B How do you say these useful phrases in your language?

FUNCTIONAL LANGUAGE
Checking in and out of a hotel

SPEAK Work in pairs. Practise the conversation. Change the words and phrases in **bold**. Use the words in the box to help you. Change numbers, times and prices, too.

| dinner | double | evening | identity card |
| madam | would you like |

Receptionist: Good **afternoon**, **sir**. How can I help you?
Guest: I have a reservation for a **single** room for **two** nights.
Receptionist: Could I have your **passport**, please?
Guest: No problem. Is **breakfast** included?
Receptionist: No, it isn't. Sorry. **Breakfast** is an extra **$14**.
Guest: What time is **breakfast**?
Receptionist: **Breakfast** is served from **7** till **11 am**.
Receptionist: **Do you need** help with your bags?
Guest: Great. Thanks.
Guest: Can I have my bill please?
Receptionist: Certainly, **Mr King**. Which room was it?
Guest: Room **305**.

68 TRAVEL AND TRANSPORT

MILLY SAM NEENA ZAC GABY

PRONUNCIATION
Intonation in questions

A Listen and repeat the questions. Does the intonation go up or down at the end? Draw ↑ if the intonation goes up. Draw ↓ if the intonation goes down.

1 How can I help you? ____
2 What's your name, please? ____
3 Could I have your passport, please? ____
4 Is breakfast included? ____
5 What time is breakfast? ____
6 Do you need help with your bags? ____

B Listen again. <u>Underline</u> the words and syllables that are stressed in Exercise A.

C SPEAK Work in pairs. Practise asking the questions in Exercise A. Remember to use the correct stress and intonation.

SPEAKING

A PREPARE Work in pairs. Write a hotel check-in conversation. Use the information below. Use some of the phrases in Functional Language.

Guest

Ask about:
- Reservation for two adults and two children
- Wi-fi
- TV
- Cost of breakfast for you and children
- Restaurant opening times
- Check-out time

Receptionist

Give information about:
- Family room with one double and two single beds
- Free wi-fi 24/7
- All rooms have a TV
- Free breakfast for children
- Breakfast: £8.99 / 7 am to 11 am
- Dinner: £24.99 / 5 pm to 11 pm
- Check-out: midday

B PRESENT Practise your conversation. Perform it for the rest of the class.

○— **Check in and out of a hotel**

▶ Turn to **page 166** to learn how to write a short article about a travel experience.

Unit 7 Review

GRAMMAR

A Choose the correct words to complete the sentences.

1 Ten years ago, you **take could** / **could take** a ferry to the island from here.
2 You can't use the tram in my town these days, but you **can** / **could** 50 years ago.
3 Before 2010, we **couldn't** / **not could** use the underground in my city.
4 When I had a scooter, I could **got** / **get** to school in 15 minutes.
5 **I could** / **Could I** ride a bicycle when I was six years old. How about you?
6 When we went to Venice, we **couldn't saw** / **couldn't see** any cars.
7 I couldn't **swim** / **swam** until I was ten years old.
8 When I was younger I **could** / **couldn't** run really fast, but I can't now!

B Complete the sentences with negative past simple form of the verbs in brackets.

1 We ___didn't travel___ (travel) to Thailand.
2 They _____ (fly) to Osaka.
3 He _____ (take) the bus to Prague.
4 The people _____ (be) friendly.
5 She _____ (stay) in a hotel.
6 I _____ (have) a good time.
7 I _____ (have) time to visit the Statue of Liberty.
8 She _____ (be) on the same flight as me.

C Use the prompts to write past simple questions.

1 you / go on holiday / last year?
   ___Did you go on holiday last year?___
2 where / you / go?
   _____
3 how / you / get there?
   _____
4 where / you / stay?
   _____
5 you / go / with friends?
   _____
6 you / do?
   _____

D Think about your last holiday. Write short answers to the questions in Exercise C.

E SPEAK Work in pairs. Ask and answer questions about your last holiday.

A: *Where did you go?*
B: *I went to Sweden. Where did you go?*

VOCABULARY

A Label the pictures (1–4) with the words in the box.

coach   ferry   scooter   tram

1 _____   2 _____

3 _____   4 _____

B Choose the correct verbs to complete the text.

We ¹**left** / **missed** New York City early in the morning and ²**arrived** / **left** in Bogotá five hours later. We ³**took** / **left** the train to the centre. We stayed in Bogotá for two weeks. On the way home, we ⁴**missed** / **arrived** the train to the airport, so we ⁵**left** / **took** a taxi instead. We then ⁶**took** / **returned** a plane to Philadelphia.

C SPEAK Work in pairs. Tell your partner about the type of transport you take every day. Then talk about the type of transport you took on your last holiday.

D Complete the phrases with an appropriate verb.

1 ___ ___ ___ lost
2 ___ ___ ___ pictures
3 ___ ___ ___ people
4 ___ ___ ___ in the sea
5 ___ ___ ___ a good time
6 ___ ___ ___ museums
7 ___ ___ ___ your camera

FUNCTIONAL LANGUAGE

Complete the conversation with the words in the box.

346   bill (x2)   minibar   room   stay   taxi

Fumi: Hello. Can I have my ¹_____, please?
Receptionist: Good morning, sir. Which ²_____ was it?
Fumi: Room ³_____.
Receptionist: Did you have anything from the ⁴_____?
Fumi: No, I didn't have anything.
Receptionist: Here you are. Here's your ⁵_____. Did you enjoy your ⁶_____?
Fumi: Yes, very much, thank you.
Receptionist: That's good. Do you need a ⁷_____?

8 FOOD AND DRINK

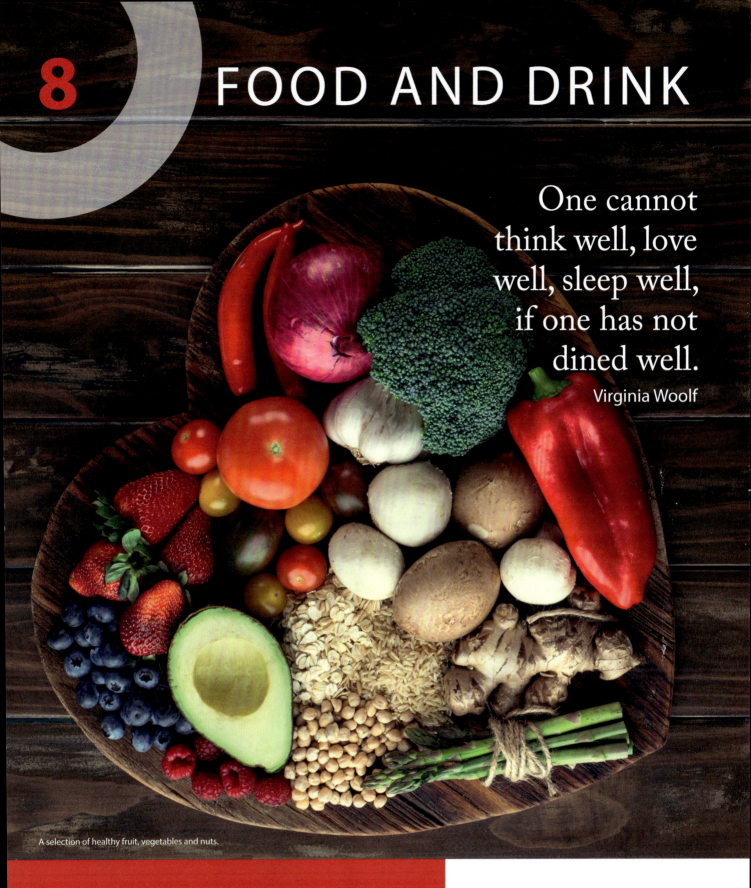

> One cannot think well, love well, sleep well, if one has not dined well.
> Virginia Woolf

A selection of healthy fruit, vegetables and nuts.

OBJECTIVES

- talk about the food you eat
- talk about the food your family eats
- talk about ingredients and recipes
- order food in a restaurant
- write an online restaurant review

Work with a partner. Discuss the questions.

1. What's your favourite food?
2. Do you prefer eating at home or going to restaurants? Why?
3. Are you good at cooking?

FOOD AND DRINK 71

8.1 I'm hungry!

Talk about the food you eat

V — food and drink   G — countable and uncountable nouns; *some* and *any*   P — plurals

VOCABULARY
Food and drink

A SPEAK Work in pairs. Discuss the questions.
1. What's your favourite food?
2. What food do you have in your fridge at home?

B Go to the Vocabulary Hub on page 150.

C SPEAK Work in groups. What kind of food is popular in your country?

GRAMMAR
Countable and uncountable nouns

A WORK IT OUT Read the conversation. Look at the nouns in bold. Which nouns are plural?

Waitress: Hi! What can I get you?
Customer: Hey. I'd like two **eggs**, a **tomato** and some **mushrooms**, please.
Waitress: OK. Anything to drink?
Customer: Er … yes. Some **coffee**, please.

B Complete the rules.

Countable and uncountable nouns
1 We *can* / *can't* count countable nouns (e.g. eggs, tomatoes, etc).
2 We *can* / *can't* count uncountable nouns (e.g. coffee, pasta, etc).

C Complete the table with the words in the box.

apples   bread   butter   a carrot   chicken   ~~coffee~~   ~~eggs~~
mushrooms   an onion   an orange   prawns   ~~a tomato~~

Countable singular	Countable plural	Uncountable
a tomato	eggs	coffee

D Go to the Grammar Hub on page 136.

E SPEAK Work in pairs. Answer the questions.
1. How often do you drink tea or coffee?
2. How much fruit do you eat every day?
3. Are there any foods you didn't like when you were a child?

PRONUNCIATION
Plurals

A 8.1 Listen and repeat. Do we always pronounce plural nouns the same way?

ca**k**es, banan**a**s, orang**es**

B 8.2 Listen and complete the table with the words in the box.

apples   ~~bananas~~   beans   ~~cakes~~   carrots   crisps   eggs
mushrooms   ~~oranges~~   potatoes   prawns   sandwiches

/s/	/z/	/ɪz/
cakes	bananas	oranges

C 8.2 Listen again and repeat.

72 FOOD AND DRINK

8.1

LISTENING

 A LISTEN FOR GIST Listen to Marta and Stefan. What is
8.3 their conversation about?

 B LISTEN FOR DETAIL Listen again and circle M (Marta),
8.3 S (Stefan) or B (both).

Who …

1 can't eat pizza because they're on a diet?   M / S / B
2 ate the chicken yesterday?   M / S / B
3 doesn't want to eat vegetables for dinner?   M / S / B
4 thinks they have a healthy diet?   M / S / B
5 doesn't eat unhealthy food?   M / S / B

C SPEAK Work in pairs. Answer the questions.

1 Do you want to try Stefan's diet? Why/Why not?
2 Do you think you have a healthy diet? Why/Why not?

A: *I don't think I have a healthy diet. I eat a lot of fast food!*
B: *Really? I never eat fast food. I think I have quite a healthy diet.*

GRAMMAR
some and *any*

 A WORK IT OUT Listen to part of the
8.4 conversation between Marta and Stefan again.
Then complete the sentences with *some* or *any*.

1 Is there _____ chicken?
2 There isn't _____ chicken. I ate it yesterday.
3 We've got _____ mushrooms and _____ broccoli.
4 We haven't got _____ apples or bananas.

B Look at the sentences in Exercise A. Complete
the table with *some* and *any*.

some and *any*	
	countable and uncountable nouns
Positive +	1 _____
Negative -	2 _____
Questions ?	3 _____

Questions with *some*
When we make an offer or a request, we use *some* and not *any*.
Do you want some bread?
Would you like some water?

C SPEAK Work in pairs. Student A – go to the
Communication Hub on **page 156**. Student B –
go to the **Communication Hub** on **page 159**.

SPEAKING

A PREPARE Think about the food you eat. Read
the questions and make notes.

1 What do you normally eat for breakfast, lunch and dinner?
2 Which foods do you eat that are really unhealthy?
3 What did you eat for dinner last night?
4 Which do you prefer – cooking dinner or eating at restaurants? Why?

B SPEAK Work in pairs. Answer the questions
in Exercise A. Try to ask for more information if
possible.

A: *I ate pepperoni pizza for dinner last night.*
B: *Really? Did you cook it at home or go to a restaurant?*
A: *I went to a restaurant with my friend.*
B: *Which restaurant did you go to?*

○— **Talk about the food you eat**

FOOD AND DRINK 73

8.2 What we eat — Talk about the food your family eats

V – containers   **P** – short and long vowel sounds   **G** – much, many, a lot of

Let's eat Around the world

How many people are there in your family? How much food do you eat in a typical week? Do you eat more packaged food or fresh food? What's your favourite food? And how much do you spend on food each week? Here, we take a look at food habits in different countries.

Ecuador

In Ecuador, most families don't eat any packaged food at all. People usually buy fresh food in local markets and they eat a lot of fruit and vegetables, as well as rice and potatoes. People usually buy food every day to cook at home. Lunch is an important meal and most children go home for lunch in the afternoon. Families usually eat together.

Average cost of food per week: $30
Popular food: rice, potatoes, chicken

The USA

Most people in the USA eat a lot of packaged food. They don't eat a lot of fresh fruit and they don't eat many vegetables. Meat is very popular here, as well as dairy products, like milk and cheese. Most Americans go to a big supermarket once a week to buy food. There aren't many markets, but some towns have a farmer's market once a week. A lot of families regularly eat at restaurants or eat fast food in front of the TV or in the car.

Average cost of food per week: $400
Popular food: corn, chicken, hamburgers

Italy

Italy is famous for its food, and for most Italians, food is a very important part of their day! Markets are very popular, but most people buy their food at a supermarket. Most people buy fresh bread every day, and they use milk mainly with coffee. Italians don't eat much packaged food, but people often buy tins of tomatoes and beans. The main meal of the day is usually lunch.

Average cost of food per week: $200
Popular food: pasta, rice, fish, bread

Source
https://www.dosomething.org/us/facts/11-facts-about-american-eating-habits

READING

A PREPARE Answer the questions. Use the places in the box to help you. Make notes.

> in a market   in a supermarket   in local shops   online

1. Where do you buy fresh food? Why?
2. Where do you buy packaged food? Why?

B SPEAK Work in pairs. Look at the photos in *Let's eat - Around the world* and answer the questions.

1. What type of food can you see?
2. What kind of people can you see in the pictures?

C READ FOR GIST Read *Let's eat - Around the world* and check your answers to Exercise B.

D READ FOR DETAIL Read again and answer the questions.

1. Which meal is important in Ecuador?
2. Where do children in Ecuador have their lunch?
3. How often do most Italians buy bread?
4. In which country do people drink a lot of milk?
5. In which two countries do people eat packaged food?

E SPEAK Work in pairs. Answer the questions.

1. Why are the diets in Ecuador, Italy and the USA so different?
2. Which diets are healthy? Why?
3. Which diet in the article is like yours? Which of the food in the pictures do you eat every week?

FOOD AND DRINK

8.2

VOCABULARY
Containers

A Label containers (1–3) with the items in the box.

> a bag of rice   a bottle of fruit juice   a tin of tomatoes

1 _____
2 _____
3 _____

B Go to the Vocabulary Hub on page 150.

C SPEAK Work in pairs. What other types of food and drinks come in containers?

A: A carton of juice.
B: A can of lemonade.

PRONUNCIATION
Short and long vowel sounds

A Underline the vowels (*a, e, i, o, u*) in the words below. Then listen to the words. How is the vowel sound different?

8.5

1 fish   2 meat

B Listen and repeat the words. Are the vowel sounds long or short?

8.6

1 beef   long / short
2 tin   long / short
3 milk   long / short
4 eat   long / short
5 crisps   long / short

C Work in pairs. Discuss the questions.

1 How often do you eat crisps?
2 Do you eat a lot of fish?

GRAMMAR
much, many, a lot of

A Look at *Let's eat - Around the world* again. Find and underline the phrases with *much, many* and *a lot of*.

B WORK IT OUT Look at the phrases you underlined in Exercise A. Complete the table with *much, many* and *a lot of*.

much, many and *a lot of*	Countable nouns	Uncountable nouns
Positive +	She eats ¹ *a lot of* bananas.	He eats ² _____ pasta.
Negative -	She doesn't eat ³ _____ apples.	He doesn't drink ⁴ _____ coffee.
Questions ?	How ⁵ _____ biscuits are there?	How ⁶ _____ rice is there?

C Go to the Grammar Hub on page 136.

D PRACTISE Use the prompts to write questions with *How much* and *How many*.

1 bread / you / eat? *How much bread do you eat?*
2 tea / you / drink? _____
3 crisps / you / eat? _____
4 meat / you / eat? _____
5 rice / you / eat? _____

E SPEAK Work in pairs. Answer the questions in Exercise D.
I don't eat much bread, but I eat a lot of pasta.

SPEAKING

A PREPARE Write questions to ask your partner about these things:

- his/her family (people, ages)
  How many people are there in your family?
- cost of food per week
  How much do you spend on food each week?
- food shopping (where? how often? what?)
- fresh food (fruit and vegetables, dairy, meat and fish)
- packaged food

B SPEAK Work in pairs. Ask your partner about the food they eat each week. Make notes.

C ORGANISE Write a paragraph about your partner.

D PRESENT Tell the rest of the class about your partner. Do people eat similar or different food?

◯— Talk about the food your family eats

FOOD AND DRINK   75

8.3 Yes, chef! — Talk about ingredients and recipes

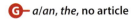 G— a/an, the, no article 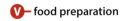 V— food preparation 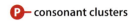 P— consonant clusters   S— decoding

READING

A Work in pairs. Are the following sentences true for you?
1. I cook dinner every night.
2. I love making unusual dishes.
3. I buy a lot of food online.

B READ FOR GIST Read the advert by *Homecook*. Which sentence best describes it?
1. It's a survey about people's cooking habits.
2. It's an advertisement about a food business.
3. It's a description of a cookery school.

C READ FOR DETAIL Read the advert again. Are these sentences true (T), false (F) or not given (NG)? Correct the false sentences.

1. *Homecook* delivers ready cooked meals to your home.   T / F / NG
2. Customers can order a box for between two and four people.   T / F / NG
3. Both Carlo and Frankie, who started the business, are Australian.   T / F / NG
4. The business gets bigger every year and now has over 100 staff.   T / F / NG
5. Customers can order a maximum of 12 meals a week.   T / F / NG
6. According to one customer, they now spend less on food with *Homecook*.   T / F / NG

D Work in pairs. Look at the words in bold in the *Homecook* advert. What part of speech are they – nouns, adjectives or verbs?

E Complete the definitions with the words in Exercise D. Use the information in the box to help you.

> **Decoding**
> Noun, adjective, verb and adverb are all parts of speech. Thinking about parts of speech helps you work out the meaning of words.

1. _____ sweet food after main meal
2. _____ cooking instructions
3. _____ one of the foods you use to make a particular meal
4. _____ to take things like letters and goods to a place
5. _____ extremely tasty or enjoyable

F SPEAK Work in pairs. Answer the questions.
1. Where do you buy fresh ingredients from?
2. Would you use *Homecook* to get fresh ingredients? Why/Why not?

Thanks for trying Homecook

Our promise
With *Homecook*, you can cook quick, **delicious** meals at home with tasty ingredients.

Our offer
We offer boxes of fresh **ingredients** for a main course for two, three or four people. You can also order starters and **desserts**. Each box comes with a recipe. Follow the recipe to create a delicious meal.

Our story
Friends Carlo Vallone and Frankie Benn started *Homecook* in 2014 in Frankie's home city of Melbourne, Australia. Carlo, from Naples, is a chef and Frankie's speciality is business.

> We started *Homecook* because we wanted to offer fresh ingredients which are ready to cook. And we did it. Last year we **delivered** over a million boxes!

How does *Homecook* work?
WE deliver thousands of boxes to homes around the country every week.
YOU choose from 12 delicious, healthy recipes each week.
WE deliver fresh ingredients and **recipe** cards for each meal you choose.
YOU cook, serve and eat!

> "The ingredients are really good quality. We save money on our food shopping now. We're really excited when the box arrives each week."
> Leanne, Geelong

GRAMMAR
a/an, *the*, no article

A WORK IT OUT Read the sentences from the *Homecook* advert. Match sentences (1–3) to rules (a–c).
1. Friends Carlo Vallone and Frankie Benn started Homecook in 2014 in Frankie's home city of Melbourne, Australia.
2. Each box comes with a recipe. Follow the recipe to create a delicious meal.
3. We deliver thousands of boxes to homes around the country every week.

> **a/an, the, no article**
> a ___ We use *a/an* the first time we talk about something. Then we use *the* to talk about it again.
> b ___ We usually use no article in front of names, places, companies and cities.
> c ___ We use *the* when there is only one or it is clear what is being talked about.

B Go to the **Grammar Hub** on **page 136**.

76 FOOD AND DRINK

8.3

VOCABULARY
Food preparation

 A Listen to Carlo's recipe for hash browns and number the instructions 1–7.

Hash browns
Ingredients:
4 large potatoes
1 white onion
1 egg
salt and pepper
vegetable oil

Instructions:

_1_ **Grate** the potatoes and squeeze out the water.

____ **Peel** and **chop** an onion.

____ **Fry** for 2–3 minutes on each side, or until crispy.

____ **Put** one tablespoon of vegetable oil in a frying pan. When it's hot, put spoonfuls of the mixture into the pan. Make them flat.

____ **Crack** an egg into a bowl and **beat** it.

____ **Serve**!

____ **Add** the potato, onion, salt and pepper to the egg and **mix** them together.

B Match the instructions (1–7) in Exercise A with the pictures (a–g).

a ____   b ____   c ____

d ____   e ____

PRONUNCIATION
Consonant clusters

A Consonant clusters are groups of two or more consonant sounds. <u>Underline</u> the consonant clusters in these words.

1 bowl   3 mushroom   5 prawn
2 crisps   4 fridge   6 snack

 B Listen and repeat the words in Exercise A.

SPEAKING HUB

A PLAN Work in pairs. Make a list of five meals which you can cook.

B PREPARE Choose one of the meals from Exercise A. List the ingredients and write a simple recipe for it.

C PRESENT Read your recipe to the class.

D DISCUSS Work in pairs. Which meals would you like to make? Which wouldn't you like to make? Why?

f ____   g ____

C SPEAK Work in pairs. What are your favourite dishes? Do you know how to cook them? Tell your partner.

A: *I love pasta. I make it all the time.*
B: *Me too. I make a sauce with fresh tomatoes. You chop the tomatoes and fry them in olive oil with some garlic.*

○─ Talk about ingredients and recipes

FOOD AND DRINK 77

Café Hub

8.4 More cheese
F— order food in a restaurant   P— stress and intonation

COMPREHENSION

A ▶ Watch the video. Complete the sentences with *Sam* or *Zac*.

1 _____ wanted to cook dinner.
2 _____ suggests they go out.
3 _____ orders chicken and rice.
4 _____ orders pasta and a large bottle of water.
5 _____ has a dessert.
6 _____ thinks _____ is strange.

B Test your memory! Tick (✓) the ten items of food you can see in the video.

C ▶ SPEAK Work in pairs. Compare your answers to Exercise B. Then watch the video again and check your answers.

A: Was there any bread?
B: Yes, I think so. Were there any bananas?

FUNCTIONAL LANGUAGE
Ordering food in a restaurant

A Complete the conversations. Write *have*, *like* or the correct form of *be*.

Zac: Hi. A table for two please.
Waiter: Do you ¹_____ a reservation?
Sam: I ²_____ afraid not. Could we ³_____ a table over there, please?
Waiter: That ⁴_____ fine, please come this way.

Waiter: ⁵_____ you ready to order?
Sam: Yes, I think we ⁶_____.
I'll ⁷_____ the chicken and rice, please. And a side salad.
Waiter: OK, one chicken, one side salad.
Zac: I'll ⁸_____ the steak and fries, please.
Waiter: OK, one steak.
Zac: No wait. Sorry. I'll ⁹_____ the pasta.
Waiter: Sure, one pasta. Would you ¹⁰_____ something to drink?
Sam: Water, please.
Zac: Can we ¹¹_____ a large bottle of water?
Waiter: No problem.
Sam: Thanks.

Waiter: Would you ¹²_____ to see the dessert menu?
Sam: I ¹³_____ OK, thanks.

Sam: Can we ¹⁴_____ the bill, please?
Waiter: Of course.

B ▶ Watch the video again and check your answers.

C SPEAK Work in pairs. Practise the conversation.

78 FOOD AND DRINK

MILLY   SAM   NEENA   ZAC   GABY

PRONUNCIATION
Stress and intonation

A ▶ 01:38–02:10 Watch the scene in the restaurant again. Notice the word stress and intonation.

Waiter: Are you ready to <u>or</u>der?
Sam: <u>Yes</u>, I <u>think</u> we are. I'd like the <u>chick</u>en and <u>rice</u>, please. And a <u>side salad</u>.
Waiter: OK, one <u>chick</u>en, one <u>side sal</u>ad.
Zac: I'll have the <u>steak</u> and <u>fries</u>, please.
Waiter: OK, <u>one steak</u>.
Zac: No <u>wait</u>. <u>Sorry</u>. I'll have the <u>pas</u>ta.

B ▶ 01:38–02:10 Watch again and repeat the conversation. Copy the stress and intonation.

C SPEAK Work in pairs. Practise the conversation in Exercise A. Remember to use the correct stress and intonation.

MENU

MAIN COURSES

Chicken and rice
Steak with mushrooms and fries
Pasta with olives and tomatoes

SIDES

Fries
Rice
Salad

DESSERTS

Fruit salad
Cheesecake
Ice cream

SPEAKING

A PLAN Look at the menu. <u>Underline</u> the food you'd like to eat.

B SPEAK Work in pairs. Write and practise a conversation in a restaurant. Do these things:
- Order food from the menu.
- Change your order.
- Do or say something strange.

C PRESENT Perform your conversation for the class.

D Have a class vote for the best conversation and the food selection.

○— Order food in a restaurant

▶ Turn to **page 167** to learn how to write an online restaurant review.

FOOD AND DRINK 79

Unit 8 Review

VOCABULARY

A Match the food items in the picture (a–m) with the words in the box.

a banana ___ a loaf of bread ___ a slice of cake ___
carrots ___ cheese ___ chicken ___ an apple ___
a mug of coffee ___ eggs ___ milk ___
mushrooms ___ an orange ___ yoghurt ___

B Choose the correct words to complete the phrases.

1. a *tin* / *bottle* of beans
2. a *carton* / *box* of fruit juice
3. a *bag* / *pot* of yogurt
4. a *tin* / *packet* of tomatoes
5. a *bag* / *carton* of rice
6. a *jar* / *tin* of mayonnaise
7. a *carton* / *packet* of crisps
8. a *tin* / *bottle* of lemonade.

C Complete the recipe with the verbs in the box.

add   beat   ~~chop~~   crack   fry   mix   peel   put

Spanish omelette

1. Peel and ____*chop*____ an onion.
2. _____ the potatoes and cut them into small pieces.
3. _____ one tablespoon of oil in a frying pan.
4. _____ the onion and potatoes together for 20 minutes.
5. _____ eight eggs into a bowl and _____ them.
6. _____ salt and pepper to the eggs and _____ them together. Then add the mixture to the onions and potatoes.
7. Cook for 10 minutes, or until brown.

GRAMMAR

A Find and correct six mistakes in the conversation.

Eloise: What do you want to cook for the party?
Gemma: Hmm. How about fishes and beefs?
Eloise: Good idea! We can do some rices too.
Gemma: But Lola doesn't eat meats. She's vegetarian.
Eloise: We can make pastas with vegetable for Lola.

B Complete the sentences with *a/an*, *some* and *any*.

1. I've got __*an*__ apple and __*a*__ sandwich for my lunch.
2. Have we got _____ mushrooms?
3. I want to make _____ pizza, but I haven't got _____ cheese.
4. Is there _____ milk in the fridge?
5. Can you buy _____ potatoes at the shop, please?

C Choose the correct words to complete the sentences.

1. Do you eat *a lot of* / *many* meat?
2. How *much* / *many* potatoes do you eat every week?
3. How *much* / *many* bread do we need?
4. We've got *a lot of* / *many* eggs. Let's make a cake!
5. There isn't *much* / *many* fruit. Can you buy some?

D Find and correct the mistakes in four of these sentences.

1. Is there recipe for this meal?
2. My home town is the New York City.
3. We need two lemons and orange.
4. They always put the ingredients at the top of the recipe.
5. My friend is very good at cooking delicious the meals.

FUNCTIONAL LANGUAGE

A Look at the conversation. Put the sentences in the correct order (1–7).

___ Waiter: Anything to drink?
___ Customer A: Yes, I'll have the chicken.
___ Customer A: Just water please.
___ Customer B: And I'll have the fish. No, wait. I'll have the steak.
_1_ Waiter: Are you ready to order now?
___ Customer A: Yes, we'd both like potatoes and vegetables please.
___ Waiter: Would you like anything with your chicken and steak?

B SPEAK Work in pairs. Student A is the waiter. Student B is the customer. Practise ordering food in a restaurant. Use the ideas in Exercise A to help you.

A: *Are you ready to order now?*
B: *Yes, I'll have the fish, please.*

80 FOOD AND DRINK

9 SHOPPING

Shoppers on Black Friday in Maine, USA.

If the shoe fits, buy it in every colour.

Anonymous

OBJECTIVES

- talk about clothes and what people are doing
- talk about what people do at different times
- talk about shopping habits and tastes
- shop for clothes
- write a social media post

Work with a partner. Discuss the questions.

1 How often do you go shopping?
2 Look at the picture. Who do you think they're shopping for? Why?
3 Do you like shopping online? Why/Why not?

SHOPPING   81

9.1 People watching

  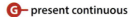

Talk about clothes and what people are doing

V – clothes   P – /ɜː/   G – present continuous

VOCABULARY
Clothes

A Work in pairs. What clothes can you see in pictures (1–4)? Use the words in the box to help you.

| cap | coat | jeans | hat | scarf | shorts | socks |
| skirt | sunglasses | trainers | trousers |

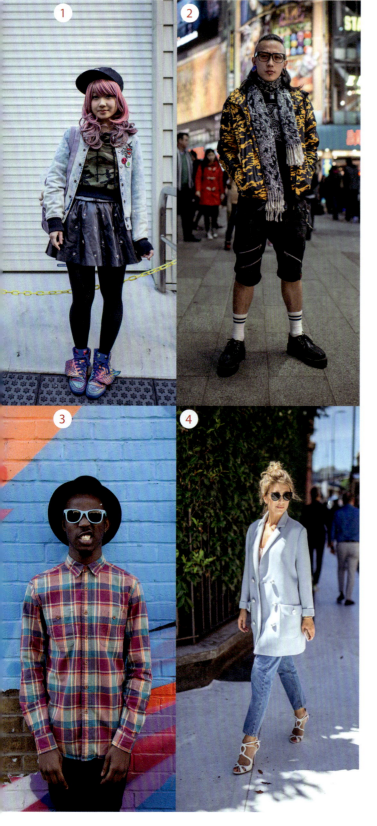

B Go to the **Vocabulary Hub** on **page 151**.

C **SPEAK** Work in pairs. Look at the pictures in Exercise A.
1 Which clothes do you like? Why?
2 Which don't you like? Why?

PRONUNCIATION
/ɜː/

A Listen and repeat. Notice that the underlined syllables are all pronounced as /ɜː/.
9.1

| <u>ear</u>ly | f<u>ir</u>st | l<u>ear</u>n | pr<u>e</u>fer | sh<u>ir</u>t |

B Tick (✓) the words that have the /ɜː/ sound. Then listen, check and repeat.
9.2

- ☐ ear
- ☐ her
- ☐ skirt
- ☐ there
- ☐ thirty
- ☐ Thursday
- ☐ we're
- ☐ work

C **SPEAK** Work in pairs. Say this tongue twister.

I prefer to wear a shirt to work on Thursdays.

LISTENING

A What do you like to do when you are alone in a café? Which sentence describes you?
- I sit quietly and read.
- I usually use my phone.
- I watch the people around me.
- I call my friends.

B **LISTEN FOR KEY WORDS** Listen to Johan's conversation. Which of the activities in Exercise A does he do?
9.3

C **LISTEN FOR DETAIL** Listen again. Match the people (1–5) with their clothes (a–e).
9.3

1 customer   a pink dress
2 angry woman   b tie
3 tall man   c pyjamas
4 short woman   d trainers
5 young girl   e hat

D **SPEAK** Work in pairs. Answer the questions.
1 Do people in your town or city wear interesting clothes?
2 Do you know any celebrities who wear unusual clothes?
3 Why do you think people wear unusual clothes?

A: *There is a charity run in my town every year. Lots of people wear funny clothes.*
B: *I think Lady Gaga wears unusual clothes.*

SHOPPING

GRAMMAR
Present continuous

A WORK IT OUT Look at the sentences from the conversation between Johan and Sophie. Underline the verbs.

1 What are you doing?
2 I'm having a coffee.
3 They're wearing really strange clothes.
4 No, the man isn't wearing pyjamas.

B Choose the correct words to complete the rules.

Present continuous
1 We use the present continuous to describe *what is happening now / routines*.
2 We make the present continuous with *be* + verb + *infinitive (without to) / -ing*.
3 In present continuous questions, *be* comes *before / after* the subject.

Present continuous spelling
- We add *-ing* to most verbs in the present continuous.
  read – read**ing**
  think – think**ing**
- With verbs ending in *-e*, we cut the *-e*, and add *-ing*.
  giv**e** – giv**ing**
- When the last three letters of a verb are consonant, vowel, consonant, we usually double the final consonant and add *-ing*.
  run – run**ning**
  stop – stop**ping**

C Go to the **Grammar Hub** on **page 138**.

D PRACTISE Use the prompts to write present continuous questions.

1 what / you / wear?
   What are you wearing?
2 you / wear / warm clothes?
   _____
3 what book / you / read / at the moment?
   _____
4 you / eat / something?
   _____
5 what / you / think / right now?
   _____

E SPEAK Work in pairs. Take turns to ask and answer the questions in Exercise D.

A: *What are you wearing?*
B: *I'm wearing blue jeans, black trainers and a white T-shirt. What are you wearing?*

SPEAKING

A PREPARE Look at the pictures (a and b). Choose a person to describe. Think about:
- what they are wearing
- what they are doing
- where they are

B ORGANISE Make notes about what you want to say.

This man is wearing sunglasses and a white shirt. He's taking a selfie with his friend.

C SPEAK Work in pairs. Describe the person to your partner. Can they guess who you are talking about?

D DISCUSS Work in groups. Discuss the questions.
1 What do you think of the clothes people are wearing in the pictures above?
2 Would you wear the same clothes? Why/Why not?
3 What kind of clothes are fashionable in your country at the moment?

○— Talk about clothes and what people are doing

SHOPPING 83

9.2 Job swap Talk about what people do at different times

V — present time expressions G — present simple vs present continuous P — /ŋ/

LISTENING

A SPEAK Work in pairs. Look at pictures (1–3). Would you like to do these jobs? Why/Why not?

B LISTEN FOR GIST Listen to the announcement. What is it about? Choose the correct answer.
9.4
  a a competition
  b a job offer
  c a sale

C LISTEN FOR KEY WORDS Listen again and complete the sentences.
9.4
1 The prize money is $_____.
2 To win the money, shoppers must do a different _____ for one day.
3 The Clothes Department is on Level _____.
4 The Clothes Department is next to the _____.
5 Registration closes at _____ pm.

D SPEAK Work in pairs. Answer the questions.
1 What do you do? Are you a student? Do you have a job?
2 Do you like what you do? Why/Why not?
3 Do you want to change what you do?

READING

A Match jobs (1–6) with what the person does (a–f).

1 doctor   a teach children
2 mechanic   b plan events, book models
3 teacher   c fix engines
4 personal shopper   d help sick people
5 fashion show director e take pictures
6 photographer   f give advice, choose
                            clothes for shoppers

B READ FOR GIST Read the social media posts. Are Bryony, Lee and Adal enjoying their job swap?

C READ FOR SPECIFIC INFORMATION Read the posts again and answer the questions. Choose Bryony (B), Lee (L) or Adal (A).

1 Who loves his job swap?   B / L / A
2 Who doesn't have a specialist to help her?   B / L / A
3 Who wants to go back to his usual job?   B / L / A
4 Who usually repairs things?   B / L / A
5 Who usually helps sick people?   B / L / A
6 Who is thinking about changing his job?   B / L / A

D SPEAK Work in pairs. Answer the questions.
1 Do you think a job swap is a fun idea? Why/Why not?
2 Which job in *Job swap* would you like to try? Why?

VOCABULARY
Present time expressions

A Read *Job swap* again. Find and underline the present time expressions. The first two have been done for you.

B Choose the correct time expression to complete the sentences.
1 Yes, I'm on the phone to the insurance company *these days / right now*.
2 I spend a lot of time at the gym *now / these days*. I'm trying to get fit for the London Marathon next year.
3 I'm *currently / today* working at St Crispin's Hospital in London. It's just for a few weeks.
4 I'm afraid Mr Stevens isn't here *at the moment / these days*. Can I take a message?

C SPEAK Work in pairs. Answer the questions.
1 What is your teacher wearing today?
2 What are you currently studying?
3 What are you doing more often these days?
4 What is your favourite TV programme at the moment?

A: *My favourite TV programme at the moment is Game of Thrones. It's amazing!*
B: *Oh, really? That's my favourite programme too!*

SHOPPING

Job swap

 Greenfield Department Store
23rd October, 8.57 am

It's job swap day! We've asked the winners of our job swap competition (Bryony, Lee and Adal) to post updates here every hour to tell us how their new job is going.

 **Bryony Williams**
23rd October, 10.05 am

I'm enjoying my job swap, but it's completely different from what I usually do. I work as a doctor, but <u>today</u> I'm organising a fashion show. It's hard work and there's a lot to do, but I'm having an interesting time. I love fashion and clothes, so I expected this to be easy, but it isn't. Today, I'm booking models and planning the event. The other job swappers have experts to help them, but I don't, so I'm feeling under pressure <u>now</u>!

Share   Like   Comment

 **Lee Cartwright**
23rd October, 10.17 am

Yesterday, I was a mechanic, but today I'm working as a personal shopper! I usually test cars and fix them, but today I'm giving people advice on buying clothes. I love my job at the garage, but I'm not enjoying this job at the moment. I can only write this now because my expert, Katrina, is talking on the phone. When she finishes, it's back to work for me. I don't want to do this anymore. I'm not having fun. I want to go back to my workshop.

Share   Like   Comment

Adal Khan
23rd October, 10.21 am

I usually teach eight-year-old children, but right now I'm taking pictures of models. Currently, I'm working as a fashion photographer! I took over 200 pictures this morning and it isn't even lunchtime yet. I'm learning so many things and I'm having the best time. As a teacher, I usually tell people what to do at school, but today Santos, my expert, is teaching me. Who knows, maybe I'm starting a new career … 😊

Share   Like   Comment

Glossary
career (n) a job that you want to do for a long period of your life
expert (n) someone with a particular skill or who knows a lot about a particular subject
swap (v) to give something to someone in exchange for something else

GRAMMAR
Present simple vs present continuous

A WORK IT OUT Read the examples in the box. Then choose the correct words to complete the rules.

Present simple and present continuous
1 We use the present continuous to talk about events that *happen every day / are happening now*.
… but today I'm organising a fashion show.
… so I'm feeling under pressure now.
2 We use the present simple to talk about *events that happen every day / events happening now*.
I work as a doctor …
I love fashion and clothes …

Time expressions
Time expressions like *all day*, *every week* and *once a year* are used with the present simple.
I visit my grandmother once a week.
Adverbs of frequency (*always*, *usually*, etc) are also used.
I usually test cars and fix them.
Time expressions like *today*, *now* and *at the moment* are used with the present continuous.
Today, I'm booking models.

B Go to the Grammar Hub on page 138.

C SPEAK Work in groups. Discuss the questions.
1 What's something that you only do once a year?
2 How often do you speak to your parents?
3 What are you watching on TV at the moment?
4 What time do you usually finish work or university?
5 What's something that you never do?

PRONUNCIATION
/ŋ/

A Listen and repeat the pairs of words. Can you hear the difference between the final sounds?
9.5
1 ban / bang
2 thin / thing
3 win / wing

B Listen and repeat. All of the words have the /ŋ/ sound.
9.6

a**ng**ry   ba**nk**   ba**nk**ing   enjoyi**ng**
fi**ng**er   havi**ng**   helpi**ng**   lo**ng**   shoppi**ng**
taki**ng**   talki**ng**   thinki**ng**

SPEAKING

Work in pairs. Go the Communication Hub on page 157.

○— Talk about what people do at different times

9.3 Shop till you drop
● Talk about shopping habits and tastes

G— object pronouns V— shops and services P— /tʃ/ and /ʃ/ S— reading for genre

READING

A Work in pairs. Answer the questions. Use the words in the box to help you.

> designer brands   discount shops   expensive things
> full price things   good quality products   local shops

1 What kind of things do you usually buy online?
2 What do you like spending money on? Why?
3 What don't you like spending money on? Why?

B Read *How to market your business* quickly. Where is it from? Who is the author writing to? Use the information in the box to help you.

> **Reading for genre**
>
> When you read something, it is important to know why the author wrote it. Think about:
> - Where is the text from (e.g. a website, magazine, etc)?
> - Who is the text for (e.g. students, doctors, etc)?

C READ FOR DETAIL Read the article again. Are the sentences true (T) or false (F)? Correct the false sentences.

1 Mike's shop sells designer clothes. T / F
2 Mike isn't getting enough customers. T / F
3 Discount shoppers spend a lot of time in shops because they love shopping. T / F
4 Luxury shoppers don't worry about the price of things. T / F
5 Quality shoppers go to local shops because they are cheap. T / F

D SPEAK Work in pairs. Answer the questions.

1 What kind of shopper would be interested in Mike's business? Why?
2 What kind of shopper are you?

A: *Mike could put his prices up. Then luxury shoppers might be interested in his business.*
B: *That's true. Quality shoppers might also be interested because they like to support local businesses.*

How to market your business

Mike owns a small shop. He spends all of his time working in it. It sells fruit and vegetables, cheese from a local farm, fresh homemade bread and delicious cakes. The shop is on a busy road, full of cafés and restaurants. The local people have a lot of money and they know how to spend it. But Mike's business is slow. He's worried. He's trying different things to sell more food, but nothing is working. So what's he doing wrong? Maybe he isn't selling to the right people. It's the first rule of business: find out who your customers are, and listen to them. So, is business in your shop slow? Read on to find out how to attract three kinds of shoppers.

💲 Drop your prices

Discount shoppers like saving money! They like spending time in shops because they want to find everything at a good price. These shoppers like big supermarkets, markets and cheap local shops. Department stores are usually too expensive for them. They aren't interested in designer brands. They often shop online and travel to find the best price. They don't like paying full price for anything, and often buy clothes or big items when there's a sale.

⭐ Offer something special

Luxury shoppers love shopping, fashion and expensive products. Shopping is a serious hobby for them. They don't mind paying a lot for their favourite designer brands! Luxury shoppers hate cheap shops and prefer smart department stores in the city centre, where they can have a coffee and meet their friends for lunch. Luxury shoppers buy what they want, when they want.

🔍 Offer quality

Quality shoppers look for products that they can use for many years and they are happy to pay a bit more for something special. They look for good quality things in shopping malls. They also like local shops because they want to support businesses in their area. They often shop at markets, or at traditional local bakeries and butchers'. They also like to touch the things they are buying and they often spend a long time looking at them.

Which kind of shopper do you think would be interested in your business?

> **Glossary**
>
> **brand (n)** a product or products that has its own name and is made by a particular company
> **designer (adj)** designer clothes are made by a famous designer and are usually expensive
> **local (adj)** in or close to the area that you live in, or to the area that you are talking about
> **luxury (n)** something expensive that you enjoy, but do not really need
> **quality (n)** how good or bad something is
> **sale (n)** an event or period of time when a shop reduces some of its prices

SHOPPING

GRAMMAR
Object pronouns

A Look at the sentences from *How to market your business*. Underline the prepositions and circle the object pronouns.

1 He spends all of his time working in it.
2 Department stores are usually too expensive for them.
3 Shopping is a serious hobby for them.
4 They like to touch the things they are buying and they often spend a long time looking at them.

B WORK IT OUT Choose the correct words to complete the rules.

> **Object pronouns**
> 1 Object pronouns usually go at the *beginning / end* of sentences.
> 2 Prepositions usually go *before / after* object pronouns.

C Go to the Grammar Hub on page 138.

D SPEAK Work in pairs. Answer the questions. Use object pronouns.

1 Do you have any brothers or sisters? How often do you see them?
2 What's your favourite film? When did you last watch it?
3 Who do you like to go shopping with? Why?

I have one brother called Tom. I see him about once a month.

VOCABULARY
Shops and services

A Read *How to market your business* again. Find and underline eight words for shops or services.

B SPEAK Work in pairs. Where could you buy the things in the box? Use the words you found in Exercise A to help you.

> apples   a cake   cheese   a cup of coffee
> meat   a pair of shoes   a pizza   a TV

C Go to the Vocabulary Hub on page 151.

D SPEAK Work in pairs. Answer the questions.

1 Do you usually buy fruit and vegetables from a market or a supermarket? Why?
2 Do you prefer buying things online or in a shop? Why?
3 Is there a shopping mall near where you live? How often do you go there?

A: I prefer buying things online because it's quick and easy.
B: Really? I prefer buying things in shops because you can see things before you buy them.

PRONUNCIATION
/tʃ/ and /ʃ/

A Listen and repeat. Can you hear the difference between /tʃ/ and /ʃ/?
9.7

/tʃ/   choose, rich, chocolate
/ʃ/   shoes, shower, finish

B Complete the table with the words in the box. Then listen, check and repeat.
9.8

> butcher's   cash   change   cheap   choose   fashion
> fresh   lunch   shop   touch

/tʃ/	/ʃ/
butcher's	cash

SPEAKING HUB

A PREPARE Work in groups. You are going to interview your classmates about their shopping habits. Think about:
- type of shops
- cost
- location

B PLAN Write questions for a shopping survey.

How often do you go shopping?
What kind of things do you usually buy online?
What do you like shopping for?

C DISCUSS Interview students in other groups. Note down their answers.

D PRESENT Get back into groups and compare your findings. Then present the information to the class.

> Lots of people shop in supermarkets because it's easy and cheap.

○─ Talk about shopping habits and tastes

Café Hub

9.4 Meeting Milly
F– shop for clothes   P– connected speech

COMPREHENSION

A SPEAK Work in pairs. Look at the picture of Milly's clothes shop. Answer the questions.
1. How often do you go shopping for clothes?
2. Do you like clothes shops like Milly's?
3. What are your favourite kinds of clothes shops?

B ▶ Watch the video. Complete the sentences. Write *Milly*, *Neena* or *Zac*.
1. _Neena_ and _Zac_ are housemates.
2. _____ and _____ are old friends.
3. _____ and _____ meet for the first time.
4. _____ and _____ are American.
5. _____ and _____ are from Seattle.
6. _____ and _____ don't try on any clothes.
7. _____ and _____ leave the shop together.

C SPEAK Work in pairs. Why can't Zac speak? How does he feel about Milly?

FUNCTIONAL LANGUAGE
Shopping for clothes

A ▶ Complete the conversations (A-F). Then watch the video again and check your answers.

A
Shop assistant: ¹_____ I help ²_____?
Customer: No, I'm just looking, thank you.

B
Customer: Can ³_____ try it ⁴_____?
Shop assistant: Sure.

C
Customer: Where ⁵_____ the changing ⁶_____?
Shop assistant: They're over there next to the scarves and shirts.

D
Customer: ⁷_____ do ⁸_____ think, guys?
Shop assistant: It looks great!

E
Customer: Have ⁹_____ got ¹⁰_____ medium?
Shop assistant: Yeah, I think so.

F
Customer: I ¹¹_____ take ¹²_____ jacket, the skirt and the shirt, please. ¹³_____ much ¹⁴_____ that?
Shop assistant: That's £85, please. Thank you.

B Work in pairs. Practise the conversations in Exercise A.

SHOPPING

9.4

MILLY

SAM

NEENA

ZAC

GABY

PRONUNCIATION
Connected speech

A Listen and repeat the questions. Is there a pause between the words connected with a ‿?
9.9

1 Can‿I try‿it‿on?
2 How much‿is‿it?

B Draw a ‿ to show the connected words. Then listen and check.
9.10

1 Can I try them on?
2 How much are they?
3 It's over there.
4 Your store is awesome!
5 Have you got an extra-large?

C Listen again and repeat. Remember to use connected speech.
9.10

SPEAKING

A PREPARE Work in pairs. Look at the pictures. What do you like / not like about the clothes?

A: *I really like the …*
B: *Do you? I think the …*

B PLAN Work in pairs. Imagine you are in Milly's shop. Student A – you are a shop assistant. Student B – you are a customer that needs help. Write a conversation.

- Offer to help the customer.
- Choose an item of clothing and ask to try it on.
- Tell the customer where the changing room is.
- Try it on and then ask for a different size.
- Give the customer a different size.
- Say you want to buy it and ask for a price.
- Tell the customer the price and ask how they want to pay.
- Buy the item and thank the shop assistant.

C PRESENT Perform your roleplay to the class.

Polka Dot Dress
£25

Tweed Suit
£225

Hat
£10

Red Leather Boots
£115

Plaid Shirt
£15

Wool Coat
£150

Leather Jacket
£170

Jumper
£15

Wool Scarf
£15

○─ **Shop for clothes**

▶ Turn to **page 168** to learn how to write a social media post.

SHOPPING 89

Unit 9 Review

VOCABULARY

A Choose the correct words to complete the descriptions.

He's wearing a ¹*suit / coat* and has brown ²*shoes / boots*. His ³*shirt / skirt* is white and his ⁴*scarf / tie* is red.

She's wearing a blue ⁵*dress / shirt*, with white ⁶*trainers / boots* and a pink ⁷*jumper / jacket*. She's also got a yellow ⁸*hat / bag*.

B Complete the sentences with the time expressions in the box.

> at the moment   currently   today   this week   this year

1 Mum doesn't want to celebrate her birthday _____.
2 I've got a doctor's appointment _____ at 3 pm.
3 I'm _____ studying history at Cambridge.
4 I live with my parents _____, but I want to move out soon.
5 I've got so much work to do _____! Five days isn't enough time.

C Complete the definitions with the words in the box.

> bakery   bank   bookshop   butcher's
> dentist's   hairdresser's   newsagent's   pharmacy

1 _____ a shop that sells books
2 _____ a shop that sells meat
3 _____ a place where you can borrow or save money
4 _____ a place where you can have your teeth examined
5 _____ a shop that sells cakes, bread, pastry, etc
6 _____ a place where you get medicine
7 _____ a place where you can get your hair cut
8 _____ a shop that sells magazines, newspapers, chocolate, etc

D SPEAK Work in pairs. Answer the questions.

1 What kind of clothes do you wear at work/university?
2 What kind of clothes do you wear at home?
3 What are you wearing today?

GRAMMAR

A Choose the correct words to complete the sentences.

1 I usually *am working / work* on Saturdays, but I *'m taking / take* this Saturday off.
2 She *'s crying / cries* because romantic films always *are making / make* her sad.
3 I usually *am going / go* camping, but this year I *'m staying / stay* in a hotel.
4 He *'s wearing / wears* white today, but he usually *is preferring / prefers* black.
5 I usually *am working / work* from home on Thursdays, but I *'m coming / come* in this week for a meeting.
6 She *'s meeting / meets* her friends tonight. I think they *'re going / go* to the cinema.

B Complete the story with the correct form of the verbs.

My name is Marc Sands and I ¹____*work*____ (work) in a clothes shop. A lot of tourists ²_____ (come) to our shop every day. At the moment, we ³_____ (have) a sale. It's only 9.30 am and people ⁴_____ (come) through the door already. The shop ⁵_____ (get) busy.

C SPEAK Work in pairs and discuss things you do every day, and say what you are doing now.

D Complete the sentences with the correct object pronoun.

1 My brother knows a lot about luxury brands. He spends a lot of money on ____*them*____.
2 Alicia is an expert on saving money. I need to listen to _____.
3 We need more staff. How can we get more people to work for _____?
4 Tariq owns a busy café in the centre of town. It is the most important thing to _____.
5 My daughter has a new party dress. She wants to wear _____ every day.
6 It's mum's birthday on Saturday. Don't forget to call _____!

FUNCTIONAL LANGUAGE

Match the beginnings of sentences (1–5) with the ends of sentences (a–e).

1 Can I   a are over there.
2 I'm looking for   b trousers are over here.
3 Yes, our   c help you?
4 Can I try   d them on?
5 Yes, the changing rooms   e a pair of trousers.

90 SHOPPING

10 THE GREAT OUTDOORS

Look deep into nature, and then you will understand everything better.
— Albert Einstein

A young traveller at Iskanderkul Lake, Tajikistan

OBJECTIVES

- talk about and compare outdoor places
- talk about places around the world
- talk about living outdoors
- make and respond to invitations
- write a product review

Work with a partner. Discuss the questions.

1 Do you prefer cities or the countryside?
2 Look at the picture. Would you like to go there?
3 Which parts of your country are beautiful?

THE GREAT OUTDOORS 91

10.1 The right location

● Talk about and compare outdoor places

 landscape features  comparatives  weak forms: /ə/ in *than*

FAMOUS FILM LOCATIONS

A lot of directors use studios or computers to make their films. But some still like to use real places. Here are some famous film locations that you can actually visit.

The village of Aït Benhaddou in Morocco is on a **hill** in the **desert**. You can see it in many films, including *Gladiator*, *Prince of Persia* and *The Mummy*. It's also a UNESCO World Heritage Site.

The locations for the three *Lord of the Rings* films are all in New Zealand. With its tall **mountains**, big **forests** and bright blue **lakes**, the Fiordland National Park was perfect for many scenes.

The **beach** of Maya Bay was the location of Danny Boyle's film *The Beach*, with Leonardo DiCaprio. It's on the **island** of Koh Phi Phi Leh near Phuket. There are 32 islands here, surrounded by the beautiful blue **sea**.

Do you know this place? They made *Avatar* in this **jungle**, on the Hamakua Coast of Hawaii. This part of the island has around 200 cm of rain every year, and it's full of tall, green trees and beautiful **rivers**.

VOCABULARY
Landscape features

A Work in pairs. Look at the pictures in *Famous film locations*. Where are they? What films did they make there?

B Read the article quickly and check your answers to Exercise A.

C Read the article again. Label the pictures with the words in **bold**.

D SPEAK Work in pairs. Can you see any of these landscape features in your country? Tell your partner.

I'm from Spain. There are lots of beautiful beaches near Barcelona.

LISTENING
The film location

 A LISTEN FOR GIST Listen to Max talking about the locations for his film. What is a location scout?
10.1

 B LISTEN FOR SPECIFIC INFORMATION Listen again. Where did they film these scenes? Why? Take notes.
10.1
   1 the beach scenes
   2 the desert scenes
   3 the jungle scenes

C SPEAK Work in pairs and discuss the questions.
   1 What are some of the good things about filming in a studio?
   2 What are some of the problems of filming in a real location (e.g. a city)?

A: *I think it's easier to film in a studio.*
B: *I agree. You don't need to worry about the weather.*

D SPEAK Work in pairs and discuss good film locations in your country. Explain your ideas.

Wadi Rum in Jordan is a great location for making films. It's a desert. They made Transformers: Revenge of the Fallen there.

92 THE GREAT OUTDOORS

10.1

GRAMMAR
Comparatives

A WORK IT OUT Look at these sentences from the TV interview with Clarice. Complete the table.

Mexico was **cheaper than** the USA.

It was **more expensive** to film in the USA **than** in Mexico.

Comparatives			
	Adjective	Comparative	Rule
One-syllable adjectives	cheap	1_____	We add [3]_____ + *than*
Adjectives with two or more syllables	expensive	2_____	We add [4]_____ + adjective + *than*
Irregular adjectives	good	better	
	bad	worse	

B PRACTISE Complete the sentences with the comparative form of the adjectives in brackets. Use the information in the box to help you.

> **Comparative spellings**
>
> For adjectives that end in *-e*, we add *-r*.
> large → larger; close → closer
>
> For adjectives that end with a consonant, we double the consonant and add *-er*.
> hot → hotter; big → bigger

1 The mountains are _____ (*cold*) than the desert.
2 Mexico is _____ (*close*) to California than Morocco.
3 Hollywood is _____ (*famous*) for films than nature.
4 Mexico is four times _____ (*big*) than Morocco.
5 Californian beaches are _____ (*crowded*) than Mexican beaches.

C Go to the **Grammar Hub** on **page 140**.

D PRACTISE Use the prompts to write comparative sentences.

1 beautiful – New Zealand / Australia
New Zealand is more beautiful than Australia.

2 hot – Buenos Aires / Rio de Janeiro
_____

3 long – the Amazon / the Nile
_____

4 dangerous – the Sahara / Everest
_____

5 cold – New York City / Moscow
_____

E SPEAK Work in pairs. Look at the sentences in Exercise D. Say whether you agree or disagree.

A: *New Zealand is more beautiful than Australia. What do you think?*
B: *I disagree. Australia has amazing beaches!*

PRONUNCIATION
Weak forms: /ə/ in *than*

A Listen to five comparative sentences. Is *than* pronounced /ðæn/ or /ðən/?
10.2

B SPEAK Work in pairs. Practise saying the sentences in Grammar Exercise B. Listen and check your partner's pronunciation. Be careful to pronounce *than* correctly.

SPEAKING

A PLAN Work in pairs. Choose two countries, two landscape features or two films to compare. Then think of adjectives to describe them.

Canada: modern, cold, big …

Thailand: beautiful, wet, traditional, interesting …

B PREPARE Write sentences comparing the two things you chose in Exercise A.

Canada is colder than Thailand.

C SPEAK Work in another pair. Student A – tell your partner your ideas. Student B – say whether you agree or disagree. Take turns.

A: *Canada is more modern than Thailand.*
B: *Hmm. I'm not sure. Bangkok is a very modern city.*

○— Talk about and compare outdoor places

10.2 Where on Earth? — Talk about places around the world

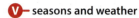 seasons and weather   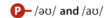 /əʊ/ and /aʊ/   superlatives

Extreme places

This week, we look at some of the most difficult places to live on Earth. What's life like there? How do people survive in these places?

Yakutsk

It's winter in Yakutsk, Siberia. It's -42°C. It's snowing and it's foggy. Welcome to the coldest city on Earth. The lowest temperature in Yakutsk was -64°C. But about 270,000 people still live normal lives in this busy, modern city. They travel to work, go to school and meet friends. It's just like in any other city, except it's impossible to stay outside for too long. 'Yes, it's very cold, but I like it here,' says Nina. She's wearing a big fur hat, boots and a long coat, but she's smiling. 'Humans can survive anywhere,' she says.

Tristan da Cunha

A population of about 265 people live in the middle of the Atlantic Ocean. They are British, but they are 9000 km from London. Their home is Tristan da Cunha. It's the world's most remote inhabited island. The weather is a bit windy, but this isn't the problem. There isn't an airport, and the nearest mainland is South Africa, 2430 km away. To get to the island, there's a boat from Cape Town. The journey takes six days.
So, how do people survive on this island? Well, there's electricity and the internet. There's a supermarket, too, but food is expensive, so most people on the island grow potatoes. Why do people stay when life isn't easy? Erik, a worker at the fish factory, says, 'It's so quiet and beautiful. We don't have the problems of the modern world here'.

Kuwait City

It's a Saturday in Kuwait City – the hottest city in the world. About 2.4 million people live here, but you don't see anyone walking around. Why? Because it's 50°C and nobody wants to be outside.
The weather here is extreme. In summer, it's hotter than the Sahara Desert. But this isn't the driest place on Earth – that's the Atacama Desert in Chile. In fact, there are a lot of thunderstorms in autumn.
What do people do here, then? During the hottest months, they live inside. Most people drive from their air-conditioned homes in their air-conditioned cars to air-conditioned offices and shopping malls. And there is another important thing. 'Water, water, water,' says Sharifa, an architect. 'We have to drink a lot!'

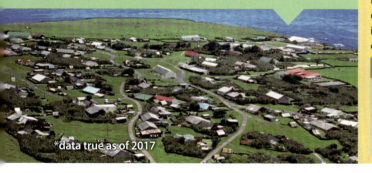

*data true as of 2017

Glossary

extreme (adj) very great in degree
fur (n) the soft hair that covers the body of some animals
inhabited (adj) a place that is inhabited is a place that has people living in it
remote (adj) far away from other cities, towns or people
survive (v) to continue to exist, especially in a difficult or dangerous situation

READING

A Work in pairs. Look at the pictures in *Extreme places* and read the introduction. What problems do you think the people living in these places have? Write notes.

B **READ FOR GIST** Read *Extreme places*. Are there any ideas you didn't think of in Exercise A?

C **READ FOR DETAIL** Read again. Choose the correct answer a, b or c to complete the sentences.

1 Yakustsk is …
   a a quiet town.
   b a small village.
   c a busy city.

2 People in Yakutsk …
   a never go outside in winter.
   b go outside in winter in warm clothes.
   c only go outside in summer.

3 In Kuwait City, the streets are empty because …
   a it's too hot to go outside.
   b not many people live there.
   c people are at work.

4 There are a lot of cars in Kuwait City because …
   a it's a very big city.
   b it's very rainy.
   c people drive everywhere.

5 To get to the island, people on Tristan da Cunha have to …
   a fly from Cape Town.
   b take a boat.
   c fly from London.

6 People on Tristan da Cunha grow potatoes because …
   a food is expensive in the shop.
   b they can't grow other vegetables.
   c there isn't a shop.

D **SPEAK** Work in pairs. Are there any extreme places in your country? Tell your partner about them.

THE GREAT OUTDOORS

10.2

VOCABULARY
Seasons and weather

A Look at the picture and answer the questions.
1 Which country do you think this is? Why?
2 Is the weather good or bad?
3 Is the weather like this in your country?

B Go to the Vocabulary Hub on page 152.

C SPEAK Work in pairs. Answer the questions.
1 What's the weather like today?
2 What's the weather like in your country in each season?
3 What's your favourite season? Why?

PRONUNCIATION
/əʊ/ and /aʊ/

A Listen and repeat. Can you hear the difference between the sounds /əʊ/ and /aʊ/?

/əʊ/ snowing, go, throw
/aʊ/ cloudy, sound, brown

B Complete the table with the words in the box. Then listen and repeat.

around   cloudy   coat   grow   home   lowest
now   outside   sound   snowing   town

/əʊ/	/aʊ/
coat	around

GRAMMAR
Superlatives

A WORK IT OUT Look at *Extreme places*. Complete the sentences with words from the text.
1 Welcome to _____ city on Earth.
2 It's a Saturday in Kuwait City – _____ city in the world.
3 But this isn't _____ place on Earth – that's the Atacama Desert in Chile.
4 It's the world's _____ inhabited island.
5 There isn't an airport, and _____ mainland is South Africa, 2430 km away.

B Complete the table. Use the examples in Exercise A to help you.

Superlatives			
	Adjective	Superlative	Rule
One-syllable adjectives	cold	1 _____	We use *the* + adjective + 3 _____
Adjectives with two or more syllables	remote	2 _____	We use *the* + 4 _____ + adjective
Irregular adjectives	good bad	the best the worst	

C Go to the Grammar Hub on page 140.

D PRACTISE Use the prompts to write superlative questions.
1 What's / high / mountain / in the world?
   What's the highest mountain in the world?
2 What's / big / ocean / in the world?
   _____
3 What's / beautiful / place / in the world?
   _____
4 What's / good / film / ever made?
   _____
5 Which / good / season to visit your country?
   _____
6 What's / bad / thing about your city?
   _____

E SPEAK Work in pairs. Ask and answer the questions in Exercise D.

SPEAKING

Student A – go to the Communication Hub on page 157.
Student B – go to the Communication Hub on page 159.

Talk about places around the world

THE GREAT OUTDOORS 95

10.3 Survival ● Talk about living outdoors

V — phrasal verbs   **G** — verb + *to* + infinitive   **P** — weak forms: /tuː/ and /tə/   **S** — identifying fact and opinion

READING

A Work in pairs. Tell your partner about the last time you got lost. What did you do?

A: I got lost on holiday in New York last year. I asked a policeman to help me!
B: Haha! I got lost in the mountains in France once. I phoned my friend for help.

B **READING FOR GIST** Read *Five ways to survive in the wild*. Who is the article written for?
1 Someone who wants to go on holiday.
2 Someone who wants to go walking in a remote place.
3 Someone who wants to buy camping equipment.

C **READ FOR DETAIL** Read the article again. Match the beginnings of sentences (1–5) with the ends of sentences (a–e).

1 People die every year
2 The cold is more dangerous
3 You can't survive for a week
4 The safest way to drink water
5 Try to find

a is to boil it first.
b than almost anything else.
c because they don't prepare well.
d without water.
e plants to eat.

D Read these sentences from the article. Are they facts (F) or opinions (O)?

Identifying fact and opinion

Texts usually contain a mix of fact and opinion.
A fact is something which is true. Facts can include statements or statistics.
Most of them are between the ages of 20 and 29.
An opinion is what the speaker personally thinks about something.
Some people think it's important to take everything you need with you, like a tent, but I don't agree.
Opinions often include phrases such as: *I think …, I prefer …, I believe …, I feel …, In my opinion …, I agree, I don't agree / I disagree.*

1 I prefer to travel with only a few things and use what nature gives me. F / O
2 I believe that the best thing to do is to make a dry place where you can sleep. F / O
3 The night is much colder than the day. F / O
4 It's always safer to boil water before you drink it. F / O
5 I feel that the best thing you can do is learn to read the night sky before you leave. F / O

E **SPEAK** Work in pairs. Put Chuck's advice in order from the most important (1) to the least important (5). Explain your ideas.

I think finding somewhere to sleep is the most important because …

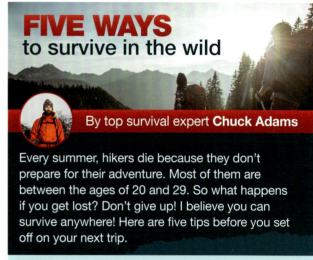

FIVE WAYS to survive in the wild

By top survival expert **Chuck Adams**

Every summer, hikers die because they don't prepare for their adventure. Most of them are between the ages of 20 and 29. So what happens if you get lost? Don't give up! I believe you can survive anywhere! Here are five tips before you set off on your next trip.

1 Build somewhere to sleep
Some people think it's important to take everything you need with you, like a tent, but I don't agree. I prefer to travel with only a few things and use what nature gives me. I believe that the best thing to do is to make a dry place where you can sleep. Put some pieces of wood against a tree and make a bed of grass on the floor. Also, one of the most dangerous things is the cold. The night is much colder than the day, so put on all of your clothes when you go to bed.

2 Make a fire
You only need two pieces of dry wood to start a fire! Check my <u>Survival in the wild</u> video on how to do this. Remember to add some big pieces of wood to keep you warmer for longer during the night.

3 Find water
Water is more important than food – you can only live for three days without water. It's better to drink water in rivers than water in lakes.
It's always safer to boil water before you drink it.

4 Find food
We get most of our food from nature. Learn how to look for plants or flowers that you can eat. You can also catch and eat small animals. Watch my <u>Survival in the wild</u> video to learn how.

5 Read the sky
Use the North Star and the shape of the moon to help find out where you are. I feel that the best thing you can do is to learn to read the night sky before you leave.

Glossary
hiker (n) someone who walks long distances in the countryside for pleasure
nature (n) the physical world, including land, sea and all living things
survive (v) to continue to exist, especially in a difficult situation
the wild (n) an environment that is natural

96   THE GREAT OUTDOORS

10.3

VOCABULARY
Phrasal verbs

A Read the information in the box. Then read *Five ways to survive in the wild* and underline five phrasal verbs.

> **Phrasal verbs**
> Phrasal verbs have two parts, usually a verb and a preposition. The preposition often changes the meaning of the verb. For example, *give up* means 'stop doing something'.
> A: *I'm tired. This race is hard.*
> B: *Don't **give up**! We're almost there.*

B Complete the definitions with phrasal verbs from Exercise A.

1. _____ to start wearing something
2. _____ to stop doing something
3. _____ to learn something
4. _____ to leave
5. _____ to try to find

C Go to the **Vocabulary Hub** on **page 152**.

D Work in pairs. Write sentences using the phrasal verbs in Exercise B.

LISTENING

A Work in pairs. Look at *Marcus James: Survival Kit*. Do you think Chuck Adams uses any of these items? Why/Why not?

MARCUS JAMES: SURVIVAL KIT

B **LISTEN FOR GIST** Listen to an interview with survival expert Marcus James. Does he agree with Chuck Adams?
10.5

C **LISTEN FOR DETAIL** Listen again. Are the sentences true (T) or false (F)? Correct the false sentences.
10.5

1. The easiest way to make fire is from dry wood.   T/F
2. Almost all hikers travel with energy bars.   T/F
3. You can live for ten days without food.   T/F
4. You should build a shelter to stay dry.   T/F
5. You should take a lot of photos.   T/F

D **SPEAK** Work in pairs. Put the items in Exercise A in order of most important (1) to least important (9). Then compare your list with another pair.

GRAMMAR
Verb + *to* + infinitive

A Listen to the interview again and complete the sentences.
10.5

1. Always **plan** _____ a few important things with you, like a penknife, a lamp and a phone.
2. For example, if you **want** _____ dry, take a raincoat.
3. You don't **need** _____ anything.
4. When you **decide** _____ hiking, tell someone where you're going.
5. And **remember** _____ warm.

B **WORK IT OUT** Look at the sentences in Exercise A and complete the rule.

> **Verb + *to* + infinitive**
> Lots of verbs in English are followed by *to* + *infinitive* / *-ing*. Examples include: *plan, want, need, decide, rememeber*.

C Go to the **Grammar Hub** on **page 140**.

PRONUNCIATION
Weak forms: /tuː/ and /tə/

A We pronounce *to* before an infinitive either /tuː/ or /tə/. Listen and repeat. Can you hear the difference?
10.6

/tuː/   to agree, to arrive, to open
/tə/   to believe, to prepare, to set off

B Listen again and complete the rules.
10.6

> **/tuː/ and /tə/**
> 1. we say /tuː/ before infinitives starting with a *vowel* / *consonant* sound.
> 2. we say /tə/ before infinitives starting with a *vowel* / *consonant* sound.

⭕ SPEAKING HUB

Work in pairs. Go to the **Communication Hub** on **page 157**.

○─ Talk about living outdoors

Café Hub

10.4 Party invitation
F – make and respond to invitations **P** – stress and intonation

COMPREHENSION

A **SPEAK** Work in pairs. Look at the picture. What are Zac, Neena and Gaby planning? What do they have to decide?

B ▶ Watch the video. Choose the correct words to complete the sentences.
1. It's Sam's birthday *today / tomorrow*.
2. Neena has a birthday *present / card* for Sam.
3. Neena thinks the cinema is *boring / expensive*.
4. Gaby thinks a party is *cheaper / easier* than a restaurant.
5. Zac checks the *weather forecast / restaurant prices*.
6. They decide *to have / not to have* a picnic.
7. Zac suggests a surprise party *in the flat / at Sam's café*.
8. Neena tells Milly to arrive at *ten to / ten past* six.
9. Sam's parents *can / can't* come to the party.

C **SPEAK** Work in pairs. Answer the questions.
1. What is the final plan for the party?
2. Why does Zac shout when Sam arrives at the flat?
3. Why do Sam, Gaby and Neena laugh at the end?

FUNCTIONAL LANGUAGE
Making and responding to invitations

A ▶ Watch the video again. Tick (✓) the invitations and replies you hear.

Inviting people	Are you free on Friday? We're having a party. ☐
	Would you like to come to Sam's party tomorrow? ☐
	We're holding a party for Sam tomorrow evening. Can you come? ☐
Saying yes	That sound's great. ☐
	We'd love to come. ☐
	Sure! I'd love to. ☐
	That would be great. ☐
Saying no	Sorry, I'm busy. ☐
	I can't come. I'm working. ☐
	I'd love to, but I'm away. ☐

B **SPEAK** Work in pairs. Student A – invite your partner using the questions in Exercise A. Student B – reply using the phrases in Exercise A. Then swap roles.

THE GREAT OUTDOORS

MILLY   SAM   NEENA   ZAC   GABY

PRONUNCIATION
Stress and intonation

A Listen and repeat the replies. Copy the stress and intonation.
10.7

1 That sounds great.
2 We'd love to come.
3 Sure.
4 I'd love to.
5 Sorry, I'm busy.
6 I can't come. I'm working.

B Listen again. <u>Underline</u> the stressed word or
10.7 syllable in the replies in Exercise A.

C SPEAK Work in pairs. Practise saying the replies in Exercise A. Remember to use the correct stress and intonation.

SPEAKING

A PREPARE Make notes about three activities to do with your partner.

- *See the new Avengers film > Friday night.*
- *Go for a walk > Sunday afternoon.*
- *Play football > next Thursday.*

B SPEAK Take turns making invitations and saying *yes* or *no*. Use the phrases in the Functional language section and your notes to help you.

A: Would you like to see a film with me this evening?
B: I'd love to, but I'm really tired.

C DISCUSS Work in pairs. Think about the last time you got an invitation. Did you go? If not, why not? Tell your partner about it.

A: I got an invitation to a work party last month.
B: Did you go?
A: No, I didn't. I was on holiday.

◯ Make and respond to invitations
➤ Turn to **page 169** to learn how to write a product review.

THE GREAT OUTDOORS

Unit 10 Review

GRAMMAR

A Look at the adverts for two flats. Use the prompts to write comparative sentences.

$150 a night | Beautiful flat, five minutes from the city centre
Flat / three bedrooms
★★★★ 3256 reviews

$60 a night | Excellent apartment, 20 minutes from the city centre
Flat / one bedroom
★★★★ 2988 reviews

1 Flat B / small / Flat A
   Flat B is smaller than Flat A.
2 Flat A / expensive / Flat B
   _____
3 Flat A / good / Flat B
   _____
4 Flat A / big / Flat B
   _____
5 Flat A / near / to the city centre / Flat B
   _____

B Complete the sentences with the superlative form of the adjective in brackets.

1 Death Valley is ___the hottest___ (*hot*) place in the USA.
2 Lake Superior is _____ (*big*) lake in Canada.
3 Manchester is _____ (*rainy*) city in the UK.
4 Quito in Ecuador is _____ (*ancient*) city in South America.
5 Mount Kilimanjaro is _____ (*high*) mountain in Africa.
6 Tristan de Cunha is _____ (*remote*) island in the world.
7 Sushi is _____ (*good*) food in the world!
8 Laos is _____ (*beautiful*) country I visited in South East Asia.

C Choose the correct form of the verbs to complete the sentences.

1 I'm planning *to go* / *going* hiking this weekend.
2 I really enjoy *to watch* / *watching* horror films.
3 Remember *to take* / *taking* a coat – it's cold outside!
4 It was raining, so I decided *to get* / *getting* the bus.
5 I keep *to wake up* / *waking up* at 6.30 am.
6 I really need *to get* / *getting* a haircut!

VOCABULARY

A Complete the descriptions with the words in the box.

beach   desert   forest   hill   island
lake   mountains   river   sea

The [1] ___desert___ here is beautiful. The [2] _____ are very tall and there's snow on them. We can't swim in the [3] _____ because it's too cold.

We're camping here in the [4] _____. There are so many trees! We swam in the [5] _____ this morning; then climbed the [6] _____ next to the campsite.

This small [7] _____ is beautiful. We swam in the [8] _____ yesterday, then sat on the [9] _____.

B Look at the pictures. Complete the phrases.

1 It's ___cloudy___.   4 It's _____.
2 It's _____.   5 It's _____.
3 It's _____.   6 It's _____.

C Complete the sentences with the phrasal verbs in the box.

found out   give up   look for   put on   set off

1 We _____ at five o'clock.
2 Don't _____! You're nearly there.
3 Can you help me _____ my keys?
4 I just _____ that I failed my exam.
5 You should _____ a scarf. It's cold outside!

FUNCTIONAL LANGUAGE

Complete the conversation with the words in the box.

busy   can't   free   sounds   would

A: Are you [1] _____ tonight?
B: Why?
A: [2] _____ you like to go to the cinema?
B: Sorry, I [3] _____. I'm [4] _____. Maybe another time.
A: How about tomorrow night?
B: That [5] _____ good. What's on?

100   THE GREAT OUTDOORS

11 THE BODY

Health is the greatest possession.
Lao Tzu

A woman doing yoga on an empty beach.

OBJECTIVES

- talk about the body and health
- talk about your experiences
- talk about sports and hobbies
- ask for information
- write a recommendation on a forum

Work with a partner. Discuss the questions.
1 Read the quote. Do you agree?
2 Look at the picture. Is exercise part of your morning routine?
3 Where do you usually do exercise?

11.1 Health tips — Talk about the body and health

V — the body G — *should* and *shouldn't* P — sentence stress

VOCABULARY
The body

A Label the picture with the words in the box.

arm ear eye foot head heart neck stomach

The Body

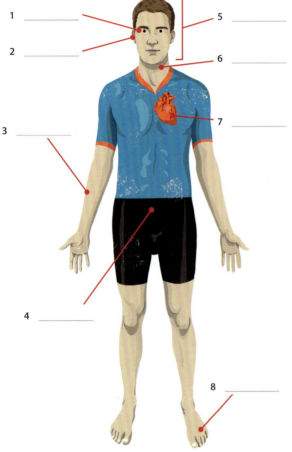

1 _____
2 _____
3 _____
4 _____
5 _____
6 _____
7 _____
8 _____

B Complete the sentences using the words for parts of the body in the box. There are two words you do not need.

blood brain hand legs nose skin

1 I run with my _____.
2 I think with my _____.
3 I smell with my _____.
4 I hold a pen with my _____.

Irregular plurals
We say *I have two feet* NOT *I have two foots*.

C SPEAK Work in pairs. Take turns to give each other instructions.

A: *Touch your neck.*
B: *OK … Point to your eyes.*

LISTENING

A Work in pairs. Look at the items (1–7) from an article in a health magazine. Which parts of the body (a–g) do you think they match? Are these things good or bad for your body? Why?

1 a mobile phone screen   a eyes
2 sleep   b brain
3 a hard bed   c blood
4 classical music   d back
5 a ball   e stomach
6 yoghurt   f heart
7 coffee   g skin

B LISTEN FOR KEY WORDS Listen to Bianca and Ella talking about an article from a health magazine. Check your answers to Exercise A. (11.1)

102 THE BODY

C LISTEN FOR DETAIL Listen again. Complete the sentences with no more than three words from the conversation.

1. Spending a lot of time _____ is bad for your eyes.
2. Sleeping on a hard _____ can help with a bad back.
3. Rolling a ball under _____ helps blood go around the body.
4. Eating yoghurt can help keep your stomach _____.
5. Putting _____ on your skin can help make it softer.

D SPEAK Work in pairs. What things are good for you? What things are bad for you?

A: *Cold showers are good for your skin.*
B: *Yes, and for your heart, too.*

GRAMMAR
should and *shouldn't*

A WORK IT OUT Look at the sentences from the conversation between Bianca and Ella. Do we use *should* to give orders or to give advice?

You should listen to classical music every day.
You shouldn't drink too much coffee ...

B Choose the correct words to complete the rule.

should and *shouldn't*
Should / Shouldn't is followed by *infinitive + to / infinitive without to*.

C Go to the Grammar Hub on page 142.

D SPEAK Work in pairs. Student A – ask for advice about your health. Student B – give your partner advice. Take turns.

A: *I've got bad skin.*
B: *You should put coffee on it.*

PRONUNCIATION
Sentence stress

A Listen and repeat the sentences. Is *should* or *shouldn't* stressed?

B Listen and repeat. Copy the sentence stress.
1. You should exercise every day.
2. You shouldn't eat much fat or sugar.
3. You should sleep eight hours every night.
4. You shouldn't use your phone at bedtime.
5. You should drink lots of water.

SPEAKING

A PREPARE Work in pairs. Look at the problems. What advice would you give each person?
1. My trousers are too tight.   *exercise more, eat less*
2. I can't see very well.
3. My head hurts.
4. I've got a sore foot.

B PLAN Write two pieces of advice for each problem in Exercise A, one with *should* and one with *shouldn't*.

1 *You should exercise more*
2 *You shouldn't eat so much.*

C DISCUSS Work in groups of four. Student A – read out a problem. Students B, C and D – give advice. Student A – choose the best advice for each problem.

Talk about the body and health

11.2 In it to win it — Talk about your experiences

 present perfect 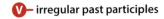 irregular past participles 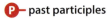 past participles

NoFear
Meet the players!

Every week on *No Fear*, 20 players climb, swim and jump as they race to the finish line. Only three people make it to the final each week. In the end, there can be only one winner! Let's meet the three fastest people from last week …

Sam McGunn, 32
Sam is a firefighter. He works hard, but in his free time he's really active. He's jumped out of an aeroplane seven times, and he's run 23 marathons! Sam is very fit, but he's never won a competition. That's why he wants to win this. His wife, Tara, and son, Ben, are here to support him. What do you think? Is Sam the strongest player on the show?

Hana Hansen, 28
Hana hasn't done any sport in her life. But she owns a large farm and works on it seven days a week, 364 days a year. She often rides horses on the farm. Her husband Raoul spends a lot of time working in other countries, so she often has to look after the animals, the house and their three young children on her own. Hana doesn't have any time for sport, but she's strong and she's a fighter. Can she beat Sam or Jude?

Jude Wexler, 31
Jude doesn't work, but he's travelled all over the world. He's climbed mountains in Africa and raced cars in the Middle East. Jude doesn't believe in hard work, he prefers to have fun. 'I travel all the time.' Have you ever flown an aeroplane? 'I have. I loved it.' Have you ever been to a gym? 'I haven't. I don't like doing exercise,' says Jude. 'To prepare for this type of challenge, you should do what you love. And I love having fun. I believe I can win.' Jude has won 14 competitions with this method. Can he make it 15?

Glossary
active (adj) someone who does a lot of different activities/sports and has a lot of energy and interests
challenge (n) something that needs a lot of skill and energy and determination to deal with or to achieve
firefighter (n) someone whose job is to put fires out and rescue people from dangerous situations

READING

A SPEAK Work in pairs. You're going to read an article about a TV programme called *No Fear*. Look at the pictures. What do you think happens in the programme?

B Read the article's introduction. Check your ideas from Exercise A.

C READ FOR GIST Read the text again. Complete the summaries with *Sam*, *Hana* or *Jude*.

1 _____ doesn't have a job and thinks the best way to win is by having fun.
2 _____ is fit, hardworking and has the support of his family.
3 _____ isn't sporty, but is strong and works all year to look after a large farm.

D READ FOR DETAIL Read again. Are the sentences true (T) or false (F)? Correct the false sentences.

1 Sam won seven competitions.   T / F
2 Sam is married with a child.   T / F
3 Hana is often home alone.   T / F
4 Hana likes to ride around her farm on her motorbike. T / F
5 Jude likes going to the gym.   T / F
6 Jude came first in 14 competitions.   T / F

E SPEAK Work in pairs. Which player do you want to win the competition? Why?

I hope Jude wins because I hate going to the gym, too.

104 THE BODY

GRAMMAR
Present perfect

A WORK IT OUT Look at the highlighted sentences from *No Fear*. Then choose the correct words to complete the rules.

> **Present perfect**
> 1 We use the present perfect to talk about *present / past* experiences.
> 2 We *say / don't say* when in the past the action happened.
> 3 We make the present perfect with subject + *have* + *past simple / past participle*.
> 4 We use *ever / never* in questions.
> 5 We use *ever / never* in negative sentences.

B Go to the Grammar Hub on page 142.

C PRACTISE Use the prompts to write present perfect sentences. Use contractions.

1 I / not be / on a TV show
   I haven't been on a TV show.
2 I / never / jump / out of a plane
3 She / climb / a mountain / three times
4 He / not try / any dangerous activities
5 They / visit / Africa / twice
6 I / never / watch / game show

D SPEAK Work in groups. Write three present perfect sentences about yourself. Two true, and one lie. Read the sentences to the group. See if they can guess the lie.

VOCABULARY
Irregular past participles

A Complete the table with the correct forms of the verbs.

Irregular verbs		
infinitive	past simple	past participle
be	was/were	been
break	broke	broken
do	1 _____	done
eat	2 _____	eaten
3 _____	forgot	forgotten
go	4 _____	gone/been
have	5 _____	had
ride	6 _____	ridden
run	7 _____	run
8 _____	saw	seen
9 _____	took	taken
10 _____	won	won

B Listen and check. Then listen and repeat.
11.4

C Go to the Vocabulary Hub on page 153.

D Go to page 121 for a list of irregular verbs.

PRONUNCIATION
Past participles

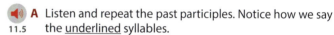
A Listen and repeat the past participles. Notice how we say
11.5 the underlined syllables.

/iːn/	/ən/	/ʌn/	/ɒn/
b<u>een</u>	brok<u>en</u>	d<u>one</u>	g<u>one</u>

B Add the verbs in the box to the table in Exercise A.
11.6 Then listen, check and repeat.

> eat<u>en</u>   forgott<u>en</u>   ridd<u>en</u>   r<u>un</u>   s<u>een</u>   tak<u>en</u>

SPEAKING

A PLAN Write four questions with *Have you ever …?*

B SPEAK Interview people in your class and make notes. Use past simple questions to get more information.

> A: *Have you ever ridden an elephant?*
> B: *Yes I have.*
> A: *Really? Where did you ride one?*
> B: *In Laos! It was amazing!*

C DISCUSS Choose two people in the class to take part in *No Fear*. Say why you chose them.

> *We chose Agata because she has done more dangerous things than anyone else.*

◯─ Talk about your experiences

THE BODY   105

11.3 Move it — Talk about sports and hobbies

G — present perfect vs past simple **P** — contractions **V** — sports **S** — understanding the sequence of past events

READING

A SPEAK Work in pairs. What do you think 'ultra-running' is?

B READ FOR GIST Read *Spotlight*. Choose the correct words to complete the sentences.

1. Ultra-running *is / isn't* running further than a marathon.
2. Ultra-running is *better / worse* for you than running marathons.
3. You *can / can't* walk when you do an ultra-run.
4. Karina *listens / doesn't listen* to music when she's running.
5. You *should / shouldn't* eat a lot during an ultra-run.
6. You *have to / don't have to* start training when you're young.

C Read again. Number the events (1–5) in the order Karina did them. Use the information in the box.

> **Understanding the sequence of past events**
>
> To understand the sequence of past events in a text, think about:
> - the order the information is stated
> - time references (e.g. *2016*, *ten years ago*)
> - sequencing words (e.g. *then*, *after that*)

a She did her first ultra-run. ☐
b Her children moved away. ☐
c She ran a marathon. ☐
d She ran in a competition in the desert. ☐
e She started running. ☐

D SPEAK Work in pairs. Would you try ultra-running? Why/Why not?

Karina Welch, ultra-runner

Are you bored of running marathons? Do you want to try something new? Ultra-running is becoming more and more popular. Ultra-runs are longer than marathons. They are usually in remote and beautiful places, like the Gobi Desert or the Rocky Mountains, so you can run and enjoy nature at the same time!

This week, we're talking to Karina Welch, an ultra-runner, who is 66.

So, Karina, when did you start running?
Twenty-five years ago, when I was in my late 40s. My children left home and I needed a way to spend my time, so I decided to start running. I began in my local park, then I ran a few marathons and finally I started ultra-running.

How many ultra-runs have you done?
I've done around 20 races. My first run was in 2009 and it was really difficult. Ultra-runs are different to marathons, but they're better for your body. You normally run in the countryside and not on hard roads.

Have you ever run a very difficult race? Where was it?
Yes, I have! Four years ago, I ran in the Marathon des Sables in the Sahara desert. I ran 250 km in six days, in very hot weather. I didn't actually run the whole time. I sometimes walked for a few kilometres, but that's normal in ultra-running. The important thing is to keep moving!

What do you do when you run for such a long time? Do you listen to music?
No, I like the silence, especially when I'm running in a very quiet place. I like listening to the birds and the wind. I usually eat a lot when I run. You need food to keep your energy levels up.

What are your tips for someone who is interested in ultra-running?
It's never too late to start! I didn't run when I was young and now I love it. Start with jogging, and slowly increase the number of kilometres. And always warm up before you run!

Finally, what do you like most about ultra-running?
I feel free. When I am running, I don't think about anything. It's just me, my legs and the sky.

> **Glossary**
>
> **jogging (n)** the activity or exercise of running at a slow steady speed
> **warm up (phr v)** to prepare for a sport or activity by doing gentle exercises or practising just before it starts

106 THE BODY

GRAMMAR
Present perfect vs past simple

A WORK IT OUT Look at the sentences from *Spotlight*. Choose the correct words to complete the rules.

I've done around 20 races.

My first run was in 2009.

Have you ever run a very difficult race? Where was it?

> **Present perfect and past simple**
>
> 1 We use the present perfect to talk about an action in the past. We *say / don't say* when it happened.
> 2 We use the past simple to talk about an action in the past. We *know / don't know* when it happened.
> 3 We use time expressions, like *ago, in 2010, last week* with the *present perfect / past simple*.
> 4 We often ask a general question about past experiences using the *past simple / present perfect*.
> 5 We then use the *past simple / present perfect* to ask for more details or to give more details (such as *where, when, how*).

B Go to the **Grammar Hub** on **page 142**.

C SPEAK Work in pairs. Take turns to ask and answer questions. Discuss where and when you did them.

1 try / snowboarding?
2 run / in a race?
3 meet / a famous person?
4 win / a sports competition?

A: Have you ever tried snowboarding?
B: Yes, I have.
A: When did you go?
B: When I was in Andorra, last year.

PRONUNCIATION
Contractions

A Listen and read. Notice the pronunciation of the contractions.
11.7

1 a I **have** never been to Moscow.
  b **I've** never been to Moscow.
2 a He **has** never run a marathon.
  b **He's** never run a marathon.
3 a We **haven't won** the competition.
  b We **have not won** the competition.

B Listen and tick (✓) the sentences you hear. Then listen
11.8 again and repeat the sentences.

1 a ☐ I have been to New York five times.
  b ☐ I've been to New York five times.
2 a ☐ Elliott has never eaten sushi.
  b ☐ Elliott's never eaten sushi.
3 a ☐ She has not run a marathon.
  b ☐ She hasn't run a marathon.

VOCABULARY
Sports

A Complete the phrases with the verbs in the box.

> do go play

1 _____ running   2 _____ karate

3 _____ football

B Go to the **Vocabulary Hub** on **page 153**.

C SPEAK Work in pairs. Tell your partner what sports you do and how often you do them.

SPEAKING HUB

A PREPARE You are going to interview your classmates about sports and hobbies. Write five main questions.

Have you ever run a marathon?
When was the last time you went to the gym?

B DISCUSS Interview three students. Write notes about their answers. Try to ask follow-up questions to get more information.

A: What sports do you play?
B: I play football once a week and sometimes play basketball with my brother.
A: Do you play for a football team?
B: No, I just play with friends for fun.

C DISCUSS Have a class discussion. What is the most popular sport or hobby? Which is the most unusual? What is the most interesting thing that someone has done or made?

I think Pablo's hobby is the most unusual. He does Zumba ... underwater!

Talk about sports and hobbies

Café Hub

11.4 Get fit
F – ask for information   P – stress and intonation

COMPREHENSION

A ▶ Watch the video. Correct the six mistakes in the poster.

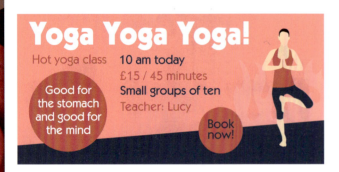

B ▶ SPEAK Work in pairs. Are the sentences true (T) or false (F)? Correct the false sentences. Then watch the video again and check your answers.

1 Milly's sitting in the park with her back against a tree. T / F
2 Neena is sitting in the kitchen. T / F
3 Neena did Yoga before and fell over. T / F
4 The *Yoga Yoga Yoga* receptionist has short hair. T / F
5 At the beginning of the class, they put their hands on their chest. T / F

USEFUL PHRASES

A Change one word in each useful phrase. Use the words in the box.

> calling   coming   eyes   fired   ~~last~~   legs

1 Oh, one final thing. *Oh, one last thing.*
2 Thanks for phoning Yoga Yoga Yoga. _____
3 What do you mean, you aren't working? _____
4 You're sacked! _____
5 Cross your arms. _____
6 Close your mouth. _____

B How do you say these useful phrases in your language?

FUNCTIONAL LANGUAGE
Asking for information

A ▶ 00.40–02.17 Complete Milly's questions. Then watch the video and check your answers.

1 What _____ is the next slow yoga class?
2 How _____ does it cost?
3 How _____ is it?
4 Are _____ any lockers for our bags?
5 How _____ people are in the class?
6 Can _____ book two places for Milly and Neena, please?

B Complete the questions. Use the questions in Exercise A to help you.

1 _____ do you open/close?
2 _____ reserve a badminton court?
3 _____ is it for one lesson?
4 _____ does it start/finish?
5 _____ teams are in the league?

C SPEAK Work in pairs. Student A – ask a question from Exercise A or B. Student B – make up an answer. Swap.

A: *What time do you open?*
B: *9 am every morning.*

THE BODY

MILLY   SAM   NEENA   ZAC   GABY

PRONUNCIATION
Stress and intonation

 A Listen and complete the questions.
1 What _____ do you open?
2 How long does it _____?
3 How much does it _____?
4 _____'s the instructor?
5 _____ many people are in the class?
6 _____ does it start?

B Listen again and repeat. Copy the stress and intonation.

C SPEAK Work in pairs. Practise asking the questions in Exercise A. Remember to use the correct stress and intonation.

SPEAKING

DISCUSS Work in pairs. Take turns to book a lesson using the information below.

Student A – call to book a lesson. Say who the lesson is for and ask about:
- time
- cost
- length of lesson
- name of instructor

Student B – look at the information in the adverts and answer Student A's questions.

Urban dance class

All ages!
Teacher: Nino
Every evening 7–8 pm
Adult: £7.50   Students: £4.00
Only 12 places per class

Boxing class
Beginners!
Small classes – five people.
Teacher: Max
3 pm to 4 pm every day
£12.50

Swimming lessons

City swimming pool
Teachers: Ahmed and Fraser
Every Saturday
10.30 am to 12.30 pm
Adult: £5   Child: £2

Tennis lessons
One-hour lessons with your coach, Andy
Maximum of two people per lesson
Every afternoon from 2 to 4 pm
Adult: £16   Child: £9

○ Ask for information

➤ Turn to **page 170** to learn how to write a recommendation on a forum.

Unit 11 Review

GRAMMAR

A Find and correct the mistake in each sentence.

1 You should to stop smoking.
_____

2 You don't should eat junk food every day.
_____

3 How often I should do exercise?
_____

4 Do you think I should to join a gym?
_____

5 She shouldn't drinks so much coffee.
_____

6 I shouldn't start going to bed earlier.
_____

B Write the words in the correct order to make sentences.

1 jumped out of / three / He's / an aeroplane / times
   He's jumped out of an aeroplane three times.

2 any / never / sport / He's / done
_____

3 She's / won / never / a competition
_____

4 you / been / Have / India / to / ?
_____

5 you / Have / the new restaurant / to / been / in town / ?
_____

6 been / Japan / times / I've / to / five
_____

7 Have / an / you / elephant / ever / ridden ?
_____

8 Mexican / never / eaten / food / She's
_____

C Use the prompts to complete the conversation. Use the present perfect and past simple where necessary.

Eloise: you / ever / try / yoga? ¹ _Have you ever tried yoga?_
Michael: Yes, ² _____.
Eloise: when / you / try / it? ³ _____
Michael: Three months ago. I / go / to a class near my house. ⁴ _____
Eloise: you / enjoy / it? ⁵ _____
Michael: Yes, ⁶ _____. I want to go again. You / ever / try / it? ⁷ _____.
Eloise: No, ⁸ _____. Maybe we can go together.

D SPEAK Work in pairs. Talk about sports and exercise and then give some advice.

A: _I want to exercise outside._
B: _You should go running._

VOCABULARY

A Label the parts of the body (1–10) with words in the box.

| arm | brain | eye | foot | hand |
| heart | leg | neck | nose | stomach |

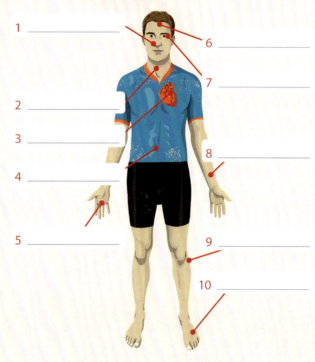

1 _____
2 _____
3 _____
4 _____
5 _____
6 _____
7 _____
8 _____
9 _____
10 _____

B Complete with the correct form of the verbs.

Ben is amazing. He's ¹*did* / **done** everything and he's ²**been** / *went* everywhere. He's ³*flew* / *flown* a plane and he's ⁴*seen* / *saw* the Pyramids. I haven't ever ⁵*win* / *won* a competition or even ⁶*ridden* / *rode* a horse. But I have ⁷*broken* / *broke* a bone, so I suppose that's something.

C Complete the table with the sports in the box.

| cycling | ~~judo~~ badminton swimming ~~football~~ |
| gymnastics basketball surfing tennis ~~running~~ |

play	go	do
football	running	judo

FUNCTIONAL LANGUAGE

Complete the questions (1–6) with the words in the box.

| any | how | cost | time | ~~when~~ | who |

1 ___When___ 's the next exercise class?
2 What _____ does the gym open?
3 _____ long is the class?
4 How much does it _____?
5 Do I need to bring _____ equipment?
6 _____ 's the class instructor?

110 THE BODY

12 MODERN LIVES

The best way to predict your future is to create it.
Abraham Lincoln

Jia Jia – a robot at a technology conference in Shanghai, China.

OBJECTIVES

- talk about future plans
- make predictions
- talk about social media habits
- show interest in something
- write a formal email

Work with a partner. Discuss the questions.

1. Where do you want to live in 10 years' time?
2. Look at the picture. Would you like a robot like this?
3. What do you want to do in the future?

MODERN LIVES 111

12.1 Life's too busy ● Talk about future plans

 going to    going to: weak and strong to   V— future time expressions

LISTENING

A Look at the picture. Work in groups and answer the questions.
- What problem does the person in the picture have?
- Are you a busy person? Why/Why not?
- How do you remember everything you have to do?

B LISTEN FOR GIST Listen to some friends talking. Who is the most organised person: Juliet, Mario or Kelly?

C LISTEN FOR DETAIL Listen again. Choose the correct answer to complete the sentences.

1 Juliet is working this weekend because
  a she always works at the weekend.
  b she was on holiday last week.
  c work is really busy at the moment.
2 Mario read an article about
  a how to work full time and study.
  b how to manage time.
  c how to get a better job.
3 According to the newspaper article, you should
  a make a short list of tasks.
  b make a long list of tasks.
  c never make a list of tasks.
4 Mario decides
  a to study this evening.
  b to learn to make lists.
  c to study in the mornings and work in the evenings.

D SPEAK Work in pairs. Do you agree with the advice? Why/Why not? What are some other ways to organise your time?

A: *I agree with Kelly. You need to understand your body clock.*
B: *To organise my time, I use an app to make lists.*

GRAMMAR
going to

A WORK IT OUT Read the sentences from the conversation. Underline the verbs. Does *going to* refer to the present or the future?

1 I'm going to try that idea at work next week.
2 I'm definitely not going to finish it.
3 Are you going to finish your essay this weekend?

B Complete the rules with *be* or *infinitive*.

going to for future intentions and plans
We use ¹_____ + *going to* + ²_____ to talk about a future plan.

C Go to the **Grammar Hub** on **page 144**.

D Complete the sentences with the correct form of *going to*. Use the verbs in brackets.

1 I'm _____ (go) to the cinema at the weekend.
2 I'm _____ (meet) friends after class.
3 I'm _____ (relax) at home tonight.
4 I'm _____ (have) chicken for dinner.
5 I'm _____ (do) my homework this afternoon.
6 I'm _____ (buy) a new car next year.
7 I'm _____ (travel) around Europe this summer.

E SPEAK Work in pairs. Make the sentences in Exercise D true for you.

A: *What are you going to do after class?*
B: *I'm going to meet my sister for lunch.*
A: *Oh, that sounds nice. I'm going to go to the gym.*

112 MODERN LIVES

PRONUNCIATION

going to: weak and strong *to*

A Listen and repeat the sentences. Notice that *to* sounds different in each sentence.

1 I'm going **to** finish my essay this weekend.
2 I'm not going **to** invite Paul and David to the barbecue.

B Read the sentences and circle /tə/ or /tuː/. Draw a ‿ to show any sounds that link together. Then listen and repeat.

1 I'm going to see the new Wes Anderson film at the weekend. /tə/ /tuː/
2 Matt's going to study in Washington DC. /tə/ /tuː/
3 I'm not going to eat anything until we get there. /tə/ /tuː/
4 He's going to open a restaurant in Cambridge. /tə/ /tuː/
5 I'm not going to stay long at the party. /tə/ /tuː/

C SPEAK Work in pairs. Practise saying the sentences in Exercise B. Listen and check your partner's pronunciation. Be careful to say *to* correctly and to link sounds with /w/.

VOCABULARY

Future time expressions

A Listen to Andrew talking to his manager, Yasmin. Tick (✓) the things Andrew is going to do this weekend.

+	Add to list
1	☐ Ask Jane about invitation
2	☐ Meet Chris
3	☐ Work at the conference

B Read the conversation between Andrew and Yasmin. <u>Underline</u> seven future time expressions.

Yasmin: So, Andrew. Are we all ready for the product launch next month?
Andrew: I think so. I still need to do a few things, like ask Jane about the invitations.
Yasmin: Are you going to speak to her soon?
Andrew: Yes. She's out at the moment, but I'm going to phone her this afternoon.
Yasmin: Great. And what about Luis and Chris? Have you arranged a meeting with them?
Andrew: I'm going to meet Chris tomorrow, but I don't know about Luis. I think he's travelling at the moment. We've emailed each other a lot, but maybe I'll actually meet him one day!
Yasmin: OK. And what about the reception tonight? Are you going to be there?
Andrew: Yes, definitely. I'm looking forward to it.
Yasmin: I wanted to ask you … can you work at the weekend? We need help with the conference.
Andrew: Er, yes, that's fine.

C Use the prompts to write questions with *going to* and future time expressions.

1 What / do / tonight?
   What are you going to do tonight?
2 How / travel / to class / next week?
   _____
3 What time / get up / tomorrow?
   _____
4 do / anything special / at the weekend?
   _____
5 go / on holiday / this year?
   _____

D SPEAK Work in pairs. Ask and answer the questions in Exercise C.

SPEAKING

A SPEAK Work in pairs. Student A – go to the **Communication Hub** on **page 157**. Student B – go to the **Communication Hub** on **page 159**.

B DISCUSS Write a list of five things you want to do soon. Share them with a partner. Ask and answer questions to find out more.

A: *When are you going to start a photography course?*
B: *Next month. I love taking pictures!*
A: *Where are you going to do it?*
B: *At the art college.*

○— Talk about future plans

MODERN LIVES 113

12.2 Everything will be shiny — Make predictions

G – *will* for predictions **V** – collocations with *get* **P** – contractions: *'ll*

What will the future be like?
No one knows, but we all like making predictions. In 1998, a young boy wrote an essay for a school competition with predictions about the year 2018. Michael Forster was ten years old when he wrote it. He didn't win the competition, but his mother saved the essay anyway and gave it to him on his 30th birthday. Some of Michael's predictions came true and others, well … read his essay below.

> In 20 years' time, it will be 2018. I will be 30 years old. The world will be very different. Everyone will wear silver clothes and will have silver hair. All houses will be metal and everything will be shiny. Cars won't drive on roads; they will fly in the air. People won't walk because they will fly around with jetpacks instead. People won't get sick, hungry or thirsty. And they won't need to get money or have a job. Robots will do everything. They will look after the people and get them everything they need. In shops, there will be robot shop assistants. Children will get to school on their jetpacks. At school, there won't be desks. Every student will have a computer. The teachers will be robots. The teacher-robots won't get angry with the students. Tottenham will win the European Cup.

Although Michael was wrong about a lot of his predictions – we don't all have silver hair, for example – some of his predictions were correct. Here at Futurelife, we love looking at past ideas about the future, so we asked Michael about his essay. 'I'm surprised that some of my ideas came true,' he said. 'We now pay machines for food at the supermarket. And many of us don't have desks; we work on computers all day.' What Michael's predictions show is that no one can predict the future, but a ten-year-old child's ideas aren't all crazy!

Glossary
essay (n) a piece of writing by a student about a subject
jetpack (n) a machine that someone wears on the back to make them fly
prediction (n) what you think will happen in the future

READING

A Work in pairs. Look at the pictures (1–3). Describe the technology in each and how it might improve the world.

B READ FOR GIST Read *Future life*. Tick (✓) the topics that Michael made predictions about.

- ☐ fashion
- ☐ video games
- ☐ virtual reality
- ☐ robotics
- ☐ houses
- ☐ education
- ☐ transport
- ☐ football

C READ FOR DETAIL Read again. Are the sentences true (T) or false (F)? Correct the false sentences.

1 Michael gave the essay to his mother on her birthday. T / F
2 Michael thought people would walk more in the future. T / F
3 Michael thought that people wouldn't need jobs in the future. T / F
4 Michael's prediction about machines in shops came true. T / F
5 Michael thought that there would be robot teachers in 2018. T / F

D SPEAK Work in pairs. Answer the questions.

1 Which of Michael's predictions came true and which didn't?
2 Do you think that making predictions is useful?

A: *Some of Michael's predictions came true. For example, every student here has a tablet.*
B: *Yes, but we don't all wear silver clothes!*

12.2

GRAMMAR
will for predictions

A Read these predictions about the future. Which ones came true? What has happened?

> Computers are tools for scientists. Nobody will want to buy one for their home.
> – **Henrik Andersson,** head of the American Telegraph Association (1943)

> People want to go out to dinner, see their friends … maybe go to the cinema. They won't stay at home watching TV.
> – **Guy Chandler,** movie producer (1946)

> Bitcoin is the future. In five years' time, Bitcoin will be the only way to buy things online.
> – **Yoichi Katayama,** author of *The Eco Futurist* (2009)

> Will we ever put a man on the moon? Maybe, but not for another 100 years.
> – **Elliott Shaw,** writer for The Boston Times (1965)

> Sadly, we won't have flying cars any time soon. They're just too expensive.
> – **Sarah Kalensky,** writer for *The Forecaster* (2017)

B WORK IT OUT Choose the correct words to complete the rules.

will for predictions
1 For positive sentences, we use subject + *will* + infinitive **with / without to**.
2 For negative sentences, we use subject + **won't not / won't** + infinitive without *to*.
3 For questions, we use **will / do** + subject + infinitive without *to*.

C Go to the **Grammar Hub** on **page 144**.

D PRACTISE Complete the sentences with *will* or *won't*.

In the future, …

1 there _____ be cars. Everyone will have jetpacks.

2 students won't go to school. They _____ study at home.

3 human teachers _____ exist. All teachers will be robots.

4 other languages won't exist. Everyone _____ speak English.

5 there _____ be any books in schools. Every student will have a tablet.

E SPEAK Work in pairs. Do you agree or disagree with the predictions in Exercise D?

VOCABULARY
Collocations with *get*

A These sentences use phrases with *get*. Find two other sentences in *Future life* that use phrases with *get*.

*People won't **get sick**, **hungry** or **thirsty**.*

*And they won't need to **get money** or have a job.*

*Children will **get to school** on their jetpacks.*

get
The verb *get* has three different meanings: **become** (*get sick*), **buy or obtain** (*get money*) or **arrive** (*get to school*).

B Go to the **Vocabulary Hub** on **page 153**.

C SPEAK Work in pairs. Ask and answer the questions.

- What time you will get home today?
- What time do you usually get tired in the evening?
- What do you want to get the next time you go shopping?

I'll get home at 8 pm today. What about you?

PRONUNCIATION
Contractions: *'ll*

🔊 **A** Listen and repeat. Notice the difference between present simple and future simple with a contraction.
12.5

They like the film. They'll like the film.

🔊 **B** Listen and tick (✓) the sentence you hear.
12.6

1 a ☐ We work together.
  b ☐ We'll work together.

2 a ☐ We leave early at the weekend.
  b ☐ We'll leave early at the weekend.

3 a ☐ We live in a big house.
  b ☐ We'll live in a big house.

4 a ☐ I travel a lot.
  b ☐ I'll travel a lot.

SPEAKING

A Work in groups. Think about the world in 2050. Make predictions about the things in the box.

> houses   technology   the weather   transport

B PLAN In your groups, write predictions about what *will* and *won't* happen in 2050.

C DISCUSS Work with students from other groups. Discuss their predictions. Do you agree with them? Why/Why not?

D PRESENT In your new group, choose three predictions you think will come true. Present your ideas to the class and explain why you think they will happen.

◯– **Make predictions**

MODERN LIVES   115

12.3 Communication — Talk about social media habits

 internet communication   diphthongs   might   predicting

VOCABULARY
Internet communication

A SPEAK Work in pairs. Look at the infographic. How many of the social networks do you use? Do you use any others?

B DISCUSS Work in pairs and discuss the questions. Make notes.

Which network …
1 has the largest number of users?
2 is most popular with younger people?
3 is useful for professional people?
4 is useful to read the news?
5 is most popular in Asia?

C Quickly read the infographic and check your answers.

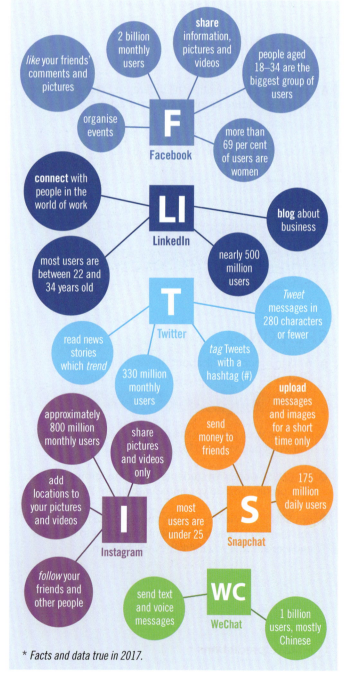

* Facts and data true in 2017.

D Match the words in the box to the icons (1–10).

| blog | chat | connect | follow | like |
| share | tag | trend | Tweet | upload |

1 _____   6 _____
2 _____   7 _____
3 _____   8 _____
4 _____   9 _____
5 _____   10 _____

E Complete the sentences with words from Exercise D.
1 When I _____ a picture, I only _____ it with my friends.
2 I _____ comedians on *Twitter*. They _____ really funny comments and videos.
3 I _____ about music once a week.
4 On *Facebook*, I usually just '_____' a few posts from family and friends.
5 I _____ with my friends on the phone not on social media.
6 I hate it when my friends _____ me in pictures.

F SPEAK Work in pairs. Which sentences in Exercise E are true for you?

PRONUNCIATION
Diphthongs

A Listen and repeat the words in the table. Notice how we say the underlined letters. (12.7)

/ɪə/	/eɪ/	/ʊə/	/ɔɪ/
n<u>ea</u>r	pl<u>a</u>ce	t<u>ou</u>rist	b<u>oy</u>

/əʊ/	/eə/	/aɪ/	/aʊ/
n<u>o</u>se	h<u>air</u>	m<u>y</u>	m<u>ou</u>th

Diphthongs are two vowel sounds that are said together. There are eight diphthongs in English – /ɪə/, /eɪ/, /ʊə/, /ɔɪ/, /əʊ/, /eə/, /aɪ/ and /aʊ/. Practising these sounds will improve your pronunciation.

B Work in pairs. Add the words and phrases in the box to the table in Exercise A. Then listen and repeat. (12.8)

| here | Facebook | follow | like |
| mouse | point | secure | share |

116 MODERN LIVES

LISTENING

A PREPARE You are going to listen to five people talking about social media. Look at the pictures and guess what their favourite social media network is.

> **Predicting**
> Before you listen, use information such as pictures, questions, what you already know, etc to help you predict the topic or guess information.

B LISTEN FOR GIST Listen to the people. How many predictions in Exercise A did you get right?
🔊 12.9

C LISTEN FOR DETAIL Listen again. Choose a, b or c to complete the sentences.
🔊 12.9

1 Shani …
  a studied business.   c teaches business.
  b runs a business.

2 Luke works in a …
  a café.   b theatre.   c school.

3 Wai likes sharing his pictures on …
  a Facebook.   b Instagram.   c LinkedIn.

4 Jean has got … grandchildren.
  a four   b five   c six

5 Maria likes that pictures only stay on Snapchat for …
  a ten years.   b two hours.   c ten seconds.

D SPEAK Work in pairs and discuss the questions.

1 Which age group do you think spends most time on social media? Why?
2 How long do you think they spend on social media each week?

GRAMMAR
might

A WORK IT OUT Look at these sentences about social media. Then choose the correct words to complete the rules.

A: I might sign up to Snapchat so I can keep up to date!
B: A lot of the people at work also use LinkedIn, so I might set up an account, too.
A: I might try some other social media networks, but at the moment, I don't really know how to use them.

> **might**
> 1 We use *might* for **definite plans / possible plans** or wishes.
> 2 We use *might* **before / after** the infinitive without *to*.

B Go to the Grammar Hub on page 144.

C SPEAK Work in pairs. Think about your own use of social media. Tell your partner what you *are going to / might* use more (or less) in the future.

A: I'm so busy. I spend a lot of time on Facebook. I might try to use it less.
B: I'm going to start using Twitter.

🔴 SPEAKING HUB

A Go to the Communication Hub on page 158.

B Work in groups. Compare the results of your survey to the information in the infographic.

Like the infographic, we found that the most popular social network was Facebook. Some people in the class use Facebook and Twitter for their work, not LinkedIn.

🔴 Talk about social media habits

Café Hub

12.4 Party time
F– show interest in something   P– stress and intonation

COMPREHENSION

A ▶ SPEAK Work in pairs. What is happening in each picture? Put the pictures in the order (1–6) you think they happen. Then watch the video and check your answers.

a ___

b ___

c ___

d ___

e ___

f ___

B SPEAK Work in pairs. Retell the story from the pictures.

FUNCTIONAL LANGUAGE
Showing interest in something

▶ Complete the conversations with the words in the box. Then watch the video again and check.

| did   great   love   matter   poor   problem |
| shame   terrible   thanks   worry |

Replying to bad news

Zac: Did you get tickets to the festival?
Sam: No, I didn't. All the tickets were sold out.
Zac: That's a [1]_____. Sorry about that.
Sam: Ah, it doesn't [2]_____.

Milly: I fell off my bike.
Gaby: Oh no! [3]_____ you. Are you OK?
Milly: I'm fine. I fall off my bike all the time.
Gaby: Really? That's [4]_____!

Replying to good news

Dad: Yeah, we're here for the weekend.
Sam: That's [5]_____!

Apologising

Milly: Hey! I'm really sorry I'm late.
Neena: No [6]_____. You missed Sam's face. He was so surprised!
Milly: I'm so sorry I'm late.
Gaby: It's all right. Don't [7]_____.

Giving compliments

Milly: That's a cool dress.
Gaby: Thanks, I [8]_____ it.
Milly: Mmmm ... and this cake is so good!
Gaby: [9]_____. I made it!
Milly: [10]_____ you? That's awesome!

118 MODERN LIVES

MILLY   SAM   NEENA   ZAC   GABY

PRONUNCIATION
Stress and intonation

A Listen and repeat the replies. Copy the stress and intonation.

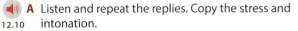

1 That's amazing!
2 I love it!
3 That's terrible.
4 Poor you.
5 That's a shame.
6 It doesn't matter.
7 No problem.
8 Don't worry.

B SPEAK Work in pairs. Student A – tell your partner some good or bad news. Student B – reply to your partner with one of the phrases in Exercise A. Remember to use the correct stress and intonation. Swap.

A: I got a new job.
B: That's amazing!

SPEAKING

A PREPARE Work in pairs. Write two conversations. Use the ideas below or your own ideas. Use the Functional language to help you.

Conversation 1
- You arrive late at the party because you got lost.
- You get lost all the time.
- You like your partner's jacket.
- You think the food is great.

Conversation 2
- You arrive late at the party because you left your bag on the bus.
- You lose things all the time.
- You like your partner's shoes.
- You think the music is great.

B PRESENT Practise your conversations. Then choose one and perform it for the rest of the class.

A: I'm really sorry I'm late.
B: It's all right – don't worry.
A: I got lost.
B: Oh no, poor you! Are you OK?

○ **Show interest in something**

➤ Turn to **page 171** to learn how to write a formal email.

Unit 12 Review

GRAMMAR

A Complete the conversation with the correct form of *going to* and the verbs in brackets.

Erin: What [1]___*are you going to do*___ (you/do) when you graduate?

Niall: I [2]_____ (work) for my uncle's company in Australia for the summer, then in September I [3]_____ (start) a course at university there.

Erin: Wow! What [4]_____ (you/study)?

Niall: Medicine. I [5]_____ (be) a doctor one day! How about you? [6]_____ (you/look) for a job?

Erin: No, I [7]_____ (travel) around Asia with some friends for a few months.

Niall: Wow! That sounds amazing. You [8]_____ (have) an amazing time.

Erin: Yes, and maybe I can visit you in Australia!

B Use the prompts to write predictions about the world in ten years' time. Then compare your ideas with a partner. Do you agree?

1   The weather / hotter

____*The weather will be hotter.*____

2   Food / more expensive

_____

3   Clothes / cheaper

_____

4   Robots / do a lot of jobs that humans do now

_____

5   Children / use pens and pencils at school

_____

6   People / drive electric cars

_____

C **SPEAK** Work in pairs. Ask and answer questions about the future. Think about:

- your plans for the summer
- predictions for your life ten years from now

D Complete the sentences with *going to*, *might* or *will*.

1   I met Gianni on *Facebook*. We aren't sure yet, but we ____*might*____ meet face-to-face soon.

2   I start as my own boss next week, so *LinkedIn* _____ certainly be the social media network that I use the most.

3   I _____ send her a message now.

4   There's a new social media network. It _____ be popular in the future, but it will be difficult to catch up with *Facebook* and *Twitter*.

5   I think people _____ probably use social media more and more in the future.

VOCABULARY

A Complete the future time expressions with *a, e, i, o* or *u*.

1   I rarely do exercise _a_ t th _e_ w _e_ _e_ k _e_ nd.

2   I'm planning to buy a house n__xt y___ __r.

3   I'd like to climb Mount Everest __n__ d__y.

4   I've got to go home s__ __n.

5   I'm going on holiday th__s s__mm__r.

B **SPEAK** Tick (✓) the sentences in Exercise A that are true for you. Discuss your answers with a partner.

C Use the words in the box to complete the phrases with *get*.

> home   hungry   lost   money
> organised   sick   ~~to college~~   wet

1   I usually get _to college_ at nine in the morning.

2   It's raining. Let's go inside – I don't want to get _____.

3   I'm not very busy today. I think I'll get _____ early tonight.

4   Let's take a map so we don't get _____.

5   The five-list plan really helps me to get _____.

6   I always get _____ at about 3 pm.

7   Don't give her too many – she'll get _____.

8   I have to work. I don't get any _____ from my parents.

D Choose the correct words to complete the text.

I'm a designer and I have my own website. I [1]*connect* / *blog* about art and design.

I sometimes use *Facebook* when I want to [2]*upload* / *chat* pictures and [3]*follow* / *share* them with my friends and family. It makes me happy when my friends [4]*blog* / *like* my pictures. I've got a *Twitter* account. I [5]*follow* / *upload* my friends. They [6]*twitter* / *tweet* a lot!

E Work in groups. Discuss the questions.

1   Who do you follow on social media? Why?

2   Do you think social media is the best way to connect with friends and family? Why/Why not?

3   What kind of things do you upload to social media?

4   Do you ever get angry when friends tag you in photos online?

5   What topic could you blog about?

FUNCTIONAL LANGUAGE

Match sentences (1–5) with replies (a–e).

1   I'm sorry I'm late.

2   I lost my phone yesterday.

3   I'm sorry, but I haven't got any money.

4   My brother's going to be on TV tonight.

5   I passed all my exams.

a   Don't worry. I can pay for this.

b   Wow! That's great.

c   That's OK.

d   Really? That's interesting. Is he an actor?

e   Oh, no. That's awful.

120   MODERN LIVES

Irregular Verbs

Infinitive	Past simple	Past participle
be	was/were	been
become	became	become
begin	began	begun
break	broke	broken
bring	brought	brought
build	built	built
buy	bought	bought
can	could	(been able to)
catch	caught	caught
choose	chose	chosen
come	came	come
cost	cost	cost
cut	cut	cut
drink	drank	drunk
eat	ate	eaten
fall	fell	fallen
feel	felt	felt
find	found	found
forget	forgot	forgotten
get	got	got
give	gave	given
go	went	gone/been
grow	grew	grown
have	had	had
hear	heard	heard
hit	hit	hit
hold	held	held
hurt	hurt	hurt
keep	kept	kept
know	knew	known
leave	left	left
lend	lent	lent
let	let	let

Infinitive	Past simple	Past participle
lose	lost	lost
make	made	made
mean	meant	meant
meet	met	met
must	had to	(had to)
pay	paid	paid
put	put	put
read	read	read
ride	rode	ridden
run	ran	run
say	said	said
see	saw	seen
sell	sold	sold
set	set	set
shut	shut	shut
sing	sang	sung
sit	sat	sat
sleep	slept	slept
speak	spoke	spoken
spell	spelt/spelled	spelt/spelled
spend	spent	spent
stand	stood	stood
steal	stole	stolen
take	took	taken
teach	taught	taught
tell	told	told
think	thought	thought
throw	threw	thrown
understand	understood	understood
wear	wore	worn
win	won	won
write	wrote	written

PHONETIC SYMBOLS

Single vowels				Diphthongs			Consonants			
/ɪ/	fish	/fɪʃ/	/ɪə/	ear	/ɪə/	/p/	pen	/pen/	/s/	snake	/sneɪk/
/iː/	bean	/biːn/	/eɪ/	face	/feɪs/	/b/	bag	/bæg/	/z/	zoo	/zuː/
/ʊ/	foot	/fʊt/	/ʊə/	tourist	/ˈtʊərɪst/	/t/	tea	/tiː/	/ʃ/	shop	/ʃɒp/
/uː/	shoe	/ʃuː/	/ɔɪ/	boy	/bɔɪ/	/d/	dog	/dɒg/	/ʒ/	television	/ˈtelɪvɪʒən/
/e/	egg	/eg/	/əʊ/	nose	/nəʊz/	/tʃ/	chip	/tʃɪp/	/m/	map	/mæp/
/ə/	mother	/ˈmʌðə/	/eə/	hair	/heə/	/dʒ/	jazz	/dʒæz/	/n/	name	/neɪm/
/ɜː/	word	/wɜːd/	/aɪ/	eye	/aɪ/	/k/	cake	/keɪk/	/ŋ/	ring	/rɪŋ/
/ɔː/	talk	/tɔːk/	/aʊ/	mouth	/maʊθ/	/g/	girl	/ɡɜːl/	/h/	house	/haʊs/
/æ/	back	/bæk/				/f/	film	/fɪlm/	/l/	leg	/leg/
/ʌ/	bus	/bʌs/				/v/	verb	/vɜːb/	/r/	road	/rəʊd/
/ɑː/	arm	/ɑːm/				/θ/	thing	/θɪŋ/	/w/	wine	/waɪn/
/ɒ/	top	/tɒp/				/ð/	these	/ðiːz/	/j/	yes	/jes/

Grammar Hub

1.1 Present simple *be*: positive and negative

	Positive	Negative
I	**I am** in this class.	**I am not** in this class.
	I'm in this class.	**I'm not** in this class.
he/she/it	**She is** South Korean.	**He is not** South Korean.
	She's South Korean.	**He isn't** South Korean.
you/we/they	**They are** from Japan.	**We are not** from Japan.
	They're from Japan.	**We aren't** from Japan.

- We use *be* to talk about states, facts and personal details, e.g. name, nationality, age or status.
- We use a noun or subject pronoun (*I*, *you*, etc) before the verb *be*.

  He's South Korean. NOT ~~Is South Korean.~~

- We often use contractions when we speak.

  I am 20 years old. → *I'm 20 years old.*

- In the negative contraction, we can also say: *You're not, He's not, She's not*, etc.

  She isn't 24 years old. OR She's not 24 years old.

> **Be careful!**
> - We use *you* for one person <u>and</u> more than one person.
>
>   *Tony, you're in this class.*
>
>   *Tony and Paola, you're in this class.*

1.2 Present simple *be*: questions

Question	Positive short answer	Negative short answer
Am I in this class?	Yes, **you are.**	No, **you aren't.**
Are you married?	Yes, **I am.**	No, **I'm not.**
Is he/she/it French?	Yes, **he/she/it is.**	No, **he/she/it isn't.**
Are we in this class?	Yes, **you/we are.**	No, **you/we aren't.**
Are you married?	Yes, **we are.**	No, **we aren't.**
Are they friends?	Yes, **they are.**	No, **they aren't.**

- In questions, the subject pronoun (*I*, *you*, etc) comes after the verb *be*.

  Am I in this class? NOT ~~I am in this class?~~

- In negative short answers we can also say: *No, you're not., No, he's not., No, she's not.*, etc.

> **Be careful!**
> - In positive short answers, we don't use contractions.
>
>   *Yes, she is. NOT ~~Yes, she's.~~*

Question word + *be* + subject + ?	
Age	**How old are** you?
Place	**Where are** you from?
Thing	**What's** your name?

1.3 *a/an* and plural nouns; *this, that, these, those*

- We use *a/an* with singular nouns.
- We use *a* with nouns that begin with a consonant sound (e.g. *s, w*) and *an* with nouns with a vowel sound (*a, e, i, o, u*).

a	**a s**andwich
	a wallet
an	**an e**mail
	an airport

- We don't use *a* or *an* with plural nouns.

	Singular	Plural
Add -s.	pen	pen**s**
Add -es to nouns that end -s or -ch.	addres**s**	addres**ses**
	wat**ch**	watch**es**
Change -y after a consonant to -ies.	countr**y**	countr**ies**
	nationalit**y**	nationalit**ies**
Some nouns are irregular.	man	men
	child	children
	person	people

	this	With a singular noun that's near	**This** is my bag here.
	that	With a singular noun that's far	**That** is Paola's bag over there.
	these	With a plural noun that's near	**These** are our bags here.
	those	With a plural noun that's far	**Those** are your bags over there.

- In questions, the verb *be* comes before *this, that, these* or *those*.

  *Is **that** your bag over there? NOT ~~That is your bag over there?~~*

122 GRAMMAR HUB

Grammar Hub

1.1 Present simple *be*: positive and negative

A Choose the correct form of *be* for each subject.

1 I   *am* / is / are
2 you   am / *is* / *are*
3 it   am / *is* / are
4 they   am / is / *are*
5 she   am / *is* / are
6 we   am / is / *are*

B Choose the correct form of *be* for each subject.

1 I ___am___ Italian.
2 We _____ married.
3 She _____ my friend.
4 It _____ 20 years old.
5 You _____ in class 4A.
6 Asim and Akil _____ Egyptian.

C Rewrite the sentences in the positive and negative. Use contractions.

		POSITIVE (+)	NEGATIVE (-)
1	He is sorry.	He's sorry.	He isn't sorry.
2	They are friends.		
3	We are from Turkey.		
4	You are famous!		
5	It is Spanish.		
6	She is in this class.		

➤ Go back to page 3.

1.2 Present simple *be*: questions

A Use the prompts to write questions and short answers.

1 you / married
   ___Are you married___ (?) ___No, I'm not.___ (-)

2 your hometown / nice
   _____ (?) _____ (+)

3 they / your new shoes
   _____ (?) _____ (+)

4 he / in a relationship
   _____ (?) _____ (-)

5 you / Turkish
   _____ (?) _____ (-)

6 you / a student
   _____ (?) _____ (+)

B Write *be* in the present simple in each gap.

1 What ___is___ your favourite food?
2 Where _____ you from?
3 How old _____ you?
4 What _____ your flight number?
5 Where _____ Max from?
6 How old _____ Cara?

➤ Go back to page 5.

1.3 *a/an* and plural nouns; *this, that, these, those*

A Complete the sentences with *a* or *an*.

1 MSU is ___a___ university in Moscow.
2 Take _____ umbrella – it's raining!
3 Tonya is _____ French student.
4 Send me _____ email later.
5 Mexico is _____ country in South America.
6 This is _____ example.

B Complete the sentences with the plural form of the nouns in bold.

1 Are these your ___keys___? **key**
2 There are two _____ for you. **sandwich**
3 Where are my _____? **headphone**
4 Harvard and Stanford are _____ in the USA. **university**
5 He has six different _____! **watch**
6 Poland and Sweden are _____ in Europe. **country**

C Look at pictures (1–6) and choose the correct words to complete the sentences.

1 Is *this* / *that* / *those* your wallet?

2 *Those* / *These* / *This* are my sunglasses.

3 *This* / *Those* / *These* are my sandwiches.

4 Are *these* / *those* / *that* bags yours?

5 *This* / *These* / *Those* suitcase is really heavy!

6 Is *those* / *that* / *this* your pen?

➤ Go back to page 7.

Grammar Hub

2.1 Possessive adjectives and apostrophes

Subject pronouns	Possessive adjectives
I	my
he	his
she	her
it	its
we	our
you	your
they	their

Be careful!

- We only add 's to the last name.

  Ivan and Hannah's family NOT ~~Ivan's and Hannah's family~~

- We don't put an apostrophe in *its* when it is a possessive adjective.

  France is famous for its cheese. NOT ~~France is famous for it's cheese.~~

- We use possessive adjectives to show that something belongs to someone.

  Ali lives with her parents.
  I live with Tom and his sister.

- We use the same possessive adjectives for singular and plural nouns.

  They're her friends. NOT ~~They're hers friends.~~

- We use possessive apostrophes to show that something belongs to someone.

  She's married to Dave's brother.

- We use 's with singular nouns.

  My sister's children are called Tanya and Kyle.

- We use s' with plural nouns.

  My grandparents' names are Ed and Jilly.

- We use 's with irregular plural nouns.

  The children's names are Moya and Daryl.

2.2 have/has got

	Positive	Negative
I/you/we/they	**I've got** a flatmate.	**I haven't got** a flatmate.
he/she/it	**He's got** a big family.	**She hasn't got** a big family.

	Question	Short answers	
I/you/we/they	**Have you got** any brothers or sisters?	Yes, **I have**.	No, **I haven't**.
he/she/it	**Has she got** long hair?	Yes, **she has**.	No, **she hasn't**.

- We use *have/has got* to talk about someone's appearance, family or possessions.

  I have got a new phone.

- We use *Have/Has* + subject + *got* to make questions.

- We often use *any* before plural nouns in the question form.

  Has she got any children?

Be careful!

Has she got any children? Yes, she has. NOT ~~Yes, she has got.~~

2.3 Using adjectives

- We use adjectives to describe things.
- Adjectives have one form for singular and plural.

  a kind woman
  two kind women NOT ~~two kinds women~~

- In sentences with a noun, the adjective comes before the noun.

  She is a good friend.

- The adjective comes after the verb *be* when we describe the subject of a sentence.

  Frederica is tall.

Be careful!

- We use *very* and *really* to make an adjective stronger.

  very tall

- We use *quite* to mean 'a little but not very'.

  quite long

- *Very*, *really* and *quite* come before the adjective.

  Her hair is very/really/quite long.

124 GRAMMAR HUB

Grammar Hub

2.1 Possessive adjectives and apostrophes

A Complete the sentences with a possessive adjective.

1 My cousin and his wife live in Paris. _____ house is very big.

2 Sofia Coppola is a director. _____ films are famous.

3 Switzerland is famous for _____ chocolate.

4 We're French, but _____ children speak English at home.

5 Ken, is _____ surname 'Clark' or 'Clerk'?

6 That's Michael with _____ wife, Laura.

7 I'm British, but _____ parents are German.

B Choose the correct options to complete the sentences.

1 My *husband's / husbands'* family lives in Brazil.

2 Their *daughter's / daughters'* name is Lillie.

3 The *children's / childrens'* grandfather is an artist.

4 My *grandparent's / grandparents'* names are Mel and Bob.

5 What are the *women's / womens'* names?

C Choose the correct words to complete the text.

[1]*I / My* am an actor, and so is my father. [2]*He / His* name is Juan. [3]*He's / His* famous in South America. [4]*I / My* mother is famous too. [5]*She's / Her* a singer. I also have two brothers. [6]*Their / They* names are Miguel and Esteban. [7]*Their / They're* singers like [8]*we / our* mother.

➤ Go back to page 13.

2.2 have/has got

A Complete the sentences using *have* or *has got*. Use contractions where possible.

1 They _____ a house in the countryside.

2 Georgiana and Stefania _____ long, blonde hair.

3 Diane _____ a twin sister called Erin.

4 My sister _____ brown eyes, but I haven't.

5 They _____ three children.

B Rewrite the sentences in Exercise A to make them negative.

1 *They haven't got a house in the countryside.*

2 _____

3 _____

4 _____

5 _____

C Use the prompts to write questions and short answers.

1 your dad / a beard

 Has your dad got a beard? (?) _____ *No, he hasn't.* _____ (-)

2 you / any lipstick

 _____ (?) _____ (+)

3 they / a car

 _____ (?) _____ (+)

4 Maria / short hair

 _____ (?) _____ (+)

5 we / any shampoo

 _____ (?) _____ (+)

6 you / your glasses

 _____ (?) _____ (-)

➤ Go back to page 15.

2.3 Using adjectives

A Reorder the words to make sentences.

1 busy / is / it / here / in

 _____

2 happy / today / Tim / is

 _____

3 is / Al's / desk / quite / messy

 _____

4 house / really / is / big / this

 _____

5 a / got / he's / car / fast

 _____

6 really / sister's / funny / your

 _____

B Correct the mistakes in each sentence.

1 Toby is a quite noisy.

2 Roxanna is a really friendly.

3 Marin is a big very man.

4 Greg is serious really.

5 Magdalena's got a very bedroom messy.

6 Alicia and Georgina are quiets young women.

7 Wow! These paintings are beautifuls.

8 This café is quiet quite.

➤ Go back to page 16.

GRAMMAR HUB   125

Grammar Hub

3.1 Present simple positive

I/you/we/they	I **finish** work at 5 pm.
he/she/it	She **finishes** work at 5 pm.

- We use the present simple to talk about habits and routines.
- We also use the present simple to talk about:
  - facts and things that are true.

    Paris is the capital of France.
  - likes and dislikes.

    Alessia likes her flat.
  - possessions with *have got* and *have*.

    He's got a pet dog.
  - fixed times.

    The film starts at 6 pm.

Spelling rules

Add **-s** to most verbs.	love	She love**s** music.
	play	He play**s** computer games.
Add **-es** to verbs that end -ss, -ch, -sh, -x, -o.	wat**ch**	She watch**es** TV.
	g**o**	He go**es** for a run.
Change **-y** after a consonant to **-ies.**	stud**y**	She stud**ies** after dinner.

Be careful!

- The *he/she/it* form of *have* is *has*.

  She has a nice flat. NOT ~~She haves a nice flat.~~

3.2 Adverbs of frequency

0% ⟵————————————————————⟶ 100%

never · · · rarely · · · sometimes · · · often · · · usually · · · always

- We use adverbs of frequency to talk about how regularly we do things.
- Adverbs of frequency go after *be* and *can*.

  *It's **usually** busy on a Saturday.*

  *I **can never** find my keys in the morning.*

- Adverbs of frequency go before other verbs.

  *I **sometimes play** football on Saturdays.*
- Look at where the adverbs go in questions.

  *How **often do** you play football?*

  *What time **do you usually eat** dinner?*

3.3 Present simple negative

	do/does not + infinitive
I/you/we/they	I **don't cook** every evening.
he/she/it	She **doesn't cook** every evening.

Be careful!

With *he/she/it* forms, we don't add -s to the verb.

It doesn't start at 8 o'clock. NOT ~~It doesn't starts at 8 o'clock.~~

- We use the present simple negative to talk about habits and routines.

  I do not do any exercise at the weekend.
- We also use the present simple negative to talk about:
  - facts and things that are true.

    I don't live in London.
  - dislikes.

    Sarah doesn't like sushi.
  - possessions with *have got* and *have*.

    They haven't got any children.
  - fixed times.

    The shop doesn't open until 6 pm.
- We use the contraction *don't* (*do not*) and *doesn't* (*does not*).

126 GRAMMAR HUB

Grammar Hub

3.1 Present simple positive

A Complete the sentences with the correct form of the verb in brackets.

1 I _____ (live) in a flat in Hong Kong.

2 My mother _____ (watch) TV every day.

3 We _____ (listen) to the same music.

4 She _____ (have) a gym class after work.

5 My dad _____ (go) to work by train.

6 The shop _____ (close) at ten o'clock.

B Rewrite the sentences. Correct the mistakes in bold.

1 They **works** in an office. _____

2 She **study** every day. _____

3 He **gos** to school at eight o'clock. _____

4 I **buys** sandwiches for lunch every day. _____

5 Our dog **watch** TV with us. _____

6 We **eats** dinner at seven o'clock. _____

7 She **live** in New York with her sister. _____

8 The train **leave** at 10.30 am. _____

➤ Go back to page 23.

3.2 Adverbs of frequency

A Reorder the words to make sentences.

1 by train / go to work / I / never

_____*I never go to work by train.*_____

2 play / we / video games / often

_____

3 always / the radio / they / in the car / listen to

_____

4 home / he / rarely / before seven / is

_____

5 busy / is / usually / Andrea / at the weekend / ?

_____

6 work late / you / do / sometimes / ?

_____

B Rewrite the sentences using the adverbs in brackets.

1 I go to the gym. (never)

_____*I never go to the gym.*_____

2 I read in bed. (often)

_____

3 Eleni plays football on Sundays. (usually)

_____

4 Dan's late for his English class. (sometimes)

_____

5 I eat sushi. (rarely)

_____

6 Lin goes to bed at 11 pm. (always)

_____

➤ Go back to page 24.

3.3 Present simple negative

A Complete the sentences with the correct form of the verb in brackets.

1 He __*doesn't have*__ (not have) coffee with breakfast.

2 I _____ (not like) jazz music.

3 You _____ (not need) a coat – it's really hot outside!

4 We _____ (not have) children.

5 Amy _____ (not go) to the cinema very often.

6 Zach _____ (not work) in an office.

7 My parents _____ (not work) anymore. They're retired.

B Rewrite the sentences in the negative.

1 Sam likes parties.

_____*Sam doesn't like parties.*_____

2 We usually have lunch in the kitchen.

_____

3 Eleni speaks Arabic.

_____

4 They have a big house.

_____

5 I listen to music on the train.

_____

6 Lin watches TV in the morning.

_____

➤ Go back to page 26.

GRAMMAR HUB   127

Grammar Hub

4.1 Present simple *yes/no* questions; short answers

	Question	Short answers	
I/you/we/they	**Do I have** a meeting today?	Yes, **you do**.	No, **you don't**.
he/she/it	**Does it have** a good camera?	Yes, **it does**.	No, **it doesn't**.

- We use present simple *yes/no* questions to ask about habits and routines.
- We use *Do/Does* + subject + infinitive without *to* to make questions.

> **Be careful!**
>
> Does she like tea? NOT ~~Does she likes tea?~~
> Yes, she does. NOT ~~Yes, she likes.~~

4.2 *have to / don't have to*

	Positive	Negative
I/you/we/they	**I have to work** at the weekend.	**I don't have to work** at the weekend.
he/she/it	**She has to wear** a uniform.	She **doesn't have to wear** a uniform.

	Question	Short answers	
I/you/we/they	**Do I have to** start at 9 am?	Yes, **you do**.	No, **you don't**.
he/she/it	**Does she have to** travel a lot for work?	Yes, **she does**.	No, **she doesn't**.

- We use *have to* + infinitive without *to* to talk about rules and things we need to do.
- We use *don't/doesn't have to* to talk about things we don't need to do.
- We use *Do/Does* + subject + *have to* + infinitive without *to* to make questions.

> **Be careful!**
>
> I don't have to work long hours. NOT ~~I haven't to work long hours.~~
> Do I have to work long hours? NOT ~~Have I to work long hours?~~
> No, you don't. NOT ~~No, you haven't.~~

4.3 Question words

Why	To ask for a reason	**Why** are you late?
What	To ask about a thing	**What** does it do?
Where	To ask about a place	**Where** do you work?
Who	To ask about a person	**Who** is your boss?
How much	To ask about a quantity	**How much** does it cost?
How long	To ask about a length of time	**How long** does the film last?
When	To ask about a time	**When** does the meeting start?

- We use question word + auxiliary verb + subject + main verb to make *Wh-* questions.

Where do you live? NOT ~~Where you live?~~
How much does it cost? NOT ~~How much it costs?~~

128 GRAMMAR HUB

Grammar Hub

4.1 Present simple *yes/no* questions; short answers

A Complete the questions with *Do* or *Does*.

1. ___Do___ you work in an office?
2. _____ they work from home?
3. _____ she work with animals?
4. _____ he like his job?
5. _____ we wear a uniform?
6. _____ it have a name?
7. _____ it get busy at the weekend?
8. _____ your sisters work in London?

B Use the prompts to write questions and short answers.

1. you / work / part time
   Do you work part time? (?) _____Yes, I do._____ (+)
2. they / live / in the city centre
   _____ (?) _____ (-)
3. she / wear / a uniform
   _____ (?) _____ (+)
4. he / travel / for his job
   _____ (?) _____ (-)
5. you / speak / French
   _____ (?) _____ (+)

➤ Go back to page 33.

4.2 *have to / don't have to*

A Choose the correct options to complete the sentences.

1. You *has to / have to* take your shoes off first.
2. You *haven't to / don't have to* wear a uniform.
3. She *don't / doesn't* have to pay the hotel bill.
4. *You do / Do you* have to get up early?
5. *Has he to / Does he have to* work nine to five?
6. A: Do I have to pay for training?
   B: Yes, you *don't / have to*.

B Complete the sentences with the correct form of *have to*.

1. Doctors _____ work long hours.
2. I _____ go to bed early. It's a weekend.
3. He _____ wear a tie. He's a chef.
4. You _____ study hard to learn a language.
5. Sally _____ study. She has an exam tomorrow.

C Complete the conversations with the correct from of *have to* and short answers.

1. A: ___Do you have to pay___ (you / pay) for food at work?
   B: Yes, _____I do_____.
2. A: _____ (I / wear) a uniform?
   B: Yes, _____.
3. A: _____ (she / finish) it today?
   B: No, _____.
4. A: _____ (they / take) a course?
   B: Yes, _____.
5. A: _____ (he study) tonight?
   B: Yes, _____.
6. A: _____ (we pay) for training?
   B: No, _____.

➤ Go back to page 34.

4.3 Question words

A Complete the sentences with the question words in the box.

how	what	when	where	who	why

1. _____ do most university students live?
2. _____ is your teacher?
3. _____ long is the course?
4. _____ class do you have now?
5. _____ do you want to work there?
6. _____ does your course start?

B Reorder the words to make questions.

1. do / where / you / study
   _____Where do you study?_____
2. much / it / how / does / cost
   _____
3. long / last / how / it / does
   _____
4. the / when / course / does / start
   _____
5. course / study / what / you / do
   _____

➤ Go back to page 36.

GRAMMAR HUB 129

Grammar Hub

5.1 *there is/are*

	Positive	Negative
Singular	**There's** a washing machine in the kitchen.	**There isn't** a TV in the living room.
Plural	**There are** four chairs in the dining room.	**There aren't** any cushions on the sofa.

	Question	Short answers	
Singular	**Is there** a microwave in the kitchen?	Yes, **there is**.	No, **there isn't**.
Plural	**Are there** any tomatoes in the fridge?	Yes, **there are**.	No, **there aren't**.

- We use *there is / there are* to say that something exists and talk about position.

  There's a coffee machine in the kitchen.
  There are more plates in the cupboard.
- We use *any* in negative sentences and questions with plural nouns and uncountable nouns.

  There aren't any plates in the cupboard.
  Is there any milk in the fridge?

> **Be careful!**
> - In a list of nouns, we use *there is* when the first is singular.
>
>   *There is a coffee maker, two cups and three plates on the table.*
> - In a list of nouns, we use *there are* when the first is plural.
>
>   *There are two cups, three plates and a coffee maker on the table.*

5.2 *can*

	Positive	Negative
I/you/he/she/it/we/they	She **can swim**.	She **can't swim**.

	Question	Short answers	
I/you/he/she/it/we/they	**Can we go** to the cinema?	Yes, you **can**.	No, you **can't**.

- We use *can* to about ability and what is possible.
- In the negative, we can also say *cannot*.

  She can't swim. OR She cannot swim.

> **Be careful!**
> *He can sing. NOT He cans sing. NOT He can to sing.*

5.3 Imperatives

- We use imperatives to tell someone to do something.

  Phone me later.
  Look at this website.
  Give me your phone.
  Open your books to page 23.
- We can use *please* to make imperatives more polite.

  Please ask at reception.
- We use *don't* to tell someone not to do something.

  Don't walk in the park at night.

> **Be careful!**
> *Give me your phone. NOT To give me your phone.*

Grammar Hub

5.1 there is/are

A Complete the sentences with *is* or *are*.

1 _____ there a microwave in the kitchen?
2 There _____ a mirror in the bathroom.
3 There _____ some eggs in the fridge.
4 There _____ some people here to see you.
5 _____ there any bedrooms upstairs?
6 _____ there a coffee machine?

B Use the prompts to write questions and short answers.

1 plates / in the cupboard
  <u>Are there any plates in the cupboard?</u> (?) _____ <u>No, there aren't.</u> (-)
2 dishwasher / in the kitchen
  _____ (?) _____ (+)
3 swimming pool / in the garden
  _____ (?) _____ (-)
4 tomatoes / in the fridge
  _____ (?) _____ (-)
5 TV / in the bedroom
  _____ (?) _____ (-)
6 socks / in that drawer
  _____ (?) _____ (+)

➤ Go back to page 43.

5.2 can

A Complete the sentences with *can* or *can't*.

1 I'm sorry. I _____ come on Saturday. I have to work.
2 _____ you open the window, please? It's very hot in here.
3 She's not here I'm afraid. _____ I take a message?
4 She _____ come out tonight, because she doesn't have any money.
5 I _____ speak Japanese, but not write it.
6 We _____ buy it now. The shop is closed.

B Use the prompts to write sentences with *can*.

1 I / play / the guitar
  _____
2 they / leave / work / whenever they want
  _____
3 she / speak / Arabic / ?
  _____
4 where / I / buy / washing powder / ?
  _____
5 I / stay / at yours / tonight / ?
  _____

➤ Go back to page 45.

5.3 Imperatives

A Complete the sentences with the verbs in the box.

| close   drink   drive   play   talk   read   sit |

1 Don't _____ football on the grass.
2 _____ the door behind you.
3 _____ on the left.
4 Don't _____ in the library.
5 Don't _____ the water.
6 _____ this – it's really interesting!
7 Please _____ down!

B Match the verbs (1–6) with the phrases (a–f) to make imperative sentences.

1 Go   **a** me more about amazing buildings.
2 Tell   **b** the window. It's hot.
3 Learn   **c** the gardens on the roof.
4 Look at   **d** your shoes off please.
5 Open   **e** some Portuguese words before you go.
6 Take   **f** away.

➤ Go back to page 47.

GRAMMAR HUB 131

Grammar Hub

6.1 Likes and dislikes

	verb + -ing	verb + noun
☺☺	I **love going** to concerts. She **loves going** to concerts.	I **love photography**. He **loves photography**.
☺	I **like watching** TV. He **likes watching** TV.	I **like rock music**. She **likes rock music**.
☹	I **don't like visiting** exhibitions. She **doesn't like visiting** exhibitions.	I **don't like pizza**. He **doesn't like pizza**.
☹☹	I **hate doing** the washing-up. She **hates doing** the washing-up.	I **hate cold weather**. He **hates cold weather**.

6.2 *was/were*

	Positive	Negative
I/he/she/it	**I was** at the theatre.	**I was not** at the theatre. **I wasn't** at the theatre.
you/we/they	**They were** at the cinema.	**They were not** at the cinema. **They weren't** at the cinema.

- We use *was/were* to talk about things that happened in the past.
- We often use these time expressions with *was/were*.

  *I was there two hours **ago**.*   *It was my birthday **on Sunday**.*   *We were out **yesterday**.*
  *They were here **last night**.*   *I was busy **at the weekend**.*

	Question	Short answers	
I/he/she/it	**Was it** interesting?	Yes, **it was**.	No, **it wasn't**.
you/we/they	**Were they** out last night?	Yes, **they were**.	No, **they weren't**.

6.3 Past simple regular and irregular verbs

Regular verbs		
Infinitive	Past simple	
ask	ask**ed**	**I asked** for help.
like	lik**ed**	**She liked** the comedy show.
stop	stopp**ed**	**You stopped** the car.
study	stud**ied**	**We studied** English last night.
Irregular verbs		
Infinitive	Past simple	
become	became	**He became** a singer.
go	went	**They went** shopping.
have	had	**We had** very little money.
send	sent	**They sent** you an email.
write	wrote	**I wrote** you a letter.
win	won	**She won** the game.

Spelling rules	Infinitive	Past simple
Add **-ed**.	join	join**ed**
Add **-d** to verbs ending **-e**.	lik**e**	like**d**
Change **-y** after a consonant to **-ied**.	stud**y**	stud**ied**
Double the consonant and add **-ed** with verbs ending in vowel + consonant.	sto**p**	sto**pped**

132   GRAMMAR HUB

Grammar Hub

6.1 Likes and dislikes

A Complete the sentences with the words in the box.

> doesn't   going   like   loves   singing

1. My dad _____ Elvis. He has all his albums.
2. I like _____ in the shower.
3. She _____ like horror movies. She gets scared.
4. You don't _____ cheese, do you?
5. Bill hates _____ to art galleries.

B Correct the mistakes in each sentence.

1. She likes ~~to~~ rock music.
2. I don't liking photography.
3. They love stay in on Friday nights.
4. We love to sitting outside.
5. How can you hating the *Star Wars* films?
6. He not like sushi.

C Use the prompts to write sentences with *love, like, don't like* and *hate*.

1. Sheila / ☺☺ / go to the theatre.
   Sheila loves going to the theatre.
2. Owen / ☹ / visit / his grandparents.
   _____
3. We / ☺ / watch / *Game of Thrones*.
   _____
4. I / ☹☹ / clean / the bathroom.
   _____
5. I / ☺☺ / dance.
   _____
6. They / ☹ / tidy / their bedroom.
   _____

➤ Go back to page 53.

6.2 was/were

A Complete the sentences with *was* or *were*.

1. Wow! That programme _____ amazing!
2. TVs _____ really expensive in the 1950s.
3. _____ Yuki there on Saturday?
4. There _____ a lot of people at the party.
5. Where _____ you last night?
6. The tickets _____ really expensive.

B Complete the text messages with *was, were, wasn't* and *weren't*.

Hi Malc! I ___was___ at an exhibition on Saturday. My friends Roma and Pete [1]_____ there, too. There [2]_____ any good paintings – we hated them all ☹! How [3]_____ your weekend?

Hal and I were at a comedy show. It was great fun! [4]_____ you out on Sunday?

Yeah. We [5]_____ at the big football game. And you?

I was at home studying. [6]_____ the football game good?

It was great.

➤ Go back to page 54.

6.3 Past simple regular and irregular verbs

A Complete the sentences with the past simple form of the verbs in the box.

> ask   like   play   stay   stop   study

1. I can't believe I failed. I _____ all night for that test!
2. I really _____ Michael Jackson when I was younger.
3. They _____ work to have lunch.
4. I think he _____ for the university rugby team.
5. She _____ Rob to come, but he was busy.
6. We _____ at home and watched *The Walking Dead* last night.

B Complete the sentences in the past simple with the verbs in brackets.

1. David Bowie _____ (die) in 2016.
2. John Lennon _____ (leave) the Beatles in 1970.
3. Chris Brown _____ (write) the hit song 'Disturbia'.
4. The movie *La La Land* _____ (win) six Academy Awards.
5. Before he was an actor, Sylvester Stallone _____ (teach) gymnastics.
6. Bob Dylan _____ (take) his stage name from the poet Dylan Thomas.

C Correct the mistakes in each sentence.

1. Real Madrid ~~winned~~ *won* the match 2–0.
2. He teached history for twenty years.
3. She writed nine books in her lifetime.
4. We taked a taxi to the restaurant.
5. She leaved work early last night.
6. You sended the letter two weeks ago!

➤ Go back to page 57.

GRAMMAR HUB   133

Grammar Hub

7.1 *could*

I/you/he/she/it/we/they	Positive	Negative
	A hundred years ago, **you could see** a lot of trams in San Francisco.	**I couldn't get** to work because of the traffic jam.

I/you/he/she/it/we/they	Question	Short answers	
	Could you run fast when you were younger?	Yes, **I could.**	No, **I couldn't.**

- We use *could* to talk about general abilities in the past.
- In the negative, we can also say *could not*.
  I couldn't drive. OR I could not drive.

> **Be careful!**
>
> He could drive. NOT ~~He could to drive.~~ NOT ~~He could drove.~~

7.2 Past simple negative

I/you/he/she/it/we/they	*didn't* + infinitive
	We didn't take the tram.

- We use the past simple negative to talk about things that did not happen in the past.
- We can also say *did not*.
  We didn't take the tram. OR We did not take the tram.

> **Be careful!**
>
> We didn't wait at the traffic lights. NOT ~~We didn't waited at the traffic lights.~~

7.3 Past simple questions

I/you/he/she/it/we/they	Question	Short answers	
	Did they travel to Beijing last year?	Yes, **they did.**	No, **they didn't.**

- We use past simple questions to ask about things that happened in the past.
- We can use question words with the past simple. These come before *did*.
  Where did they go?
  When did she leave?
- The verb *be* forms questions in a different way to other verbs.
  Was it expensive? NOT ~~Did it be expensive.~~
  See **Grammar Hub 6.2** on **page 132** for more information.

> **Be careful!**
>
> Did they go to New York? NOT ~~Did they went to New York?~~
> Where did you go? NOT ~~Where you went?~~

Grammar Hub

7.1 could

A Use the prompts to write sentences with *could*.

Eighty years ago …

1 ✓ ride / a horse / into town

You could ride a horse into town.

2 ✗ take / a bullet train / across Japan

_____

3 ✓ find / trams / in San Francisco

_____

4 ✓ see / red double-deckers / in Mumbai

_____

5 ✗ fly / quickly / across Europe

_____

6 ✗ be / stuck / in a traffic jam

_____

B Complete the paragraph using **could** or **couldn't**.

Two hundred years ago you [1]_____ travel around London on public transport because … there wasn't any! In 1800, the city was still quite small with only about one million people and most people [2]_____ walk from their home to their place of work. If you wanted to travel further, you [3]_____ take a carriage pulled by horses, but only the very rich [4]_____ have their own private carriage. People [5]_____ cross the River Thames by taking a boat called a 'wherry'. Londoners [6]_____ take an underground train until 1863 when the first station opened.

➤ Go back to page 63.

7.2 Past simple negative

A Complete the sentences with the past simple form of the verbs in brackets. Use contractions.

1 It's OK. They ___*didn't miss*___ (not miss) their flight.

2 I _____ (not arrive) home until midnight last night.

3 He _____ (not like) the food on the plane.

4 We _____ (not take) the train because it was very expensive.

5 Sarah _____ (not feel) well on the ship.

6 The children _____ (not enjoy) the journey. They were so bored!

B Complete the sentences with the negative form of the verbs in the box.

> meet   pay   take   travel   ~~read~~   write

1 We ___*didn't read*___ *Journey to the Centre of the Earth* at school.

2 Jules Verne _____ about a real person.

3 Nellie Bly _____ to India.

4 She _____ a lot of luggage with her.

5 She _____ for the trip. The *New York World* paid.

6 Nellie _____ Elizabeth Bisland on her journey.

➤ Go back to page 65.

7.3 Past simple questions

A Use the prompts to write questions and short answers.

1 they / go / with their friends

Did they go with their friends? (?)
Yes, they did. (+)

2 you / visit / a lot of cities

_____ (?)
_____ (–)

3 she / meet / many people

_____ (?)
_____ (+)

4 your company / pay / for the flight

_____ (?)
_____ (+)

5 they / visit / the Eiffel Tower

_____ (?)
_____ (–)

6 you / sleep / on the plane

_____ (?)
_____ (–)

B Complete the questions with *you* and a verb from the box.

> eat   get   go   ~~have~~   stay   swim   travel   visit

1 _____*Did you have*_____ a good holiday?

2 Where _____ on holiday this year?

3 How _____ there? By plane?

4 _____ any interesting museums?

5 _____ any local food?

6 _____ in the sea?

7 How long _____ for?

8 _____ by bus or train?

➤ Go back to page 66.

GRAMMAR HUB   135

Grammar Hub

8.1 Countable and uncountable nouns; *some* and *any*

Singular countable nouns	Plural countable nouns	Uncountable nouns
an apple	apples	bread
a banana	bananas	butter
a carrot	carrots	cheese
an egg	eggs	chicken
a mushroom	mushrooms	fish
an orange	oranges	lettuce
a potato	potatoes	milk
a tomato	tomatoes	rice
		water

- Countable nouns are nouns you can count.
- Most nouns are countable. They can be singular or plural.

  a banana   six bananas
- Uncountable nouns don't have a plural form and we can't count uncountable nouns.

  beef NOT ~~beefs~~ OR ~~one beef, two beefs~~

	Singular countable nouns	Plural countable nouns	Uncountable nouns
	a/an	*some*	*some*
Positive	I've got **a banana** in my bag. I had **an apple** for breakfast.	There are **some apples** in the fridge. I've got **some tomatoes** for the salad.	I can buy **some milk** on the way home.
	a/an	*any*	*any*
Negative	I haven't got **a banana**. No, I don't want **an ice cream**, thank you.	There aren't **any prawns** left. We haven't got **any mushrooms** I'm afraid.	Sorry, I don't have **any tea**.
	a/an	*any*	*any*
Question	Do you want **a banana**? Is there **an onion** in this recipe?	Have we got **any mushrooms**? Are there **any sausages** left?	Have you got **any cake**? Is there **any yoghurt** in the fridge?

> **Be careful!**
> - With questions, we often use *some* when we make an offer.
>   *Do you want **some** bread?*
> - We use *some* not *any* when we make a request.
>   *Can I have **some** rice, please? NOT ~~Can I have any rice, please?~~*

8.2 *much, many, a lot of*

	Countable nouns	Uncountable nouns
Positive	*a lot of*	*a lot of*
	There are **a lot of carrots** in this recipe!	She drinks **a lot of coffee**.
Negative	*not many*	*not much*
	We don't have **many tomatoes**.	There isn't **much milk** left.
Question	*How many?*	*How much?*
	How many potatoes do we need?	**How much pasta** do you want?

- We use *a lot of* with countable and uncountable nouns.
- We use *many* with countable nouns.
- We use *much* with uncountable nouns.

> **Be careful!**
> - We use **a lot of** for a large amount.
>   *There are **a lot of** eggs in this recipe.*
> - We use **quite a lot of** for a medium amount.
>   *There is **quite a lot of** milk in this recipe.*
> - We use **not many/much** for a small amount.
>   *There isn't **much** sugar in this recipe.*

8.3 *a/an, the,* no article

a/an	We use *a/an* the first time we talk about a singular noun.	I've got **a recipe** for lasagne. There's **an onion** in the cupboard over there.
the	We use *the* with singular nouns when it is clear what we are talking about or when there is only one.	Fry **the onion** for five minutes. Where's **the waitress**?
	We use *the* with plural nouns when it is clear what we are talking about.	**The ingredients** for this recipe are unusual.
no article	We use no article with the names of people, companies, cities and countries (except *the UK, the USA, the Netherlands*).	This is **Erica**. She's a chef from **Sydney, Australia**.
	We use no article when we talk about things in general.	Do you like **pizza**? **Crisps** are not very healthy.

136 GRAMMAR HUB

Grammar Hub

8.1 Countable and uncountable nouns; *some* and *any*

A Choose the correct options to complete the sentences.

1 I'm a vegetarian so I don't eat *meat / meats*.
2 Would you like some *crisp / crisps*?
3 She never drinks *coffee / coffees* after 9 pm.
4 What's your favourite *pizza / pizzas*?
5 Can you buy some *bread / breads* on your way home?
6 Is there *an onion / onions* in this recipe?

B Complete the sentences with *some, any, a* or *an*.

1 Did you buy _____ carrots at the supermarket?
2 Are there _____ good restaurants near here?
3 Would you like _____ more tea?
4 There's _____ pasta in the cupboard.
5 Do you want _____ orange?
6 There's _____ bottle of water in the fridge.

➤ Go back to page 72.

8.2 *much, many, a lot of*

A Complete the paragraph with *a lot of, much* or *many*.

Although we're not vegetarians, we eat [1]_____ vegetables. I like tomatoes, but there aren't [2]_____ in our local market at the moment because it's winter. At breakfast we usually have cereal and [3]_____ fruit. Fresh fruit is really good for you. We don't eat [4]_____ meat, but we sometimes have chicken on Sundays. My son loves potatoes so we always have [5]_____ potatoes with our Sunday dinner. We all like a delicious dessert, but we don't eat [6]_____ chocolate.

B Complete the sentences with *much* or *many*.

1 How __*much*__ money have you got?
2 How _____ people are coming to dinner?
3 How _____ water do you drink every day?
4 How _____ do you spend on food every month?
5 How _____ sugar do you want in your coffee?
6 How _____ bottles of water do we need?
7 How _____ packets of biscuits have you got?

➤ Go back to page 75.

8.3 *a/an, the,* no article

A Choose the correct options to complete the paragraph.

Kings Biscuits is [1]*the / a / an* company that makes [2]*the / – / an* chocolate biscuits. [3]*The / A / –* company is in [4]*the / a / –* New York, but it sells biscuits all across [5]*the / a / an* USA.

B Complete the paragraphs with *the, a, an* or *–*.

[1]_____ Jamie Oliver is [2]_____ English chef who is famous in [3]_____ UK and across [4]_____ world. He has a lot of restaurants and [5]_____ popular TV shows. [6]_____ People love cooking and eating his Italian recipes.

[7]_____ Wellington Froots is [8]_____ company that grows and delivers fresh [9]_____ fruit and vegetables. Friends Isabella Sheridan and Akiko Okamura started their business in Isabella's home city of [10]_____ Wellington, in [11]_____ New Zealand. [12]_____ company delivers [13]_____ new box of locally-grown, fresh ingredients to its customers every week.

C Correct the mistakes in each sentence.

1 My dad's got an fantastic recipe for carrot cake!
2 Let's go to a new French restaurant on Broad Street.
3 Ramen is a popular noodle dish from the Sapporo, Japan.
4 Could you get me a grater? It's in that cupboard over there.
5 The junk food is bad for your health.
6 Could you buy the onion on your way home? I need one for this recipe.

➤ Go back to page 76.

GRAMMAR HUB 137

Grammar Hub

9.1 Present continuous

	Positive	Negative
I	**I'm talking** to my friend.	**I'm not feeling** very well.
he/she/it	**She's wearing** shorts and a t-shirt.	**She isn't working** today.
you/we/they	**They're playing** cards.	**They aren't wearing** uniforms.

	Question	Short answers	
I	**Am I saying** it correctly?	Yes, **you are.**	No, **you aren't.**
he/she/it	**Is she wearing** a backpack?	Yes, **she is.**	No, **she isn't.**
you/we/they	**Are you doing** it together?	Yes, **we are.**	No, **we aren't.**

Spelling rules	infinitive	*-ing*
Add **-ing**.	look	look**ing**
Drop the **-e** with verbs ending **-e**.	giv**e**	giv**ing**
Double the final consonant with verbs ending consonant, vowel, consonant + **-ing**.	sto**p**	sto**pping**
	trave**l**	trave**lling**

- We use the present continuous to talk about things happening now.
- In the negative, with *you*, *he*, etc we can also say: *You're not + -ing, He's not + -ing, She's not + -ing, It's not + -ing, We're not + -ing, They're not + -ing.*

  It isn't raining. OR It's not raining.
- In negative short answers, with *you*, *he*, etc we can also say: *No, you're not., No, he's not., No, she's not., No, it's not., No, we're not., No, they're not.*

  Are they driving to work at the moment? No, they aren't. OR No, they're not.

9.2 Present simple vs present continuous

- We use the present simple to talk about habits and routines.

  He wears a suit to work every day.
- We also use the present simple to talk about things that are true in general.

  They usually dress up for a party.
- We use the present continuous to talk about things happening now.

  Take a coat – it's raining outside.
- We also use the present continuous to talk about things happening around now.

  I'm working in Berlin for a month. I usually work in New York.

Be careful!

- We often use the present simple with the time expressions *all day*, *every week*, *once a year*, and adverbs like *always*, *often*, *usually* and *never*.
- We often use the present continuous with the time expressions *(right) now* and *at the moment*.

9.3 Object pronouns

Subject pronoun	Object pronoun
I	me
he	him
she	her
it	it
we	us
you	you
they	them

- We use object pronouns after a verb or after a preposition.

  After a verb: *Can you **show me** a different dress, please?*
- After a preposition: *It's Dinu's birthday. I'm buying a present **for her.***

138 GRAMMAR HUB

Grammar Hub

9.1 Present continuous

A Complete the conversations with the present continuous form of the verbs in brackets. Use contractions where possible.

1 A: Where are you?
  B: We _____ (get) off the bus right now.

2 A: _____ he _____ (come) now?
  B: Yes, very soon.

3 A: Where's Ahmed?
  B: He _____ (have) lunch.

4 A: Are you at work?
  B: No, I _____ (sit) in the park.

5 A: What _____ you _____ (read) at the moment?
  B: *The Secret History* by Donna Tartt. It's amazing!

6 A: What are you up to?
  B: I _____ (watch) the rugby.

B Use the prompts to complete the text messages. Use contractions where possible.

What ___*are you doing*___ (you / do) now?

1 _____ (I / watch) TV. What about you?

2 _____ (I / walk) the dog.
3 _____ (she / wear) her new collar. Is Elle with you?

No, she isn't here. She's with Wes.
4 _____ (they / go) to the gym now.

5 _____ (you / go) too?

No, I'm too tired.

➤ Go back to page 83.

9.2 Present simple vs present continuous

A Choose the correct option.

1 The department store *opens / is opening* at nine o'clock every day.

2 I *don't usually give / am not usually giving* fashion advice.

3 He *wears / 's wearing* a Hugo Boss suit and Prada shoes.

4 It looks like she *enjoys / 's enjoying* the fashion show.

5 In the USA, students usually *don't wear / aren't wearing* a uniform to school.

6 Today, I *work / 'm working* on a report for Gemma.

7 It usually *snows / is snowing* at this time of year.

8 I can't meet tomorrow. I *work / 'm working* from home on Tuesdays.

B Complete the conversations with the present simple or present continuous forms of the verbs in brackets.

1 A: Can _____ (I / speak) to Rosanna Francis?
  B: Sorry, _____ (she / not / be) here. Can I take a message?

2 A: Hey! Where _____ (you /be)?
  B: _____ (I / leave) now.

3 A: _____ (you / watch) the news?
  B: No. Why? What _____ (be / happen)?

4 A: Where _____ (be / you / from)?
  B: I _____ (be / from) a small town in Northern Spain.

5 A: What _____ (you / cook)?
  B: I _____ (be / make) spaghetti.

➤ Go back to page 85.

9.3 Object pronouns

A Complete the sentences with the object pronouns in the box.

me you him her it them

1 My sister loves clothes. I always go shopping with _____.

2 I love blue. It's the best colour for _____.

3 Alison loves shoes. She spends a lot of money on _____.

4 Tom's very friendly. His customers like _____.

5 Jin want's a new smartphone. She's saving up for _____.

6 I bought _____ a cup of coffee, Doug. Be careful – it's hot!

B Complete the sentences with subject or object pronouns.

1 I need some new clothes, but _____ don't want to spend a lot of money on _____.

2 My sister gives great fashion advice. _____ always enjoy clothes shopping with _____.

3 Daniel hasn't got a lot of money, so _____ don't think _____ can afford those shoes.

4 I follow Mark Greenwood on Instagram. _____ 's a fashion blogger.

5 Jo has three sisters. _____ always borrowed each other's clothes when _____ were younger!

➤ Go back to page 87.

GRAMMAR HUB   139

Grammar Hub

10.1 Comparatives

		Adjective	Comparative
One syllable	Add **-er**.	high	higher
More than one syllable	Add **more** + adjective.	beautiful	more beautiful
Irregular	Use irregular comparative.	good	better
		bad	worse
		far	further

Spelling rules		
Add **-er**.	cheap	cheap**er**
Add **-r** with adjectives that end in **-e**.	larg**e**	larg**er**
Double the consonant and add **-er** with adjectives that end vowel + consonant.	h**ot**	ho**tter**

- We use comparatives to say how two or more things are different.

  *Mount Everest is **higher** than Ben Nevis.*
  *Thailand is **more beautiful** than Alaska.*

- Some two-syllable adjectives can form one-word comparatives.

  dirty ➞ dirtier   quiet ➞ quieter
  narrow ➞ narrower

- Comparatives are often followed by *than* but not always.

  *Avatar was better **than** The Beach. OR The Beach was good but Avatar was better.*

10.2 Superlatives

		Adjective	Superlative
One syllable	Add **the** + **-est**.	cold	the coldest
More than one syllable	Add **the most** + adjective.	remote	the most remote
Irregular	Use **the** + irregular superlative.	good	the best
		bad	the worst
		far	the furthest

Spelling rules		
Add **-est**.	cheap	cheap**est**
Add **-st** with adjectives that end in **-e**.	larg**e**	larg**est**
Double the consonant and add **-est** with adjectives that end vowel + consonant.	h**ot**	ho**ttest**

- We use superlatives to say that something is top or bottom of a group.

  *The Atacama is **the coldest** dry desert in the world.*
  *What's **the most** remote place in your country?*

- Some two-syllable adjectives can form superlatives without *most*.

  dirty ➞ the dirtiest   quiet ➞ the quietest
  narrow ➞ the narrowest

- We often put *the* before superlatives but not always.

  Megan is my best friend. NOT ~~Megan is my the best friend.~~

10.3 Verb + *to* + infinitive

	verb + *to* + infinitive
decide	We **decided to go** hiking in the mountains.
forget	Don't **forget to take** your mobile phone.
help	The map **helped** us **to find** the way.
learn	They're **learning to use** a compass.
need	You **need to build** a place to sleep.
plan	I'm **planning to hike** through the jungle next summer.
prefer	She **prefers to travel** by car.
remember	**Remember to set off** early.
try	She's **trying to start** a fire.
want	I **want to know** more about survival.

- Many verbs are followed by *to* + infinitive.

> ### Be careful!
>
> *I plan **to go** to Rome next summer.*
> *NOT ~~I plan going to Rome next summer.~~*
> *NOT ~~I plan go to Rome next summer.~~*

140 GRAMMAR HUB

Grammar Hub

10.1 Comparatives

A Write the comparative form of each adjective.

1 old _____older_____   4 expensive _____

2 big _____   5 bad _____

3 dirty _____

B Match to make sentences.

1 Moscow is colder than   a crowded than the countryside.

2 December is hotter   b New York.

3 The city is more   c beautiful than Ireland?

4 Riding a motorbike is more   d than the Eiffel Tower.

5 Is Romania more   e dangerous than driving a car.

6 The Burj Khalifa is taller   f than July.

C Correct the mistakes in each sentence.

> colder
1 The mountains are ~~more cold~~ than the desert.

2 Mount Everest is biger than Mount Kilimanjaro.

3 K2 is the more dangerous than Mount Everest.

4 The Nile is more long than the Amazon.

5 It's difficulter to film in the jungle than in a city.

6 The UK is bigger as Ireland.

7 Ireland is famouser for mountains than beaches.

➤ Go back to page 93.

10.2 Superlatives

A Write the superlative form of each adjective.

1 tall _____the tallest_____

2 hot _____

3 sunny _____

4 beautiful _____

5 good _____

B Choose the correct options to complete the sentences.

1 Aconcagua is the *most tall / tallest* mountain in South America.

2 The Pacific is the *most big / biggest* ocean in the world.

3 I think the Newfoundland is the *most beautiful / beautifullest* dog in the world!

4 Mawsynram is the *most wet / wettest* place on Earth.

5 Hanoi is the *most ancient / ancientest* city in Vietnam.

6 Parinacota is the *most high / highest* city in Chile.

C Complete the sentences with the correct superlative form of the adjective in brackets. Add *the*.

1 Yakutsk is _____ (cold) city in the world.

2 Is Monaco _____ (expensive) country to live in?

3 Death Valley is _____ (hot) place on Earth.

4 Tristan Da Cunha is _____ (remote) island on the planet.

5 The Tata Nano is _____ (cheap) car in the world.

6 Valletta is _____ (sunny) place in Europe.

➤ Go back to page 95.

10.3 Verb + *to* + infinitive

A Complete the sentences with *to* and the verbs in the box.

> bring (x2) carry go make read travel

1 I forgot _____to bring_____ my raincoat with me.

2 I'm trying _____ the map, but it's really dark.

3 They should get some wood. They need _____ a fire to keep warm.

4 Did you remember _____ a bottle of water with you?

5 She's planning _____ on holiday to Greece next year.

6 We helped _____ the boxes into the house.

7 I don't like flying – I prefer _____ by train.

B Reorder the words to make sentences. Add *to* in the right place.

1 you / need / boil the water / don't
_____You don't need to boil the water._____

2 for / they / decided / go / a / walk
_____

3 planning / we're / the / world / travel
_____

4 before dark / get / hope / there / we
_____

5 needs / some camping equipment / she / buy
_____

6 in the jungle / must learn / they / survive
_____

7 do / a survival course / I / don't want
_____

➤ Go back to page 97.

GRAMMAR HUB 141

Grammar Hub

11.1 *should* and *shouldn't*

	Positive	Negative	
I/you/we/they	**You should drink** lots of water.	**You shouldn't smoke**.	
	Question	Short answers	
he/she/it	**Should I buy** a return ticket?	Yes, **you should**.	No, **you shouldn't**.

- We use *should* to give advice.
- We use *should/shouldn't* + infinitive without *to*.

> **Be careful!**
>
> You should rest. NOT ~~You should to rest~~. NOT ~~You should resting~~.

11.2 Present perfect

	Positive	Negative
I/you/we/they	**I've climbed** Mount Everest.	We **haven't visited** the Burj Khalifa.
he/she/it	**She's ridden** an elephant.	He **hasn't been** to Africa.

	Question	Short answers	
I/you/we/they	**Have you (ever) been** to New York?	Yes, **we have**.	No, **we haven't**.
he/she/it	**Has she (ever) eaten** sushi?	Yes, **she has**.	No, **she hasn't**.

- We use the present prefect to talk about past experiences.
- We use *have/has* + past participle.
- With the present perfect, we don't say when the action happened.

  I've ridden a motorbike. NOT ~~I've ridden a motorbike yesterday~~.

- We can use *ever* in questions to mean 'before now'.
- We can use *never* in negative statements.

  I've **never** jumped out of an aeroplane.

> **Be careful!**
>
> - We use *been* not *gone* to talk about places we have visited.
>
>   I have never **been** to China. NOT ~~I have never gone to China~~.
>
> - Be careful with the past participles of common irregular verbs.
>
>   bring → brought   buy → bought   do → done
>   go → gone/been   make → made   think → thought
>   write → written

See **Irregular Verbs** on **page 121** for more information.

11.3 Present perfect vs past simple

- We use the present perfect to talk about an action in the past, but we don't say when it happened.

  Yes, I've **been** to Canada. NOT ~~Yes, I've been to Canada in 2015~~.

- We use the past simple to talk about an action at a specific time in the past.

  She went to Greece **in 2016**. NOT ~~She has been to Greece in 2016~~.

- We use time expressions with the past simple, *not* the present perfect.

  I went to Hawaii three years **ago**. NOT ~~I've been to Hawaii three years ago~~.

  We took the train to work **yesterday**. NOT ~~We've taken the train to work yesterday~~.

> **Be careful!**
>
> - We often ask a general question about past experiences using the present perfect.
> - Then we use the past simple to ask for or give more details.
>
>   A: Have you ever been to France?
>   B: Yes, I have.
>   A: When did you go?
>   B: Two years ago.

142   GRAMMAR HUB

Grammar Hub

11.1 *should* and *shouldn't*

A Complete the sentences with *should* or *shouldn't*.

1 That's a bad cough. You really _____ see a doctor.

2 You _____ smoke – it's really bad for your health.

3 If you want to lose weight, you _____ exercise more.

4 If you're sick, you _____ go to work today. You could make other people sick.

5 You look really tired. You _____ go to bed early.

6 A: _____ I take my medicine now?
   B: Yes, you _____.

B Use the prompts to write sentences with *should* or *shouldn't*.

1 ___*You shouldn't eat*___ (you / not / eat) late at night.

2 _____ (we / not / listen) to loud music.

3 _____ (I / go) to the gym more often?

4 When _____ (I / take) my medicine?

5 _____ (she / not / have) four coffees every day.

6 _____ (they / drink) lots of water.

7 _____ (he / not / watch) so much TV.

➤ Go back to page 103.

11.2 Present perfect

A Complete the sentences with the past participle form of the verbs in the box.

~~appear~~ climb do forget been visit

1 I've ___*appeared*___ on a TV show twice.

2 Have you ever _____ a mountain?

3 She's never _____ her first aeroplane jump.

4 They haven't _____ any dangerous activities.

5 We have _____ Korea three times.

6 Have you ever _____ to Greece?

B Complete the sentences with the present perfect form of the verb in brackets. Use contractions where possible.

1 He _____ (not do) any sport in his life.

2 They _____ (never go) to Iceland.

3 We _____ (swim) in the Mediterranean Sea.

4 _____ (you ever drive) a sports car?

5 I _____ (meet) Taylor Swift.

6 She _____ (never play) tennis on grass.

➤ Go back to page 105.

11.3 Present perfect vs past simple

A Choose the correct tense to complete the sentences.

1 She *'s been / went* to Denmark last year.

2 They *'ve travelled / travelled* to Chile a long time ago.

3 *Have you cycled / Did you cycle* to work yesterday?

4 *Have you ever been / Did you ever go* to Vietnam?

5 We *'ve driven / drove* across Europe last summer.

6 *Have you tried / Did you try* snowboarding when you were in Switzerland?

B Complete the text messages with the present perfect or past simple form of the verb in brackets.

> **Virginia:** [1] _____ (go) skiing last week?

> **Teresa:** Yes, we [2] _____.
> [3] _____ (ever go) skiing?

> **Virginia:** No, I [4] _____.
> I [5] _____ (do) any winter sports.

> **Teresa:** Really? I [6] _____ _____ (try) both skiing and snowboarding. They're great fun!

➤ Go back to page 107.

GRAMMAR HUB   143

Grammar Hub

12.1 *going to*

	Positive	Negative
I	**I'm going to travel** around Japan after university.	**I'm not going to work** in an office when I graduate.
he/she/it	**She's going to book** the tickets next week.	**She isn't going to visit** Kyoto during her trip.
you/we/they	**We're going to stay** in hostels.	**We aren't going to book** anything until we get there.

	Question	Short answers	
I	**Am I going to get** in trouble for this?	Yes, **you are**.	No, **you aren't**.
he/she/it	**Is he going to make** a reservation for both of us?	Yes, **he is**.	No, **he isn't**.
you/we/they	**Are you going to speak** to her next week?	Yes, **we are**.	No, **we aren't**.

- We use *going to* to talk about future plans and intentions.
- In the negative, with *you*, *he*, etc, we can also say: *You're not going to*, *He's not going to*, etc.

  She isn't going to book anything until next month. OR *She's not going to book anything until next month.*
- In negative short answers, with *you*, *he*, etc, we can also say: *No, you're not.*, *No, he's not.*, etc.

  Are they going to visit the Guggenheim? No, **they aren't.** *OR No,* **they're not.**

12.2 *will* for predictions

	Positive	Negative
I/you/he/she/it/we/they	Rock music **will be** popular forever.	Students **won't go** to school in the future.

	Question	Short answers	
I/you/he/she/it/we/they	**Will they visit** Mars in our lifetime?	Yes, **they will**.	No, **they won't**.

- We use *will* + infinitive without *to* to make predictions.

  Germany will win the next World Cup.
  In 10 years' time, most people will drive electric cars.
- In the positive, we often contract *will* to *'ll* in informal writing and speech.
- In the negative, we can also say *will not*. This is more formal.

  Schools **will not** *teach the same subjects in the future.*

> **Be careful!**
> - We often use *will* after *Do you think . . . .*
>   *Do you think the party* **will be** *fun?*

12.3 *might*

	Positive	Negative
I/you/he/she/it/we/they	**I might stop** using Facebook.	**She might not read** my tweets.

- We use *might* to talk about something that is not definite but possible.
- We use *might* + infinitive without *to*.

144   GRAMMAR HUB

Grammar Hub

12.1 *going to*

A Reorder the words to make sentences.

1 go / going to / backpacking around Europe / she's

   She's going to go backpacking around Europe.

2 study / at university / going to / I'm / art history

   _____

3 going to / the tickets / when / are you / book / ?

   _____

4 a new job / start / I'm / looking for / going to

   _____

5 build / they're / themselves / going to / it

   _____

B Complete the sentences with the correct form of *be going to* and the verbs in brackets. Use contractions where possible.

1 _____*Are you going to have*_____ (you / have) a big birthday party?

2 _____ (she / finish) her essay this weekend.

3 When _____ (they / travel) to Bucharest?

4 What time _____ (you / get up) tomorrow?

5 _____ (it / not / be) cold tonight.

6 _____ (we / not / arrive) until late.

➤ Go back to page 112.

12.2 *will* for predictions

A Reorder the words to make sentences.

In the year 2025 …

1 there / flying / cars / be / will

   _____

2 won't / be / school / there / books / any

   _____

3 cities / other / have / planets / on / we'll

   _____

4 robots / do / work / all / the / will / us / for

   _____

5 come / true / will / our / predictions / all

   _____

6 with / people / will / around / jetpacks / fly

   _____

B Use the prompts to write questions and short answers with *will*.

1 we / finish / on time?

   _____*Will we finish on time?*_____ (?) _____*Yes, we will.*_____ (+)

2 she / read / your diary

   _____ (?) _____ (+)

3 you / work and study / at the same time

   _____ (?) _____ (-)

4 his predictions / come true

   _____ (?) _____ (-)

5 he / get / a better job

   _____ (?) _____ (+)

6 Chris / be / at the party

   _____ (?) _____ (-)

➤ Go back to page 115.

12.3 *might*

A Complete the sentences with *might* or *might not*.

1 I _____ be able to come on Saturday, because I've got to help my friend move house.

2 Do you want me to give Tom a message? I _____ see him at the conference.

3 I'll try, but I _____ be able to get everything finished in time.

4 I _____ be home late tonight because I've got lots of work to finish.

5 You should call Sarah. She _____ think you've forgotten her!

B Complete the sentences with the correct form of *might* and a verb in the box.

| come   get   have   ~~see~~   send   wait |

1 OK, great. I _____*might see*_____ you later then.

2 You're right. I _____ her an email to check the flight time.

3 It's hot in here. I _____ outside.

4 I _____ the bus, because it's cheaper than a taxi.

5 She _____ time to finish everything.

6 I _____ tonight. I'm not feeling very well.

➤ Go back to page 117.

Vocabulary Hub

1.1 Countries and nationalities

A Match countries (1–12) with the words in the box.

> Brazil Chile China Egypt France
> India Italy Japan Portugal
> Spain Thailand Turkey

1 _____ 7 _____
2 _____ 8 _____
3 _____ 9 _____
4 _____ 10 _____
5 _____ 11 _____
6 _____ 12 _____

B Complete the table with the words in the box.

> British Greek Russia Poland ~~South Korean~~
> Swedish Switzerland Vietnamese

Country	Nationality
	-ian/-an
Colombia	Colombian
South Korea	1 _South Korean_
2 _____	Russian
	-ish
Finland	Finnish
3 _____	Polish
Sweden	4 _____
	-ese
Sudan	Sudanese
Vietnam	5 _____
	Other
The Netherlands	Dutch
Greece	6 _____
7 _____	Swiss
the UK	8 _____

➤ Go back to page 2

2.2 Describing appearance

A Complete the table with the words in the box.

> bald a beard glasses large
> a moustache short slim tall

Face / head:	
Height:	
Build:	

B Match the descriptions (1–5) with the pictures (a–e).

1 She's tall and has got curly hair. ____
2 She's got long, straight hair and glasses. ____
3 He's got red hair and a moustache. ____
4 He's got fair hair and blue eyes. ____
5 He's short and bald. ____

➤ Go back to page 14

Vocabulary Hub

3.1 Everyday activities

Match photos (1–9) with the activities.

___ listen to music   ___ watch TV   ___ have a shower   ___ go to the cinema   ___ go for a run
___ have coffee with friends   ___ go to bed   ___ read a book   ___ have lunch

➤ Go back to page 22

4.1 Work and jobs

Match the photos (1–8) with the words in the box.

___ dentist   ___ designer   ___ hairdresser   ___ journalist   ___ mechanic   ___ nurse   ___ police officer   ___ shop assistant

➤ Go back to page 32

Vocabulary Hub

5.1 Rooms and furniture; prepositions of place

A Label the rooms (a–e) with the words in the box.

bathroom   bedroom   dining room   kitchen   living room

B Look at the picture again. Number the words 1–16.

___ armchair   ___ lamp
___ bath   ___ plant
___ bed   ___ shower
___ chair   ___ sink
___ coffee machine   ___ sofa
___ cooker   ___ table
___ cupboard   ___ toilet
___ fridge   ___ washing machine

➤ Go back to page 42.

5.2 Places in a town or city

Match photos (1–12) with the places.

___ café   ___ cinema   ___ gym   ___ hospital   ___ library   ___ market   ___ museum
___ park   ___ restaurant   ___ supermarket   ___ theatre   ___ underground station

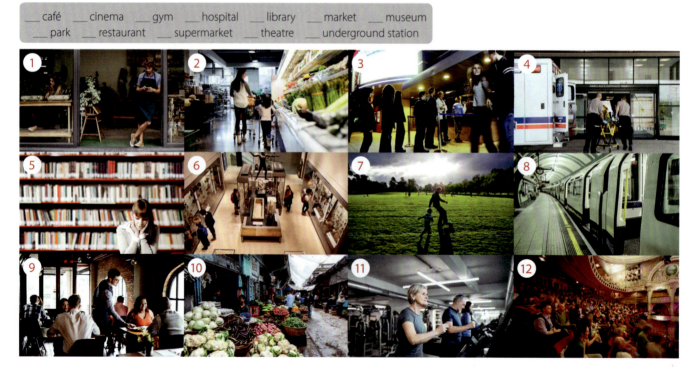

➤ Go back to page 44.

Vocabulary Hub

7.1 Transport

Match pictures (1–12) with the words in the box.

___ bicycle ___ boat ___ bus ___ car ___ ferry ___ motorbike ___ plane ___ cruise ship ___ taxi ___ train ___ tram ___ underground

➤ Go back to page 62.

7.2 Travel phrases

Complete the email using the past tense of the verbs in the box.   arrive   leave   miss   return   take

To: Samantha

Dear Samantha,
We're back! We visited my parents last week. Our journey home was terrible. It took a long time. We ¹_____ my parents' house on Saturday evening. We ²_____ a bus and then a train to Caracas. We ³_____ in the city at lunchtime on Sunday. Unfortunately, the traffic on the way to the airport was really bad, and we ⁴_____ our flight! So we ⁵_____ to the city and stayed in a hotel. In the end, we got home on Wednesday, four days after leaving my parents' house!
Speak soon.
Rose

➤ Go back to page 65.

VOCABULARY HUB 149

Vocabulary Hub

8.1 Food and drink

A Label the images (1–15) with the words in the box.

> an apple   butter   cake   cheese   chicken
> crisps   eggs   lettuce   mushrooms   pasta
> potatoes   prawns   rice   tea   tomatoes

1

2

3

4

5

6

7

8

9

10

11

12

13

14

15

B Complete the table with words from Exercise A.

Dairy	
Meat and fish	
Fruit and vegetables	
Drinks	
Other	

➤ Go back to page 72.

8.2 Containers

Complete the labels (1–8) with words from the box.

> a bag   a bottle   a box   a carton
> a jar   a packet   a pot   a tin

1 _____ of water

2 _____ of cereal

3 _____ of milk

4 _____ of biscuits

5 _____ of yoghurt

6 _____ of rice

7 _____ of beans

8 _____ of jam

➤ Go back to page 75.

Vocabulary Hub

9.1 Clothes

A Match pictures (1–18) with the words in the box.

___ boots ___ coat ___ dress ___ gloves ___ hat
___ headscarf ___ jumper ___ scarf ___ shirt
___ shoes ___ shorts ___ skirt ___ socks ___ sunglasses
___ T-shirt ___ tie ___ trainers ___ trousers

1 2 3
4 5 6
7 8 9
10 11 12
13 14 15
16 17 18

B Complete the descriptions with words from Exercise A.

I like Nobel Peace Prize winner Malala Yousafzai's style. It's traditional and beautiful. She usually wears a ¹_____, a long ²_____, a pair of ³_____ and some simple shoes.

I prefer simple styles, like Mark Zuckerberg's. He usually wears a ⁴_____, a pair of blue jeans and a pair of sporty ⁵_____.

Emma Watson is so stylish. She looks great when she wears a black ⁶_____ and a pair of black ⁷_____.

➤ Go back to page 82.

9.3 Shops and services

Match the words in the box with pictures (1–12).

___ bakery ___ bank ___ bookshop ___ butcher's ___ department store ___ dentist's
___ hairdresser's ___ library ___ market ___ newsagent's ___ pharmacy ___ supermarket

➤ Go back to page 87.

VOCABULARY HUB 151

Vocabulary Hub

10.2 Seasons and weather

A Label the images with the words in the box.

autumn   spring   summer   winter

1 _____   2 _____   3 _____   4 _____

B Match phrases (1–8) with pictures (a–h). Some phrases can go with more than one picture.

1 It's cloudy.   ___
2 It's cold.   ___
3 It's foggy.   ___
4 It's hot.   ___
5 It's raining.   ___
6 It's snowing.   ___
7 It's sunny.   ___
8 It's windy.   ___

➤ Go back to page 95.

10.3 Phrasal verbs

Choose the correct phrasal verbs to complete the text.

Around two years ago, my husband and I went hiking in Austria. When we ¹*set off / gave up*, it was quite cold, but then it got hotter and I ²*put on / took off* my jacket. The mountain air felt so nice! We walked for a really long time. In fact, we got lost! We ³*found out / looked for* our car, but we couldn't find it. We met a man and we tried to talk to him. We wanted to ⁴*find out / look for* where the nearest village was, but he didn't understand us. In the evening, it got really cold. I ⁵*put on / took off* my jacket, but it wasn't enough. We were frightened and we were ready to ⁶*set off / give up*, but then we found a village! The police officer told us that our car was only three minutes' walk from the police station!

➤ Go back to page 97.

Vocabulary Hub

11.2 Irregular past participles

Complete the sentences with the past participle form of the verbs in the box. There are two verbs you do not need.

`be  do  go  have  ride  see  take  win`

1 I've never _____ a horse and I don't want to.
2 She's _____ three running races.
3 I've _____ to more than ten countries.
4 They've _____ the sun rise in Africa.
5 I've never _____ a meal that cost more than £100.
6 He's _____ a picture of a famous person.

➤ Go back to page 105.

11.3 Sports

A Label the pictures with the words in the box.

`badminton  basketball  cycling  golf  gymnastics  judo  skating  skiing  surfing  swimming  tennis  yoga`

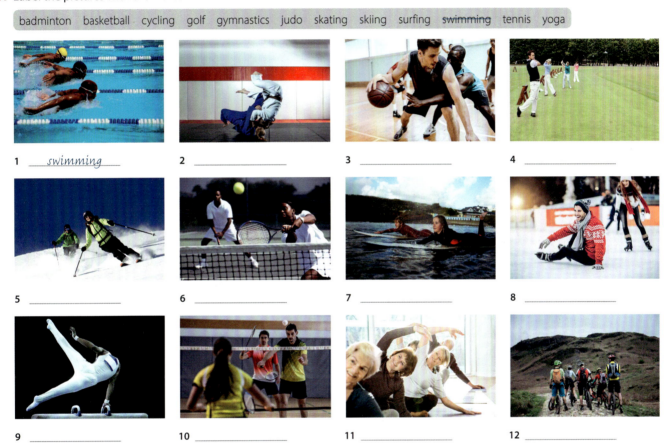

1 _swimming_
2 _____
3 _____
4 _____
5 _____
6 _____
7 _____
8 _____
9 _____
10 _____
11 _____
12 _____

B Match the sports in Exercise A with the correct verb – *do*, *go* or *play*.

Play	
Do	
Go	

➤ Go back to page 107.

12.2 Collocations with *get*

A Write the phrases with *get* in the correct place.

`get home   get hot   get lunch   get some coffee
get there   get tired`

Become	Buy or obtain	Arrive

B Think of two more phrases for each meaning of *get*. Add them to Exercise A.

➤ Go back to page 115.

VOCABULARY HUB 153

Communication Hub

2.2 Student A and B

Student A – look at the photos. Choose one person and describe them to your partner.
Student B – listen and guess who your partner is describing.
Then switch roles.

➤ Go back to page 15.

5.3 Student A and B

DISCUSS Work in pairs. Answer the questions about buildings (1–6). Use the adjectives in the box to help you.

1 Describe the buildings.
2 What happens inside?
3 Which building is your favourite? Why?
4 Which building don't you like? Why?

amazing   beautiful   big   boring   cool   interesting   funny   modern   old   small   strange   tall   terrible   ugly

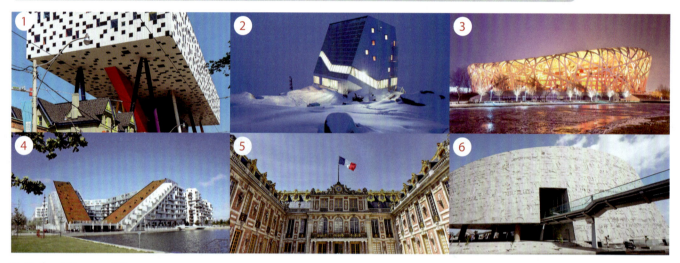

➤ Go back to page 47.

6.1 Student A and B

A SPEAK Work in pairs. Read the *City Guide* and choose one thing to do together at the weekend. Explain what you like and don't like to help you decide.

A: *Let's go out this weekend!*
B: *Good idea. What's on?*
A: *There's a rock concert in the park on Saturday.*
B: *Oh, I don't like rock music. Let's go to a nightclub. I love dancing.*
A: *Sorry, I'm a terrible dancer!*

B SPEAK Have a class vote. Which events are popular?

➤ Go back to page 53.

City Guide

Cinema
French film festival ★★★
A festival of French cinema, with famous films like *Amélie*, *That Man from Rio* and *Two Days in Paris*.

Art
Van Gogh – the last years ★★★★★
An exhibition of Van Gogh's paintings from 1888 to 1890.

Clubs
70s disco ★★★★
The 70s disco craze continues. Dance all night to your favourite tunes!

Communication Hub

7.2 Student A and B

Work in pairs. Follow these instructions to play the game:
- Use a dice and counters to play the board game.
- Complete the sentences with the past simple form of the verbs in brackets.
- Every time you get the answer right, roll again!

25 SPIN AGAIN!	26 They (not take) the train to Spain; they (go) by bus.	27 You missed the train. Go back to **6**.	28 I (not see) the Colosseum when I (be) in Rome.	FINISH
24 There's a storm. Go back to **8**.	23 I (go) to Thailand last year.	22 We (not fly) to Mexico; we sailed.	21 You're in a traffic jam. Go back to **12**.	20 SPIN AGAIN!
15 We (not book) into a hotel; we (stay) with friends.	16 You forgot your passport. Go to **3**.	17 SPIN AGAIN!	18 We (not go) to Malaysia by train; we (go) by car.	19 They (take) the ferry.
14 He (not go) to Rome.	13 He (miss) the train.	12 You've only got hand luggage. Go to **18**.	11 SPIN AGAIN!	10 They (not arrive) in Bogotá until 5 am.
5 SPIN AGAIN!	6 They (not take) much luggage.	7 They (miss) their flight to France.	8 She (leave) at 8 am.	9 Your flight arrived 30 minutes early. Go to **18**.
4 SPIN AGAIN!	3 I (travel) to Dubai by plane.	2 You've got a first-class ticket. Go to **8**.	1 She (take) a train to London.	START

▶ Go back to page 65.

7.3 Student A and B

SPEAK Work in pairs. Use the pictures to tell the story of Max and Sarah's holiday.

▶ Go back to page 67.

Communication Hub

2.1 Student A

A Read about another famous family. Answer Student B's questions about the family.

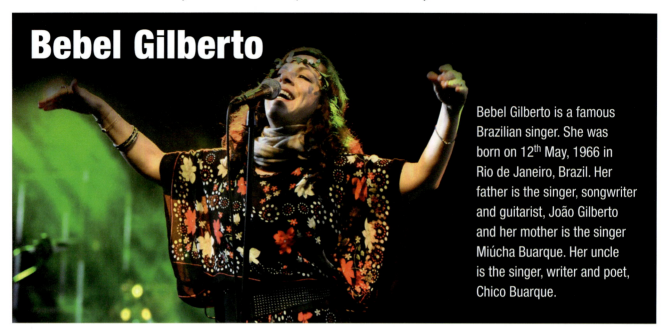

B Ask Student B questions about a famous family. Write the answers.

1 What's his name? _____
2 What is his dad's name? _____
3 What is his sister's name? _____
4 Why are they famous? _____

➤ Go back to page 13.

8.1 Student A

Look at the picture. Ask Student B what's in their fridge. Answer Student B's questions. What is the same? What is different?

➤ Go back to page 73.

Communication Hub

10.2 Student A

A Use the prompts to make superlative questions.

1 small / city / in the world?
2 hot / city / in Europe?
3 wet / place / on Earth?
4 high / city / in South America?
5 old / city / in Africa?
6 remote / city / in the world?
7 big / jungle / in the world?

B SPEAK Ask Student B your questions and write down the answers. Answer Student B's questions using the information box below.

> Tokyo, Japan – 37 million people
> Argos, Greece – 6th century BC
> Winnipeg, Canada – minus 45C (1966)
> El Azizia, Libya – 58°C
> Lhasa, Tibet – 3600 m
> Singapore
> The Sahara Desert – 9 million km²

A: What's the biggest city in the world?
B: The biggest city in the world is Tokyo, Japan. Thirty-seven million people live there.

➤ Go back to page 95.

12.1 Student A

Look at Andrew's list of five things he has to do. Ask and answer questions to find the missing information.

A: What's Andrew going to do on Friday?
B: He's going to …

> 1 This afternoon – phone James Smith.
> 2 _____ on Friday.
> 3 Send out the conference invitations next week.
> 4 Tomorrow morning – _____.
> 5 Today – _____!

➤ Go back to page 113.

9.2 Student A and B

A You are going to interview your partner about their job/studies. Write questions using the prompts (1–7).

1 What / do?
2 Where / (work/study)?
3 What / do / every day?
4 What / enjoy / about / (job/course)? What / not enjoy?
5 Where / live / at the moment?
6 What / interest / in?
7 What / do / today?

B SPEAK Interview your partner using the questions from Exercise A. Make notes.

C SPEAK Work in small groups. Imagine two students in the class are going to swap jobs for a day. Use your notes from Exercise B to help you choose which students should swap jobs. Explain why.

> Fumi is interested in art and Alex works in a museum. Maybe they should swap jobs.

> Good idea!

➤ Go back to page 85.

10.3 Student A and B

A Work in pairs. Which of the following places do you think is the most difficult to survive in? Why?

> a forest   an island   a jungle   a mountain

B PLAN Work in pairs. Imagine you are lost in one of the places in Exercise A. What are the dangers? What can help you? Choose three items to take with you.

Location	
Dangers	
Things to take	

C ORGANISE Write a survival plan.

SURVIVAL PLAN
We can use the penknife to cut up fruit.
We can use the matches to light a fire – wild animals won't like the fire!

D PRESENT Tell the class your ideas.

➤ Go back to page 97.

COMMUNICATION HUB   157

Communication Hub

12.3 Student A and B

A SPEAK Interview your classmates about how they use social media. Make notes. Ask for more information.

SOCIAL MEDIA HABITS

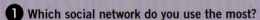

1 Which social network do you use the most?
 a Facebook   b Twitter
 c LinkedIn   d other

2 How often do you 'like' things?
 a fewer than 5 times a day
 b 5–10 times a day
 c 11–20 times a day
 d more than 20 times a day

3 What do you share the most?
 a pictures   b videos
 c news stories   d funny stories

4 How many people do you follow?
 a fewer than 50   b 50–100
 c 101–300   d more than 300

5 How often do you chat?
 a fewer than 5 times a day
 b 5–10 times a day
 c 11–20 times a day
 d more than 20 times a day

6 In the future, how much do you think you'll use social media?
 a more   b less
 c the same amount   d not at all

B ORGANISE Work in groups. Compare your answers. Organise them into statistics.

Most people share news stories.
Nobody tweets every day.

➤ Go back to page 117.

2.1 Student B

A Ask Student A questions about a famous family. Write the answers.

1 What's her first name? _____
2 Where is she from? _____
3 What are her parents' names? _____
4 Why is she famous? _____

B Read about another famous family. Answer Student A's questions about the family.

Matthew Centrowitz Jr

Matthew Centrowitz Jr is an Olympic athlete from the USA. In 2016, he won a gold medal for the 1500 metres. His father, Matt Centrowitz Sr, is also an Olympic athlete who won a gold medal in the 1979 Pan-American games. Matthew Centrowitz Jr's sister Lauren Centrowitz, is also an athlete.

➤ Go back to page 13.

Communication Hub

8.1 Student B

Look at the picture. Ask Student A what's in their fridge. Answer Student A's questions. What is the same? What is different?

➤ Go back to page 73.

10.2 Student B

A Use the prompts to make superlative questions.

1 big / city / in the world?
2 old / city / in Europe?
3 cold / city / in North America?
4 hot / place / in the world?
5 high / city / in Asia?
6 expensive / city / in the world?
7 big / desert / in the world?

B SPEAK Ask Student A your questions and write down the answers. Answer Student A's questions using the information box below.

> Vatican City, Rome – 800 people
> Athens – 22°C average temperature in summer
> Mawsynram, India – 11,871 mm of rain every year
> La Rinconada, Peru – 5101 m
> Luxor, Egypt – 3200 BC
> Auckland, New Zealand – 2153 km from Sydney
> The Amazon rainforest – 5.5 million km²

A: What's the smallest city in the world?
B: The smallest city in the world is the Vatican City in Rome. Eight hundred people live there.

➤ Go back to page 95.

12.1 Student B

Look at Andrew's list of five things he has to do. Ask and answer questions to find the missing information.

A: What's Andrew going to do this afternoon?
B: He's going to …

> 1 This afternoon – _____.
> 2 Email the design company on Friday.
> 3 _____ next week.
> 4 Tomorrow morning – arrange a meeting with Max.
> 5 Today – write the PRS report!

➤ Go back to page 113.

1 Writing — Fill in a form with personal details

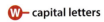
capital letters

A Look at the visitor card. Where would you fill in a card like this?

a At a university
b On a plane
c At work

B Complete the visitor card with the words in the box.

| 07713 8765543   1997   10 months |
| Poland   ~~Polish~~   student |

Visitor card

- Family name: Kowalska
- Given name(s): Marta Irena
- Nationality: _____Polish_____
- Date of birth: day [1][0] month [0][3] year [ ][ ][ ][ ]
- Country of birth: _____
- Occupation: _____
- Passport number: ZS 0067389
- Address in the UK: 24 Bridge Street, Leeds, LS5 7RT
- Email: mkowalska23@polemail.com
- Phone number: _____
- What is the main reason for your visit?
  business / tourism / (other)
  I am here to do a course at a university in Leeds.
- Duration of visit: _____

C Complete the rules in the box with words from the visitor card in Exercise B.

Capital letters
You use capital letters for:
• the names of countries — Poland
• the names of towns and cities — _____
• nationalities — _____
• people's names — _____
• the personal pronoun 'I' — _____

D Look at the student registration form. Find and correct five mistakes with capital letters.

Student registration

- Family name: puente
- Given name(s): Ricardo
- Nationality: mexican
- Date of birth: day [1][7] month [0][2] year [1][9][9][7]
- Country of birth: usa
- Occupation: student
- Address in the UK: 11 Lark Close, london, SW5 9JT
- Email: m.puente@hotmail.com
- Phone number: 07665 456829
- What is the main reason for studying English?
  business / tourism / (other)
  i want to study at university in the UK.
- Duration of visit: 2 weeks

WRITING

Imagine you are on a plane. Complete the visitor card. Remember to use capital letters correctly.

Visitor card

- Family name: _____
- Given name(s): _____
- Nationality: _____
- Date of birth: day [ ][ ] month [ ][ ] year [ ][ ][ ][ ]
- Country of birth: _____
- Occupation: _____
- Passport number: [ ][ ][ ][ ][ ][ ][ ][ ]
- Address in the UK: _____
- Email: _____
- Phone number: [ ][ ][ ][ ][ ][ ][ ][ ][ ][ ][ ]
- What is the main reason for your visit?
  business / tourism / (other)
  I am here to do a course at Leeds University.
- Duration of visit: _____

2 Writing — Write an email to a friend

W — *and*, *but* and *or*

A Read the email. Who is it to?

a   a close friend   b   an old friend   c   a colleague

How's things?
Sent: Friday 10th November 2017, 2.19 pm
To: jbloggs@screen.nett
From: Aiden_28@logbox.com

Hi Joe,

How are you? Long time no see!

How are things? I live in London now with my girlfriend. Do you still live here? How's your family?

Look forward to hearing your news!

Best wishes,

Aiden

B Tick (✓) the topics you think Joe will write about in his reply. Then read and check.

- food ☐
- family ☐
- job / school ☐
- friends ☐
- home ☐
- clothes ☐

RE: How's things?
Sent: Friday 10th November 2017, 4.37 pm
To: Aiden_28@logbox.com
From: jbloggs@screen.nett

Hi Aiden,

I'm very well, thanks. It's great to hear from you!

Yes, we are still in London, but we're not in the flat anymore. We live in a house because … we've got two beautiful children now!

We've got a son, Ben, and a daughter, Maya. Ben is three and Maya is four- it's a noisy house! Ben looks like his mum (lucky him!) but he's got my personality. He isn't tidy or serious, but he's only three! Maya's got blonde hair and blue eyes like me. Here's a picture for you of all of us on holiday this year!

How about you, Aiden? How are things with you and your family?

Best wishes,

Joe

C Read the email in Exercise B again and underline examples of *and*, *but* and *or*.

D **WORK IT OUT** Choose the correct words to complete the rules.

and, *but* and *or*

1. We use ***and* / *but* / *or*** when we want to add more or similar information in positive statements.
2. We use ***and* / *but* / *or*** when we want to add more or similar information in negative statements.
3. We use ***and* / *but* / *or*** when we want to add different or unexpected information.

E Complete the sentences with *and*, *or*, or *but*.

1. I've got two pets, a cat _____ a dog.
2. I haven't got any children _____ pets!
3. I live in a house with my friends Amy _____ Emma.
4. I have a horrible flatmate. She isn't friendly _____ tidy!
5. My flatmate loves football _____ I hate it.

F **SPEAK** Work in pairs. Look at the emails in Exercises A and B and answer the questions.

1. How do you start an email to a friend?
2. How do you end an email to a friend?
3. Which phrases are useful when it's the first contact in many months or years?

WRITING

A **PLAN** Imagine you are responding to the email in Exercise A. Make notes about:

How to start the email
How to answer the questions
How to finish the email.

B **WRITE** Write your email. Use the email in Exercise B to help you. Remember to:

Start and end your email appropriately
Answer the questions
Use *and*, *or*, *but* to join sentences together.

WRITING 161

3 Writing
● Write a blog post about your day

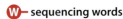
sequencing words

A Work in pairs. Look at the photo in the blog post. Guess the answers to the questions. Explain your ideas.
1 Where's she from?
2 What's her job?
3 Why is she famous?

A DAY in the LIFE of...
about | archive | contact

Ciara Everard Irish 800 m champion
7th January 2017 | Leave a comment

I'm an athlete. On weekdays, I always get up at 8 am. First, I go for a run. I'm usually out for 30 minutes – not long. Then I go home, have a shower and have breakfast – banana pancakes and a cup of tea. I'm not a morning person, so I usually need some coffee, too!

From 10 am to lunchtime, I'm in the gym. I don't like it, but I know it's good for me! After that, I go home and make lunch. I usually have an omelette, some fish and toast. In the afternoon, I'm always really tired, so I sleep for about 30 minutes. At 3 pm, I get up, read my emails and do some work.

At 5 pm, I go for my evening run. Then I do exercises and have an ice-bath. At 7 pm, I go home and make dinner. I usually prepare my meals at the weekend so I don't need to cook every night.

In the evening, I relax and watch TV. Finally, I have a snack and go to bed at 11 pm.

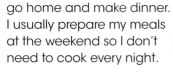

B Read the blog post and check your answers to Exercise A.

C Read the blog post again. Complete Ciara's diary.

Day	Time	What?
Mon 26th	8.00 am	*get up and go for a run*
	8.30 am	
	10.00 am	
	1.00 pm	
	2.30 pm	
	5.00 pm	
	7.00 pm	
	11.00 pm	

D Work in pairs. Would you like a life like Ciara's? Why/Why not?

E Read the first sentence in the box. Then find and underline five sequencing words in the blog post about Ciara Everand.

Sequencing words
We use sequencing words (*first*, *after that*, *then* and *finally*) to help the reader understand the order of things in a text.
- We use ¹_____ to say what we do first.
- We use ²_____ or ³_____ to say what we do after another thing.
- We use ⁴_____ to say what we do last.

F Complete the rules in the box with the sequencing words you underlined in Exercise E.

WRITING

A **PREPARE** You are going to write a blog post about your day. Write a diary like Ciara's. Include 6–10 activities you do in a normal day and the times you do them.

B **WRITE** Use your diary to write a short blog post about your day. Add details and use sequencing words (*first*, *after that*, *then* and *finally*) to explain the order.

C **REVIEW** Work in pairs. Compare your blog posts.

162 WRITING

4 Writing — Write an email asking for information

W — Punctuation: question marks, commas and full stops

A Work in pairs. Complete the adverts with the words in the box.

weekend   company   ten-week   course

Start up your own ¹ _____
One day training course with experienced business teacher
Contact Trevor East: teast@ivory.nett

² _____ **language courses**
Are you interested in languages?
Learn with us.
Don't wait – call now to get started.
Alena Chin: alenac@onthewall.com

Summer computer skills ³ _____
Do you want to learn computer skills?
Classes every day.
Contact Ed Soames: edso@screen.nett

⁴ _____ **CV writing course**
Five-week course (Saturdays and Sundays only)
Perfect for graduates or people who want to change jobs
Contact Anne Roberts: anne@roberts.nett

B Read the email. Which advert is it for?

Inquiry about your course
Sent: Friday 10th November 2017, 2.19 pm
To: edso@screen.nett
From: SKhan@logbox.com

Dear Mr Soames,
I am writing to ask about your summer computer skills course.
Firstly, what are the dates of the course? I am free in May, June and July and the first part of August. Secondly, when do the classes start – are they in the morning or in the afternoon? And finally, how much does the course cost?
I look forward to hearing from you.
Regards,
Samira Khan

C Look at the email in Exercise B again. Circle question marks, commas and full stops.

D Look at the question marks, commas and full stops that you circled in the email. Choose the correct options to complete the rules.

Punctuation: question marks, commas and full stops

We use *question marks / commas / full stops* at the end of sentences.
We use *question marks / commas / full stops* at the end of questions.
We use *question marks / commas / full stops* to separate words in a list or after sequencing words.

E Number the stages of the email in Exercise B.

___ Asking about when the course starts and ends
_1_ Greeting and name of the person you're writing to
___ Standard 'end of letter' phrase
___ Reason for writing
___ Asking about the times of classes
___ Salutation and name of writer
___ Asking about the cost of the course

F Complete the table with the phrases in the box.

All the best   Best wishes   Dear Monica   Dear Mr Ikeda
~~Dear Mrs Bennett~~   Kind regards   Yours sincerely

Starting an email	Finishing an email
Dear Mrs Bennett	

G Order the two groups of phrases in Exercise F from most formal to least formal.

WRITING

A PREPARE Imagine you want to apply to one of the courses in Exercise A. Choose a course and write three questions to ask in an email.

B WRITE Write an email asking for information. Use the email in Exercise B to help you.

C REVIEW Work in pairs. Check your partner's email for:
- spelling and punctuation
- grammar
- organisation

5 Writing

● Write a description of a place

W— using adjectives

A Work in pairs. Look at the picture in the review. Answer the questions.
1 What can you see? Describe the building.
2 What do you think this building is?
3 Where do you think it is?

B Read the online review. Check your answers to questions 2 and 3 in Exercise A.

C Read the review again. Choose the correct answers a, b or c.
1 What is the Villa Borghese?
   a a museum
   b a park
   c a café
2 What can you see in the museum?
   a paintings and furniture
   b cars and transport
   c furniture and clothes
3 Why does the writer like the café?
   a because it's warm inside
   b because it's popular
   c because the food is good

D Read again. Underline the adjectives that the writer uses to describe these things:
• the park
• the paintings
• the museum building
• the rooms in the museum
• the sandwiches

Using adjectives

When you write, use a variety of adjectives to make your writing more interesting.

Villa Borghese is a **famous** park in Rome. It's quite **big** and it's **beautiful**.

Villa Borghese is a famous park in **Rome**. It's quite big and it's beautiful. It's a great place to spend a couple of hours.

There's a museum in the park, the Borghese Gallery. There are some amazing paintings in the museum. The building is very interesting, too. It's an old, white house with a lot of windows. Inside the house, the rooms are beautiful. They've got some old furniture in them.

There's a café inside the gallery, but I like the café in the park. It's very popular. You can sit outside and have lunch under the trees. The sandwiches are delicious!

⤴ Share   👍 Like   💬 Comment

E Read about the Eiffel Tower. Change the adjectives *nice* and *good* for more interesting adjectives.

The Eiffel Tower is a nice tower in Paris, France. It's very popular with tourists. It's a nice place to spend an hour. It's tall and it's a very nice shape. There aren't any windows, and there aren't any walls. It's grey. I think it's really nice. You can go to the top of the Eiffel Tower. The views of the city are good. There's a restaurant on the first floor. The food is good.

WRITING

A **PREPARE** Choose a building, place or landmark in your city (or in a city that you know well). Think about these questions:
1 What is the building?
2 Where is it?
3 What does it look like?
4 What is your opinion of it?
5 What can you see and do there?
6 Can you eat or drink anything there?

B **PLAN** Think about your answers in Exercise A. What adjectives can you use to describe topics 1–6 in Exercise A?

C **WRITE** Write your description. Use a variety of adjectives to make your writing more interesting.

6 Writing

● Write a review of an event

W— using narrative sequencers

A Work in pairs. Look at the picture. What do you think happens at this event?

B Read the review. Check your answer to Exercise A.

C Choose the correct words to complete the sentences.

According to the review, …

1 the tour leader was *funny* / *serious*.
2 the tourists *learnt* / *didn't learn* about Melbourne.
3 it lasted for *30 minutes* / *60 minutes*.
4 the weather was *good* / *bad*.
5 it was *cheap* / *expensive*.
6 it was a *good* / *bad* experience.

D Read the review again. Number the topics 1–6 in the order they are written about.

___ The weather   ___ The writer's opinion
___ The location   ___ The cost of the event
_1_ The type of event   ___ Details of the event

E Look back at the review. Underline the narrative sequencers. Use the information in the box to help you.

> **Using narrative sequencers**
>
> • To begin the story, we use *first* or *to start with*.
>   **First**, we met in the city centre.
>   **To start with**, we got some headphones.
> • To continue the story, we use *then*, *next* and *after that*.
>   **Then**, we went to Main Street.
>   **Next**, we learnt about the city.
>   **After that**, we had lunch.
> • To end the story, we use *finally* or *in the end*.
>   **Finally**, the concert ended.
>   **In the end**, we called a taxi.

F Complete the story with narrative sequencers. Use the information in the box to help you.

Last weekend was really busy. Saturday evening was Comedy Night at The Old Fire Station. ¹_____, we watched a comedian – I can't remember his name. ²_____, we saw the famous Ali Wong. She was great. We laughed a lot! ³_____, there was a band for about 45 minutes. ⁴_____, the evening ended with a routine by Kyle Kinane. He was very funny, too. It was a great evening's entertainment and fantastic value – it cost $30 each.

WRITING

A PREPARE You're going to write a review for an event you went to. Think about the event and make notes under the headings in Exercise D.

B WRITE Use your notes to write your review. Use narrative sequencers to help you organise your ideas.

Guru Dudu Silent Disco Walking Tour

★★★★

goodreviews, 18th January 2018

I went to my first disco 20 years ago. I went to my first silent disco last week. Well, my first silent disco walking tour!

The tour started outside the Federation Square in Melbourne. First, we each got some wireless headphones and followed Guru Dudu, our tour leader and DJ, through the streets of the city. Then, we met some local people who talked about the history of the city. After that, we walked, danced and laughed as Guru Dudu played dance music and made jokes through our headphones. It was a great way to see the city. It was warm and sunny, and everyone had fun. Finally, the tour ended back where it started. The whole thing lasted an hour. It really was the best city tour ever! And it was great value at just $24 a ticket. I really recommend it!

Reviewed by Tom

WRITING 165

7 Writing

Write a short article about a travel experience

W— *so* and *because*

A Work in pairs. What makes a holiday good or bad?

B Read *Travel spotlight: Tulum*. Which of the things in Exercise A are mentioned?

Travel spotlight: TULUM

Last month, I travelled to Tulum, in Mexico. It's quite easy to get there. I flew to Cancún, and then took a bus. I wanted to be near the sea, so I stayed in a small hotel on the beach. It was really beautiful. For three days, I read books and swam in the clear, blue sea.

Tulum is a small town, but there are lots of things to do, so it isn't boring! During the day, you can visit historic places near the beach or go kite surfing. You can also visit the Sian Ka'an nature park and see birds, animals and fish. I went on a day trip to Chichen Itza because I like history.

At night, you can eat dinner in one of the great restaurants in town, or you can go salsa dancing in a club. The food at the hotel was really good – I ate fresh fish every day!

Tulum is a great place for a nice beach holiday with some interesting places to visit. A return flight to Cancún costs around $500. The best time of year to go to Tulum is between December and April because it's sunny, but not too hot.

C Read again and answer the questions.
1 Where did the writer go? _____
2 How did she travel there? _____
3 Where did she stay? _____
4 What did she do during the day? _____
5 What can you do at night? _____
6 What was the food like? _____
7 When is the best time to visit? _____

D Complete the sentences with *so* or *because*. Use the information in the box to help you.

> **so and because**
> - We use *so* to talk about the result of something.
>   *I wanted to be near the sea, **so** I stayed in a small hotel on the beach.*
>   *But there are lots of things to do, **so** it isn't boring!*
> - We use *because* to explain the reason for something.
>   *I went on a day trip to Chichen Itza **because** I like history.*
>   *The best time of year to go to Tulum is between December and April **because** it's sunny, but not too hot.*

1 The writer flew to Cancún ___because___ it's near Tulum.
2 She stayed in the hotel _____ it was on the beach.
3 She is interested in history, _____ she went to Chichen Itza.
4 She ate fish every day _____ it was really fresh.
5 It isn't too hot between December and April, _____ it's the best time of year to go.

WRITING

A **PREPARE** You are going to write a travel blog about a place that you know. Make notes about the place. Use the questions in Exercise C to help you.

B **PLAN** Add more information to your notes. Use the travel blog in Exercise B to help you.

C **WRITE** Write your article. Use *so* and *because*.

8 Writing

● Write an online restaurant review

W — pronoun referencing

A SPEAK Work in pairs. Answer the questions.
1. Do you like eating out?
2. How often do you eat out?
3. What's your favourite type of restaurant?
4. Do you ever write online reviews about restaurants you visit?

B Read the two restaurant reviews. Who didn't have a good time?

Posted on 03/01/19 at 10:32am
Primavera ★

We chose Primavera because **it** had amazing reviews and we love Italian food. When we arrived, the music was really loud. I called the waitress and asked **her** to turn **it** down. **She** just walked away! It wasn't much better when we ordered our food. When the starters arrived, my fish wasn't cooked so I sent **it** back. My boyfriend said there was too much garlic on **his** prawns – he didn't even finish **them**! For the main course, we had a salad and a steak. **They** were OK but nothing special. We didn't have a dessert. Overall, **it** cost too much and the food wasn't good. We didn't enjoy our meal and we won't go again.

Nor, Singapore

Share   Like   Comment

Posted on 17/03/19 at 03:25pm
Allium ★★★★

I wanted somewhere special for my wife's 30th birthday, so I chose the French restaurant, Allium. **It**'s very popular and so it wasn't easy to get a table. The piano player was really good and the service was great. There were fresh flowers on every table. **They** smelled lovely. For starters, we ordered the soup and the mushrooms. Then for the main course, I had the chicken and my wife had beef. We both had the lemon parfait for dessert. It was quite an expensive meal, but the food was great so **it** was good value. Our waiter, Pascal, was really good, too, so we left **him** a big tip! We loved Allium. I really recommend **it** for a special occasion.

Dieter, Germany

Share   Like   Comment

C Read the reviews again and answer the questions. Choose Nor (N) or Dieter (D).
1. Who wasn't happy with the staff?   N / D
2. Who thinks the food was good?   N / D
3. Who liked the music?   N / D
4. Who thinks their meal was too expensive?   N / D
5. Who doesn't recommend it?   N / D

D Complete the sentences with a pronoun. Use the information in the box to help you.

> **Pronoun referencing**
> The first time we talk about something, we use a noun. After that, we use pronouns to avoid repeating the noun and to make our writing flow.
> When we arrived, **the music** was really loud. I called **the waitress** and asked (her) to turn (it) down.

1. We enjoyed our meal. ____ was delicious.
2. The waitress and the manager were unfriendly. ____ didn't help us at all.
3. The waiter only came to our table after I called ____ three times.
4. The starters were amazing. I can't recommend ____ highly enough.
5. My wife loved the restaurant. ____ wants to go back soon.
6. We liked our waitress and left ____ a good tip.

WRITING

A PREPARE Think about a good or bad experience you had at a restaurant. Make notes. Think about:
- who you were with
- the name of the restaurant
- what it looked like
- the type, choice and quality of the food
- the staff
- the cost

B WRITE Write a review of your restaurant. Use your notes from Exercise A to help you. Remember to use pronouns and to write about what you liked and didn't like.

C REVIEW Work in pairs. Read each other's reviews. Do you want to go to the restaurant your partner went to?

9 Writing
Write a social media post

W— checking your work

A Work in pairs. Answer the questions.
1. What social media sites do you use?
2. Do you follow anyone on social media? Who?
3. Do you ever post pictures of yourself or friends/family on social media?
4. What kinds of pictures do people usually post on social media?

B Look at the pictures and read the social media posts. Match posts (a–d) with pictures (1–5). There is one picture you do not need.

C Read the posts again and answer the questions.
1. Why is the woman trying on sunglasses?
2. What are Daria and her friend looking for?
3. What are the people doing at the beach?
4. Why is the man having breakfast in a café?

D Find and correct two mistakes in each sentence. Use the information in the box to help you.

> **Checking your work**
> Always check your work for mistakes after you write something. Make sure you:
> - use the correct punctuation (capital letters, apostrophes, full stops).
> - avoid common spelling mistakes, for example *fourty* forty.
> - use the correct grammar, for example, *I'm watching* watch a film at the moment.

1. Were at the market and I eat an ice cream.
2. Like you thees shoes?
3. What you do at the moment?
4. I having a party beacause it's my birthday.

E Read post c again and correct:
- three punctuation mistakes
- three grammar mistakes
- three spelling mistakes

WRITING

A PREPARE Find a picture of yourself. (If you don't have one, imagine a picture that you want to describe.) Make notes about:
- where you are
- who you are with
- what you are doing

B WRITE Write a social media post about your picture. Use the posts in Exercise B to help you.

C REVIEW Check your work for mistakes. Use the strategies in the box to help you. Then swap with a partner and check their work.

a I'm having breakfast at my favourite café today. And I'm with my favourite person – my wife Lucy! The eggs here at Kevin's are delicious. It's the perfect start to my birthday! ❤
#goodtimes

b We're at the market. I'm looking for some new sunglasses because it's really sunny here. What does everyone think of these? They're really funny! Everyone is looking at us! 😆😆 #Spain

c Im spending the day with my lovely freind daria – we're shopping, obviously! I buyed a new top in a great little shop. Now we looking for a place to have lunsh. Does anyone know a restaurant in Mango Grove that have good food.
#bestfriends

d It's Saturday! Can you see where we are? That's right – at the beach! It's a beautiful day. The kids are eating ice creams. Rita's sleeping and I'm just relaxing! 😎

168 WRITING

10 Writing — Write a product review

W — adverbs of manner

A Work in pairs. Look at the pictures. Answer the questions.

1. Do you own any of these items?
2. Where did you buy them?
3. Are they good quality?

 1 a torch

 2 a penknife

 3 a backpack

 4 a pair of walking boots

5 a tent

6 a first aid kit

7 a small camping stove

B Read three customer reviews. Which of the items in Exercise A are they for?

> 1 **I bought this to use at night on a camping trip.** I've already got one, but this one is smaller and stronger. But it's also expensive and the batteries die very quickly. The most important thing is that it has a strong light! And it works quite well, so I recommend it for beginner campers or hikers.
> Published 1 week ago by Bob Smith

> 2 **I got this to use when I go fishing.** It's fantastic and it does a lot of different things. It cuts nicely. It also has scissors and a tin opener. Use it carefully, though. It can be dangerous! I'd recommend this to everyone!
> Published 5 days ago by Greg Barnett

> 3 **I got this for our family holiday.** We understood the instructions easily, but it's too small. It says it's for four people, but I don't think that's true. It's also made quite badly. And they have the worst customer service, too! After just one week, it broke, and now I can't get my money back. Don't buy this!
> Published 2 days ago by Elizabeth Brown

C Which is a five-star (★★★★★) review, which is a three-star (★★★) review and which is a one-star (★) review? Why?

D Read the reviews again. Make notes about each using the table below.

	Review 1	Review 2	Review 3
What is the product?			
What are its bad points?			
What are its good points?			
Would the reviewer recommend it?			

E Find two adverbs of manner in each online review. Which adverb is irregular? Use the information in the box to help you.

> **Adverbs of manner**
>
> Adverbs of manner tell us how something happens.
> *It cuts nicely.*
> We add *-ly* to an adjective to make a regular adverb.
> *quick – quickly*
> For adjectives ending in *-y*, we cut the *-y* and add *-ily*.
> *easy – easily*
> Some adverbs are irregular.
> *hard – hard*
> *good – well*
> Adverbs come after the main verb.
> *We understood the instructions easily.*
> *Use it carefully.*
> We use words like *quite*, *very* and *really* to add more information.
> *It's made quite badly.*
> *It works really well.*

F Complete the sentences by making adverbs from the adjectives in brackets.

1. The torch broke _____ (easy).
2. The boots arrived very _____ (quick).
3. Everything goes _____ (perfect) into one bag.
4. The stove didn't work very _____ (good).
5. Please use the penknife _____ (careful) because it's very sharp.
6. The instructions say quite _____ (clear) there aren't any scissors in the first-aid kit.

WRITING

A PREPARE Imagine you have bought one of the items in Exercise A. Write down some good and bad things about it.

B WRITE Write a review of your product. Use the questions in Exercise D to help you. Use some adverbs of manner. Write about 50 words.

C REVIEW Work in pairs. Read each other's reviews. Can you find any mistakes? How many adverbs of manner can you find?

11 Writing — write a recommendation on a forum

W — *too*, *also* and *as well*

A SPEAK Work in pairs. Do you ever give or read advice on chat forums? Which ones? What do you write about? Tell your partner.

B Work in pairs. Read the post on a fitness website. What sports or activities do you think Martin should try?

Hi everyone. I'm 23 and I want to get fit. Can anyone recommend a sport or activity for me? I like doing things on my own and team sports, but I don't want to spend a lot of money. What should I try? Thanks!

Martin | 15 June, 4.17

C Read the replies to Martin's question. Do they match any of the things you thought of in Exercise B?

Hi Martin! You should try yoga. It's really good fun! You don't need any special equipment or clothes. One problem is that lessons are sometimes expensive. I found a yoga class in my town and I go twice a week. Now I can touch my toes!

Luis | 15 June, 4.25

Hi there! I think you should try running. I've started a running club in my town. It's great! We go running together every week. Of course, you can also go running on your own. The best thing about running is that you can do it at any time you want! But be careful! Running is difficult, and it can hurt your knees as well. You should start slowly.

Caitlin | 15 June, 4.27

What about football? I started five years ago and I love it. My friends and I play every week on a Saturday morning. Football is really good exercise, and it's fun, too! One problem is that you need to buy boots and sports clothes. You also need other people to play. You can't do it on your own. But I think it's more fun to do exercise with friends!

Marta | 15 June, 4.27

D Read again and answer the questions. Make notes.
1 What sports and activities do the writers think Martin should try?
2 What good things do the writers say about the sports or activities?
3 What bad things do the writers talk about?

E Work in pairs. Whose advice do you think is best? Why?

> **Adding information with *too*, *also* and *as well***
> We can use *too*, *also* and *as well* to add information to an idea.
> *Too* and *as well* come at the end of the sentence.
> *Also* comes before the main verb, but after the verb *be*.

F Work in pairs. Read again. Find and underline sentences with *also*, *too* and *as well*.

G Rewrite the second sentence using the word in brackets. Use the Language information box to help you.
1 Golf is expensive. You need a lot of time. (also)
   You also need a lot of time.
2 Swimming is good for your heart. It's good for your arms and legs. (as well)
   _____
3 You can play basketball in winter. You can play it in summer. (too)
   _____
4 Rita is good at tennis. She's good at badminton. (too)
   _____

WRITING

A PREPARE Read the post below. What sport or activity should Janice try? Make notes. Use the steps in Exercise D to help you.

> I am a 53-year-old woman. I'd like to try a sport or activity. I don't like team sports and I have problems with my back. Does anyone have any advice for me? What should I try? Thanks!
> **Janice**

B Write your recommendation. Use *also*, *too* and *as well* to add information.

12 Writing — Write a formal email

structuring emails

A Read the invitation. What is it for?

1 an anniversary   2 a birthday   3 a wedding

15th May

Join us on our special day

hosted by Ray and Marcia
15th May, 12.00–18.00
Old Creek Golf Club
20 Ocean Drive, Tampa, Florida, USA

The ceremony will take place at 12 noon. After the ceremony, there will be a lunch at the Clubhouse, followed by a reception. Formal dress.

For more details, please contact our wedding planner, Kelly Olson:
kelly@floridaweddings.nett

B Work in pairs. Read again and answer the questions.

1 Whose wedding is it?
2 When is the wedding?
3 Where is the wedding?
4 Who do you contact for more details?

C Read Justin's email to the wedding planner. Number the steps 1–6.

Dear Ms Olson,
I am writing to ask you for some information.
My wife and I are going to attend Ray and Marcia's wedding in Tampa on 15th May. We would like to book a double room in a hotel nearby. Please could you recommend somewhere?
Also, we are going to arrive at Tampa airport late at night. Is there public transport at that time? Or should I take a taxi?
I look forward to hearing from you.
Kind regards,
Justin Blake

___ Ask for a recommendation
___ Start a formal email with the title and the surname of the person you're writing to
___ Friendly phrase before the end of the email
___ Reason for writing
___ Ask about transport
___ End a formal email with the full name of the writer

D Complete the email with the words in the box.

cost   could   dear   information   look   regards   writing

1_____ Mr Young,
I am 2_____ to ask for some 3_____ about a reception room in your hotel.
I am going to be 30 years old this year, and I want to have a big party to celebrate. I am going to invite around 150 people. Please 4_____ you tell me how much the room costs?
Also, could you tell me how much food would 5_____ for the guests?
I 6_____ forward to hearing from you.
Kind 7_____,
Gemma Lai

Structuring emails

We usually write formal emails to people we don't know, often to ask for information.
We start formal emails with *Dear* + *Mr/Mrs/Ms* + surname.
We often give a reason for writing and then ask some questions.
Before the end of the email, we use a friendly phrase (*I look forward to seeing / hearing from you.*)
You can end formal emails with any of these phrases: *Yours sincerely, Regards, Kind regards.* Then your full name.
We don't usually use contractions in formal emails.
I am writing to ask for information **NOT** *I'm* writing to ask for information.

WRITING

A PREPARE Read the invitation. What is it for?

6th Aug

10 years!

Hosted by Sophie and Nadim   6th August, 18.00–22.00
10 Jack McClure Place, Northbridge, New South Wales, Australia

Come and celebrate ten fantastic years together!
We hope you can all come!
PS The Tired Traveller is a great small hotel nearby. Write to Mr and Mrs Foster for reservations.

B Write an email to *The Tired Traveller* hotel to make a reservation. Write about the following:

- What kind of room would you like?
- How long do you want the room for?
- When and how are you going to arrive?
- What else do you want to know?

C Work in pairs. Read each other's emails. Did your partner use formal language?

Audioscripts

UNIT 1

🔊 Lesson 1.1, Listening, Exercise A
1.1 **H = Helen   V = Veronica   P = Pilot**

H: Excuse me, is this row 15?

V: Yes. I'm in seat 15A.

H: My seat is 15B. Hi, I'm Helen.

V: Nice to meet you. I'm Veronica Martinez.

H: That's a nice name. I like Spanish names.

V: Thanks, but I'm not Spanish. I'm Mexican. I'm from Mexico. Where are you from?

H: I'm Canadian, but I live in Mexico. My company's office is in Mexico City.

P: Good morning, ladies and gentlemen. This is the 9.45 flight to Mexico City …

🔊 Lesson 1.2, Listening, Exercise A
1.9 **L = Lee   C = Carlos**

L: Hello?

C: Hi, Lee, it's Carlos. Where are you? Are you still in Tokyo?

L: Oh, hi, Carlos! No, I'm not. I'm 1300 miles from Tokyo. I'm in China now.

C: Wow! Where are you in China?

L: I'm in Beijing.

C: Cool. What's it like there?

L: It's very busy in the centre. There are lots of new buildings and long streets. It's a big city.

C: Is the food good?

L: Yes, it is. I really like Chinese food.

C: What's your next destination?

L: I don't know. Maybe Shanghai, or maybe the countryside.

C: Sounds fun! Send me more photos!

L: I will!

🔊 Lesson 1.3, Listening, Exercise B
1.10 **N = Narrator   G = Guard**
W = Woman   M = Man

N: 1

G: Excuse me, madam. Is this your bag?

W: Yes, it is.

G: I need to look inside. Oh, is this a bottle of water?

W: Yes, it is.

G: Sorry, bottles aren't allowed.

W: Oh, of course. I'm sorry.

G: Is there a laptop or a phone in this bag?

W: No, there isn't.

G: OK. You can go. Oh, wait! Are these your keys?

W: Oh, yes, they are. Thank you so much!

N: 2

G: Excuse me, sir. Is that your bag?

M: Yes, it is.

G: Can you bring it here, please.

M: Sure.

G: Is your phone in this bag?

M: Yes, it is.

G: You need to take it out, please.

M: Oh, OK.

G: Thank you … One more thing …

M: Yes?

G: Are those your bags?

M: No, they aren't. I think they belong to that family over there.

G: I see. You can go.

UNIT 2

🔊 Lesson 2.2, Listening, Exercise B
2.5 **W = Woman**

W: My brother doesn't look like me. We've both got long red hair, but everything else is different. He's short, and I'm not. I'm very slim, but he isn't. He's got glasses. I haven't. And he's got a beard. I definitely haven't got a beard.

🔊 Lesson 2.3, Listening, Exercise A
2.7 **F = Fiona   K = Keisha**

F: I like this picture.

K: This is on our first day. These are the people in my study group.

F: Everyone looks so happy.

K: Yes. They're all really friendly and lovely.

F: Fantastic! So, who is who?

K: The girl with dark, curly hair is Zoe. She's my best friend. She's a very funny person.

F: Are any of your flatmates in this picture?

K: Yes! Jody is my flatmate. She's got long hair.

F: Has she got black hair?

K: No, that's Alice. She's quite quiet, but I like her. This is Jody – she's got long, blond hair.

F: Is she tidy? It's good to have tidy flatmates.

K: Yes, she is. She's quite serious and very tidy! I'm the messy one in our flat!

UNIT 3

🔊 Lesson 3.1, Listening, Exercise B
3.1 **T = Tom   V = Venus**

T: Hello, and welcome to Twenty-Two Minutes with me, Tom Fenn. Our guest today is Venus Mack, who is phoning in from California. Good morning, Venus.

V: Hey, Tom. Hey, UK. Good evening from Los Angeles.

T: You have two minutes to tell us about your typical day.

V: OK, well, my name's Venus Mack, I'm 25 years old and I'm a late night DJ for a radio station here in L.A.! I live in a small house, and – uh – a typical day? My day is unusual because I get up at four o'clock in the afternoon. That's right! Four pm. So, first, I go for a long run. My dog, Bowie, comes, too. Then, I go home, have a shower and have breakfast – breakfast at 6 pm, right? – it's usually fruit and coffee. I leave home at around 6.30. I go to work by car. Everyone drives here in L.A.! I get to work at 8 pm. I love my job! I meet a lot of musicians, and some of them are on my show. This week it's a band – from the UK – called Reuben. My show starts at 10 pm and ends at 2 am. After the show, I work with my producer, Joel, and prepare for the next show. I finish work at 6 am and then I go to a café and have coffee with friends, and maybe some dinner, and then I go home to give Bowie his breakfast. I go to bed at around 9 am.

T: Fantastic! Thanks, Venus.

🔊 Lesson 3.2, Listening, Exercise B
3.4 **I = Ian   A = Ali**

I: So, are you ready for screen-free week, Ali?

A: Screen what?

172   AUDIOSCRIPTS

Audioscripts

I: Screen-free week. No internet, no mobile phone, no TV for a week.

A: What? You're joking!

I: Ali, how many hours a day are you on your phone?

A: How many hours a day? I don't know. About nine? From early in the morning to late at night.

I: You look at it when you wake up?

A: Yeah, my phone is my alarm clock! Then, I look at the news and read my texts and emails.

I: What about during the day, at work?

A: Well, I use maps on my phone all the time for work. I've got an app. It's brilliant! It tells me if there are problems on the roads.

I: What about after work?

A: Yeah, I use my phone a lot in the evening – I talk to my friends – well, *text* my friends or play games with them online. At the weekend, we watch football on TV, and we chat online – we have a group chat – about the games. On Saturday and Sunday, it's non-stop football! I love football!

I: So, what about screen-free week?

A: No way! Impossible! I need my phone!

🔊 Lesson 3.3, Listening, Exercise A
3.9 **C = Carlos   M = Moira**

C: Moira, are you free tomorrow night?

M: I don't know. Why?

C: Well, tomorrow is 16th September – Independence Day in my country – and there's a party at my friend's house. Do you want to come?

M: Oh, that sounds like fun! I'd love to come. We have Independence Day in my country, too. How do you celebrate it in Mexico?

C: All the shops and banks close and everyone takes a holiday because it's party time! There are parties everywhere. People play music in the streets. Everybody dances and sings.

M: Oh, it's the same in Madagascar. We all dance and sing in the streets, too. There's usually a big parade in town – and we eat special food!

C: In Mexico, there's a big parade in Mexico City, and in the evening, we go and watch the fireworks! It's really noisy!

M: Oh, I love fireworks!

C: And we put up red, white and green decorations. That's the colour of our flag.

M: Madagascar's flag is red, white and green, too! We don't put up decorations, but we wear traditional clothes and dance … and sing …

C: We don't wear traditional clothes, but we shout 'Viva Mexico!' and we dance!

M: I want to go to Mexico next September!

C: Well, come to the party tomorrow and it will be just like Mexico!

UNIT 4

🔊 Lesson 4.2, Listening, Exercise A
4.5 **S = Salah   H = Hussam**

S: How's your new job?

H: It's great. I don't have to work nine to five. I can choose my own hours.

S: That's great, so when do you work?

H: I usually start work at midday. Why? When do *you* start?

S: I start really early in the morning. Sometimes before six!

H: Urgh! I couldn't do that!! I usually take it easy in the morning because I don't go to bed until midnight or later.

S: When do you have lunch?

H: I have lunch any time I feel like it. Some days, I have lunch at 1 pm, other days I eat late in the afternoon.

S: What time do you usually finish work?

H: I finish when I want to. I don't have to ask my boss. It's my decision.

S: That's amazing. So you can leave whenever you like?

H: No, I don't leave. I stay where I am.

S: I don't understand.

H: I don't work in an office. I'm self-employed now. I work from home.

🔊 Lesson 4.3, Listening, Exercise A
4.7 **T = Tom   L = Lily**

T: Hello. Can I help you?

L: Hi. Yes, please. I work in an office, but I want to change jobs. I'd like to do a course.

T: Well, you've come to the right place. We offer over 800 courses. My name's Tom. Come and sit down.

L: Thank you. I'm Lily.

T: Nice to meet you, Lily. Now, what subject do you want to study?

L: I want to train to be a teacher.

T: Ah, an excellent job! We have a very good teacher training course. I'm a teacher myself.

L: Oh?

T: Yes, I teach an art history course and …

L: I want to teach art history!

T: That's great! I can definitely help you.

L: Do I have to go to university?

T: Yes, you do.

L: That's a problem. I have to stay at work while I study. I need the money.

T: I recommend distance learning. You study when you want. You work from home and you send your homework to us by email.

L: That sounds good. I want to get a qualification. Does this course offer one?

T: Yes, of course! This is a degree course. You pay for access to our online materials and we provide you with your own teacher. The teacher of this art history course is … erm, well … me actually.

L: OK!

T: At the end of each course, you take an exam. You can pay for one year at first and see how you like it. Then, after two more years, you can get a degree.

L: That sounds great. Now, how much …

UNIT 5

🔊 Lesson 5.1, Listening, Exercise C
5.4 **S = Sadie   L = Luke**

S: Hello? Is this Luke Westman?

L: This is Luke speaking.

S: My name's Sadie Parfitt. I'm calling about your beach house.

L: Sure! Where are you from?

S: I'm from the south of England.

L: OK, that's great.

S: Er … yes. So, are there any beds in your house?

L: Beds? Yes, there are. There are two beds. There's a bed in the bedroom and another bed opposite the kitchen.

AUDIOSCRIPTS   173

Audioscripts

S: Very good. And is there a cooker?

L: Yes, there's a cooker. It's in the kitchen. There's a fridge, a coffee machine and a washing machine, too.

S: I see. Is there a swimming pool?

L: Yeah, sure there is. It's huge … It's called the Pacific Ocean!

S: Sorry? There is a swimming pool?

L: No, ma'am. It's a joke. It's the ocean. No, there isn't a swimming pool.

S: Ah! Yes, a joke. Lovely. So, is there a garden?

L: A garden? No, there isn't a garden – there's a beach. It's a caravan by the beach.

S: A caravan? The advert said a 'fantastic home' …

L: It *is* a fantastic home!

S: OK … Well, are there any chairs in the dining room?

L: No, there aren't any chairs. It's a dining area, not a dining room. There's a table, and four people can sit at the table, but there aren't any chairs.

S: I see.

L: So, tell me about your house. How many bedrooms are there?

S: My house? Oh, I don't have a house.

L: But … this is a house swap. We swap houses. You stay in my house and I stay in your house …

S: No, sorry, I don't have a house. So when can I stay in your caravan?

L: OK, ma'am. Thank you for calling. Goodbye now. Thanks.

UNIT 6

Lesson 6.2, Listening, Exercise B
6.4 **G = Grandad   C = Carrie**

G: Hey, Carrie. Let's watch that new nature programme on TV. It starts in five minutes.

C: Oh, I can't, Grandad. Mum says I have to do my homework. But we can watch it later.

G: Later? It finishes at seven.

C: I can get it on demand. We can watch it on my tablet.

G: On demand?

C: Yeah. You know, you don't have to watch TV programmes at a specific time on TV any more. You can watch them online, whenever you like.

G: So, can I watch the football match from yesterday?

C: Yes! You know, most people watch TV on demand now. Last night, I watched three episodes of my favourite TV programme.

G: Amazing! When I was young, my favourite TV programme was on once a week. On Tuesday nights. It was a music show.

C: How many TV channels were there?

G: Hmm … There weren't many TV channels. Three, I think.

C: Three? Now there are hundreds. Was it boring?

G: No, it wasn't.

C: Were TVs cheap back then?

G: No, they weren't. They were expensive. TV wasn't an everyday thing. We were the first family in our street to get one. It was in 1951, when I was ten. That's nearly 70 years ago! TV was special in the 1950s. We all watched TV together – the whole family. It was the same in every home in the country.

C: Everyone at the same time? That's funny. Were they happy?

G: Yes, they were. It was normal!

C: Mum and Dad often watch TV on their laptops and Susan has a tablet. We all watch TV alone.

G: People today spend more time alone. It was very different when I was young. Parents, children, grandparents were all together more. TV was a shared experience.

C: Was that nice, Grandad?

G: Yes, it was. I wasn't lonely. People did things together. It was fun.

UNIT 7

Lesson 7.3, Listening, Exercise B
7.6 **C = Colleague   E = Emma**

C: Hi, Emma. Did you have a good holiday?

E: Yeah! It was amazing, thank you!

C: Where did you go?

E: To China.

C: China? Wow! That's interesting. What did you do? Did you visit the Great Wall?

E: Yes, I did. It was … well, great! Do you want to see some photos?

C: Sure … So, why did you choose China?

E: Well, I didn't choose it, actually. I went on a 'mystery holiday'.

C: What do you mean, a 'mystery holiday'?

E: I used a company that organises your holiday for you. But they don't tell you anything about it until you get to the airport.

C: Huh? So how did it work?

E: I told them about my interests, how long I wanted to go for, and my budget – I said I could spend about £1500 – then they chose the hotels and activities … and basically created a holiday for me.

C: So, did you know your destination? Did you know the holiday was in China?

E: No, I didn't. I didn't know anything except the date and the airport. When I arrived at the check-in desk, I got a letter with the details. I found out that I was on a flight to Beijing. It was a complete surprise!

C: That's so cool! Was it cheap?

E: No, it wasn't. It was quite expensive, actually. But they organised the flights, hotels, transport, entertainment – they did everything!

C: So where did you stay?

E: In hotels, but I also stayed with a Chinese family in Shanghai. And I slept on a train, too – the overnight train to Shanghai.

C: Did the company organise that?

E: Yes, but I didn't know anything about it before. When I was in Beijing, I got an email about my next destination. Then in Shanghai, I got another email, and so on.

C: What else did you do?

E: I went sightseeing in Beijing, went on a boat trip on a river and climbed mountains in the forest.

C: Did you see any pandas?

E: Yes, I did. Hold on … Here's some pandas that I went to see in Chengdu.

C: Wow! I love pandas! You did so much. But why did you decide to do a mystery holiday?

174   AUDIOSCRIPTS

Audioscripts

E: Well, I wanted an adventure. Every day was a surprise and different. It felt new and exciting. And I didn't have to organise a thing!

C: It sounds great! I want to try a mystery holiday, too!

UNIT 8

Lesson 8.1, Listening, Exercise A
8.3 M = Marta   S = Stefan

M: Stefan, what are you doing?

S: I'm looking for something to eat for dinner tonight, but we don't have anything I can eat.

M: What do you mean? There's lots of food in there. Why don't we have pizza?

S: Oh, no! No, no. I can't have pizza.

M: Why not? You love pizza.

S: I do, I do … but I'm on a diet and pizza is one of the things I can't eat.

M: Is this the diet in your magazine? I told you – you *don't* need to lose weight.

S: I know, but I want to. Anyway, it's a very healthy diet.

M: OK, so what *can* you eat then?

S: Oh, lots of things: beef, chicken, fish …

M: Vegetables?

S: Of course!

M: So why not pizza?

S: Ah, well I can't eat bread. So, no pizza. Now, what's in the fridge? Is there any chicken?

M: Er … So, about the chicken …

S: Where is it? I'm sure we had some chicken …

M: There isn't any chicken. I … er … ate it yesterday.

S: Oh, OK. Right. Well, I can eat vegetables. Now, what have we got … Ah, yes! We've got some mushrooms, and some broccoli. Oh, and we've got a carrot, too … That's good.

M: Mushrooms, broccoli and a carrot? We can't eat mushrooms, broccoli and a carrot for dinner! What else is there?

S: Er … we might have some fruit … There's an orange! It's a bit old, but it's OK. Hmm … we haven't got any apples or bananas … we need to get some fruit next week …

M: We can't just eat fruit for dinner! I'm not sure about this diet. Why do we need to change? I think we have a healthy diet. We eat a lot of fresh food.

S: Hmm … Maybe …

M: … and we never eat unhealthy food like cake or crisps.

S: Hmm … Yes, you're right! This diet is a terrible idea.

M: Great. So, let's make dinner. Pizza?

UNIT 9

Lesson 9.1, Listening, Exercise B
9.3 S = Sophie   J = Johan

S: Hey, Johan.

J: Hey!

S: How are things? What are you doing?

J: I'm well, thanks. I'm having a coffee at the café in the park.

S: Ah, I miss the café in the park. Is Tom there?

J: No, just me. Excuse me – espresso, please? Oh, sorry! How embarrassing! I just ordered a coffee from a customer. I thought he was a waiter – he's wearing a white shirt and a tie, and carrying some cups.

S: Oops! Is the park busy?

J: Yes, it's very busy. Ooh! There's a woman near me. I *think* she's a runner – she's wearing a t-shirt and trainers. She's very angry. She's trying to get a bottle of water but no one is serving her.

S: Mm.

J: Oh, Sophie, you should see this – there's a tall man and a short woman coming this way. They're wearing *really* strange clothes. She's in pyjamas!

S: What? They're in pyjamas?

J: No, the *man* isn't wearing pyjamas. He's dressed like a pirate! He's in a black jacket, a bandana and a hat with three corners.

S: That's odd! I wonder why they're dressed like that …

J: Hang on, I'll ask … Excuse me, why are you wearing those clothes? Ah, I see, thanks. Apparently, they're doing a charity run.

S: Oh, I see!

J: Aww! How cute …

S: What's happening now?

J: There's a little girl in a pretty pink party dress with a pink ribbon in her hair. She's holding her mother's hand. I think it's her first party. She looks very sweet!

Anyway, tell me about you. What are you doing?

S: Well, it was really cold this morning, so …

Lesson 9.2, Listening, Exercise B
9.4 A = Announcer

A: Hello, shoppers and welcome to Greenfield Department Store. Would you like to win one thousand dollars? Then enter our job swap competition! Swap your job for one day and you could win the money. To enter our job swap competition, go to the clothes department on level two, which is by the café. Make sure you enjoy a coffee and a sandwich while you're there! Registration opens this morning at ten o'clock and stays open until four o'clock this afternoon, so make sure you register your name and contact information today.

UNIT 10

Lesson 10.1, Listening, Exercise A
**10.1 P = Presenter   C = Clarice
Mk = Mark   J = Janek   Ma = Maria**

P: With us today is Clarice Steinburg, a location scout. Clarice worked on this year's top film, *The Adventurer*, which won eight Oscars! Clarice, welcome! Tell us about your job. What does a location scout do?

C: Well, I find the best places to make a film. I don't mean a studio; I mean actual locations, like a building, a city or a landscape.

P: I see, I see … Well, Clarice, we've got a lot of questions for you tonight from people here in the audience. First up is Mark from London. What's your question, Mark?

Mk: Yes. Hi, Clarice. *The Adventurer* is a great film, and the locations are amazing.

C: Thank you.

AUDIOSCRIPTS   175

Audioscripts

Mk: A lot of the story takes place on a beach in California. Which beach is it?

C: Well, we didn't actually film in California. We filmed the beach scenes in Mexico.

P: Mexico? Why was that?

C: It's very difficult to film in California because it's really crowded and there are people everywhere. Often, the beaches are busier than the city! It's difficult to close a busy beach for days to make a film.

P: So, it was better to film in Mexico?

C: That's right. The beaches in Mexico are quieter than in California.

P: Was it expensive?

C: No. Actually, it was more expensive to film in the USA than in Mexico. Even with the cost of flights and hotels, Mexico was cheaper than the USA.

P: OK. We're ready for another question. Janek?

J: Thank you. The part in the desert is amazing. Is that Mexico, too?

C: No, we shot that bit in Morocco.

P: Wow! Why Morocco? That's so far from California!

C: Yes, Morocco is much further than Mexico! But there are some old buildings in the part of the desert where we filmed, and the sand is very red, so it's more interesting.

P: Next question. Maria?

Ma: Hi, Clarice.

C: Hi!

Ma: I loved *The Adventurer*. The scenes in the jungle are really beautiful. Where did you film them? I want to go there!

C: I'm sorry. We filmed those right here in Los Angeles!

P: No! There aren't any jungles in L.A.!

C: I know! We created that location on a computer! It was all in a studio in downtown Los Angeles. It's very difficult to film in a real jungle.

🔊 **Lesson 10.3, Listening, Exercise B**
10.5 G = Greg   M = Marcus

G: We're here with survival expert Marcus James to hear his advice on how to survive in the wild. Marcus, thank you for joining us.

M: You're welcome. Thanks for having me on the show.

G: So Marcus, if you're lost and you need to stay warm or cook some food, what's the best way to start a fire? Two pieces of dry wood?

M: Well, Greg, the easiest thing to do is to carry a box of matches or a lighter in your backpack, and use that to light a fire.

G: Oh, yes … I suppose so. So how about some other tips? For example, what are the safest plants to eat? How can I catch animals?

M: Again, 95 per cent of hikers have energy bars in their backpack. They don't need 'macho survival techniques'. Always plan to take a few important things with you, like a penknife, a lamp and a phone. Then, you don't have to catch animals! And, did you know, Greg, you can actually survive for up to three weeks without food? And that's a fact!

G: Really? So, what about Chuck Adams? Is his advice wrong?

M: It's not bad – I just don't think it's the most useful advice. For example, if you want to stay dry, take a raincoat. You don't need to build anything.

G: What's the most useful advice in your opinion?

M: The best advice I can give you is to be prepared. When you decide to go hiking, tell someone where you're going. On the hike, check your map and compass. Take lots of photos on your phone. They can help you find your way back later. And if you get lost, leave signs so people can find you. For example, leave clothes or a blanket on a tree. And remember to keep warm. The truth is, most people don't die because they get lost – they die because they don't prepare.

UNIT 11

🔊 **Lesson 11.1, Listening, Exercise B**
11.1 B = Bianca   E = Ella

B: This article is called 'Look Good, Feel Good'. It's got some nice clothes and some good health tips. You want a healthier lifestyle, don't you, Ella?

E: Mmm?

B: Actually, there are some really nice clothes in this article. What should I wear tonight? Those are lovely trousers. Should I wear trousers tonight, Ella? Or a dress? I think I'll wear a dress. It's a party, after all.

E: Mmm.

B: Anyway, here's some good advice on how to look after your body. Oh, you shouldn't spend too much time on your phone – the screen is bad for your eyes.

E: Mmm?

B: I like this one. Sleep is good for your heart. I think your heart is very healthy, Ella. You're always asleep! And sleeping on a hard bed helps with a bad back. Interesting.

E: Mmm?

B: And do you know how to improve your brain? You should listen to classical music every day.

E: Oh?

B: Yes! It says it here. Ha! I didn't know Mozart could make you more intelligent!

E: Mmm.

B: Ooh! Rolling a small ball under your foot is good for you. It helps the blood go around your body.

E: Really?

B: You should eat yoghurt to keep your stomach healthy. Everyone knows that! Coffee is good for you. Is it? Oh, I see. You should put it on your skin. It makes it soft.

E: Mmm.

B: But you shouldn't drink too much coffee – it keeps you awake. Ella? Coffee keeps you awake. Ella? Are you awake?

E: Mmm? Oh, yes, please.

---

176   AUDIOSCRIPTS

B: What do you mean 'yes, please'? Are you listening to me?

E: Of course I am. You just offered me some cake.

B: I said 'awake'. You never listen to me. I'm giving you all of this great health advice for free and as usual, you're *not listening*!

E: Mhm. Sorry, what did you say?

UNIT 12

🔊 Lesson 12.1, Listening, Exercise B
12.1 J = Juliet   M = Mario   K = Kelly

J: Guys! I'm so sorry I'm late. I needed to finish some things at work.

M: It's Saturday, Juliet. Why are you working at the weekend?

J: Oh, things are really busy at the moment. It's terrible. I'm at work all day, then I have to leave at five to pick up the children. Then in the evenings, I'm always busy with them. Well, actually, I'm usually in the car because I have to take them to their dance classes, or football, or swimming.

M: I read an article in the *Guardian* about time management. It had some useful tips.

K: Yeah, I saw that, too.

J: Well, I need some tips. Something has got to change. Tomorrow, I'm going to make a long list of everything I need to do.

M: No, don't make long lists!

J: Why not?

M: Because you can't finish everything. The article said you have to make a list of five things.

J: Only five?

M: That's right. But I never make lists. What's the point?

K: I like making long lists because that way I remember everything. But maybe I should try the five-list idea.

J: I make lists, too, but I'm going to try that idea at work next week. My biggest problem is that I can't say no, so I have too much to do.

M: I'm like that, too. I agreed to work full time this week, but then I'm studying for my degree in the evening. I need to finish an essay. It's due in on Monday, but there just aren't enough hours in the day. I don't know what I'm going to do.

K: Are you going to finish your essay this weekend?

M: I think I can find time to plan it tonight, but I'm definitely not going to finish it. It's difficult to study when I'm tired.

K: You need to understand your body clock. When do you work best? I'm definitely a morning person.

M: Yes, I think I am, too.

J: Maybe you should ask your boss if you can work in the evenings, so you can study in the mornings?

M: That's a great idea! I'm going to see him tomorrow, so I can ask him then.

K: Or maybe you could take a day off? It's impossible to do everything, so don't worry about it!

M: But you're really organised, Kelly. I'm not! I find it hard to prioritise.

K: Just make a list, then decide which are the most important things.

M: Why make a list when everything is a priority. I can't decide what's most important, so I do nothing!

J: I know just what you mean!

🔊 Lesson 12.3, Listening, Exercise B
12.9 N = Narrator   S = Shani   L = Luke
W = Wai   J = Jean   M = Maria

N: Shani Zahra

S: I use Facebook for news about friends and family and sometimes Twitter, to see what's trending, but I don't post much. I studied business at university and now I work for a large bank so my number one social network is LinkedIn. I like to see what's happening in the business world. I blog about business and one day I'd love to teach it.

N: Luke Fox

L: I connect with friends on Instagram – or face to face at our local café. I follow loads of people on Twitter. I love it! A friend of mine is an actor and he tweets about the acting world and the theatre. He's so funny! And I follow the latest news stories. I teach 8-year-old children and they know all the news. I might sign up to Snapchat so I can keep up-to-date!

N: Wai Zhu

W: I don't mind Facebook, but I much prefer Instagram. I like taking pictures and Instagram is a great place to share them. I also use WeChat a lot. It's really popular back home in China, so I use it to keep in touch with my friends and family. A lot of the people at work also use LinkedIn, so I might set up an account, too. I don't want to miss out!

N: Jean Walker

J: I only use Facebook. Sometimes I use it to catch up with my five friends, but usually it's to see my family. I've got four children and six grandchildren. They put photos on Facebook and I get to see what they're doing. Sometimes I 'like' a photo, but I can't do much more than that, I'm afraid. I might try some other social media networks, but at the moment I don't really know how to use them.

N: Maria Ricci

M: I check Facebook every two hours. It's a great way to keep in touch with old school friends you haven't seen for ten years. However, for photos, I like Snapchat best because pictures only stay online for ten seconds after I send them.

AUDIOSCRIPTS 177

Macmillan Education
4 Crinan Street
London N1 9XW
A division of Springer Nature Limited

Companies and representatives throughout the world

Language Hub Elementary Student's Book ISBN 978-1-380-01675-1
Language Hub Elementary Student's Book with Student's App
ISBN 978-1-380-01670-6

Text, Design and Illustration © Springer Nature Limited 2019
Written by Peter Maggs and Catherine Smith.

With thanks to Edward Price and Carol Goodwright for additional authoring and to Signature Manuscripts for the Grammar Hub pages.

The authors have asserted their right to be identified as the authors of this work in accordance with the Copyright, Designs and Patents Act 1988.

The right of Sue Kay and Vaughan Jones to be identified as authors of the Speaking Pages in this work has been asserted by them in accordance with the Copyright, Designs and Patents Act 1988.

First published 2019

All rights reserved. No part of this publication may be reproduced, stored in a retrieval system, or transmitted in any form or by any means, electronic, mechanical, photocopying, recording, or otherwise, without the prior written permission of the publishers.

Designed by emc design ltd
Illustrated by Rasmus Juul, Rose Frith represented by Lemonade Illustration Agency, Peter Lubach (Beehive illustration)
Cover design by Restless
Cover image by Plainpicture/Cultura/dotdotred
Picture research by Emily Taylor
Café Hub videos produced by Creative Listening.
Café Hub video scripts written by James and Luke Vyner.

The authors and publishers would like to thank the following for permission to reproduce their photographs:

Alamy Andor Bujdoso p117(tr), Danita Delimont p96(br), Dominic Dibbs p165, EyeEm p168(4), Hero Images pp86, p114(2) ImageBROKER p43(bl), Lebrecht Music and Arts Photo Library p65(b), David Pearson p151(3), Stefano Politi Markovina p151(7), Rosalrene Betancourt p44(bl), Andrej Sokolow/dpa p151(tcr), Theatrepix p56(tl); **BrandX** p151(6,11); **Steve Cole** p17(cr); **Comstock Images** p58-59(background); **Corbis** p169(4); **Getty Images** pp12(tr), 27(party), 28-29(background), 33(4), 147(3.1.1), 147(3.1.2), 147(3.1.5), 147(3.1.6), 147(4.1.4), 147(4.1.7), 148(5), 148(6), 149(2), 149(5), 150(2,5,8,10,11,13), 151(1,5,8,9), 153(6,7,8,9), 154(2.2.1, 2.2.5, 2.2.6), 166(Chichen Itza), 4kodiak p77, Mireya Acierto p107(2), Aga fotostock p147(4.1.6), Tony Anderson p151(10), Sally Anscombe p114(tm), ArabianEye p94(cr), ArcaidImages pp47(4), 50, Archive Photos Creative p54(3), Yuri Arcurs p148(1), Petri Artturi Asikainen pp21, 82(1,2), Aurora Creative p33(3), Gregory Bajor p149(3), Liam Bailey p31, Barcroft Media p114(1), Thomas Barwick pp34(tl), 170(tl, tm), 171(tl), David M. Benett p151(tr), benimage p169(5), Markus Bernhard p17(bcr), Bettmann Archive p65(d,e), Bildagentur p47(5), Blend Images pp66(br), 82(3), 151(4), 168(3), Phil Boorman p163, Caiaimage/ Paul Bradbury p35(1), Brand New Images pp24(topdog), 59(br), BraunS p24(tr), James Brittain p52(2), Gary Burchell p113, Peter Burnett p106, Caiaimage pp16, 22(tr), 34(tr), 54(4), 87, Ramsey Cardy p158, Cescassawin p46(1), Steve Chenn p153(1), Creative Crop p150(15), Christopherarndt p44(tl), Stewart Cohen p2(tl), Corbis pp61, 63(3), 65(a), Cultura pp33(1), 74(bl), 96(chuck), 104(tcr), 170(caitlin), 171(br), Jake Curtis pp24(tl), 83(b), Datacraft Co Ltd p5(2), Nick David pV1(c), Jacques Demarthon p51, Digital Vision ppV1(b), 78-79, 90(tr), 91, 147(3.1.3), Zach Dischner p166(wind surfing), dj murdok photos p12-13(background), Michael Dodge p56(tr), Nick Dolding p95, Dorling Kindersley pp7(saw), 89(boots, jacket), 99(gifts), Richard Drury p24(lisab), E+ ppV1(a), 7(water), 42(bl), 93, 153(10), Johannes Eisele p26(tr), 111, Eric Raptosh Photography p17(t), Andrew Errington p153(5), EyeEm pp3(b), 8-9(background), 24(tl), 38-39(background), 66(bm), 67(br), 68-69(background), 90(tl), 101, 117(tl), FangXiaNuo p148(4), FoodPix p18(Croissant), Marvin Fox p3(tl), Tony C French p15(r), 22(tl), fStop p108-109(background), Mitchell Funk p62(2), Jamie Garbutt p114(tr), Geber86 pp84(3), 107(1), 112, 153(3), Gilaxia p118-119(crowd), Baptiste Giroudon p52(3), Steve Glass p25(br), GoodLifeStudio p147(4.1.1), Sylvain Grandadam p102-103, Dennis Hallinan p54(1), HannamariaH p152(1-4), Daniel Hernanz Ramos p63(6), Hero Images pp67(Kate956), 85(tl), 148(2), Gary Houlder p147(4.1.8), Neil Holmes pp70(2), 149(9), Howardkingsnorth p63(5), Hulton Archive Creative p54(2), The Image Bank pp27(balinese dancers), 148(3), Image Source pp85(cl), 153(4), IndiaPictures p62(1), Interim Archives p64, iStockphoto pp89(dress, suit), 148(9, 10), 150(3, 14), 151(2), 169(1), 164, 167, Jetta Productions p35(2), JGI/ Jamie Grill p23, J J D p14(1), Joegolby p53, John Warburton-Lee Photography p27(parade), Johner RF p52(4), Jupiterimages p27(card), Maya Karkalicheva p170(marta), Steve Kelley p27(fireworks), Barry King p12(bl), Howard Kingsnorth p92(bl), KingWu p5(3), Glyn Kirk p83(a), kulicki p118-119(background), Thomas

Kurmeier p154(5.3.1), Kyoshino p18-19(background), Andrew Lipovsky p67(LisaChorley), Lonely Planet Images pp45, 66(t), 94(tl), 117(tm), LOOK p154(5.3.2), Lorado p104(t), Macduff Everton/Botanica p15(l), Megan Maloy p147(3.1.9), Daniel MacDonald p154(2.2.2), Martin-dm p66(girl with backpack), Irina Marwan p26(br), Maskot p154(2.2.7), Miss Passion Photography p41, Dean Mitchell p151(12), Moment pp65(c), Moment p149(12), Momo productions p24(milos), Tara Moore pp17(br), 168(5), m.p.imageart p154(2.2.3), Peter Muller p24(celine), Mytruestory Photography p67(bl), National Geographic pp148(7), 166(restaurant), National Geographic Magazines p74(tl), Nikada p5(1), Liam Norris p147(3.1.7), Ed Norton p67(tl), Numbeos p108(bl), OJO p33(2), Gabriel Olsen p12(br), Ourtneyk p71, PeopleImages p170(tr), Photonica p42(tr), Pixdeluxe p7(b), Pixland p161, PongMoji p84(1), Portra ehf p104(bcl, br), Portland Press Herald p81, Martin Putty p1, Presley Ann p12(bm), PYMCA pp70(3), 149(11), Redferns p156, José Reis Jr p92(bcl), Lilly Roadstones pp117(bm), 170(Luis), Robert Harding World Imagery pp11, 94(bl), 153(12), Tim Robberts pp67(TravelBob), p114(3), Kirill Rudenko p82(4), Michael Schwalbe p149(4), Pascal Le Segretain p151(cr), Selimaksan p55, Nick Sinclair p168(1), Alexander Spatari p68-69(b), StockFood p150(6), Stone Sub p52(5), Phillip Suddick p107(3), Tadamasa Taniguchi p24(fumi), Fredrik Telleus p170(martin), Tetra images p154(2.2.8), Alys Tomlinson p52(6), Universal Images Group pp2(map), 52(1), 146(maps), 154(5.3.6), Betsie van der Meer pp153(11), 168(2), Klaus Vedfelt p14(2), 37, Vetta pp36, 84(2), Mark Viker p7(toiletries), Visit Britain p148(12), Visual China Group p26(bl), Tom Werner p32, Westend61 p24(scotgirl), 96(tr), 147(4.1.3, 4.1.5), 148(11), 152(bl), 154(2.2.4), WestLight p39(folders), James Whitaker p85(bl), WIN-Initiative p149(6), xijian p117(bl), Zeigler p72-73; **Hinterhaus** Productions p100(tl); **ImageSource** pp48-49(background), 147(4.1.2), 150(1); **iStockphoto** pp7(phone), 18(camera, phone), 42(br), 100(bl), 105; **Photodisc** pp7(bat), 18(umbrella), 98-99(background), 169(3); **Rex features** Morgan Treacy/INPHO/Shutterstock p162; **Shutterstock** Hartmut Albert p92(tcl), Africa Studio p88-89, Andrmoel p166(b), Cesc Assawin p154(5.3.3), Elenovsky p89(shirt), Angelo Gilardelli p89(hat), Jag_cz p149(10), Kaprik p46(3), Art Konovalov pp70(4), 149(14), Korkusung p4(1), Teddy Leung p149(1), Felix Lipov p154(5.3.5), Elijah Lovkoff p149(13), Milanzeremski p74(cr), S/Mimo p89(scarf), Mishu88 p149(8), Filip Olejowski p89(coat), Pavel L Photo and Video p63(4), Photka p169(1), Denis Rozhnovsky p147(3.1.8), Volha Stasevich p154(5.3.4), Steve Photography p92(tl), StockPhotosArt p46(2), Sova Vitalij p153(2), Kirayonak Yuliya p24(tm); **Springer Nature Limited** pp7(keys), 18(keys); **Stockbyte** pp7(scissors), 169(2) Stockbyte/PunchStock pp70(1), 149(7); **SWNS Group** p14(a,b); **Thinkstock** pp7(laptop), 18(laptop, headphones, skateboard), 89(jumper), 147(3.1.4), 148(8), 150(4,7,9,12), 169(1).

Commissioned photographs in the Café Hubs by Creative Listening.

The authors and publishers are grateful for permission to reprint the following copyright material:

p14 Extract from 'One is dark-skinned and one is white, one has brown eyes and the other blue - but Bobby and Riley are million-to-one TWINS' by Jennifer Newton. Originally published in MailOnline, 5th July 2015. © Associated Newspapers Ltd. Reprinted with permission of Solo Syndication p36 Extract from The Open University. © The Open University 2018. All Rights Reserved. Reprinted with permission of The Open University.p162 Extract from 'A day in the life: Ireland's 800m Olympic hopeful Ciara Everard' by The42 Team. Originally published in The 42, 12th January 2016. Content copyright © Journal Media Ltd. 2018. Reprinted with permission of The 42.

These materials may contain links for third party websites. We have no control over, and are not responsible for, the contents of such third party websites. Please use care when accessing them.

The inclusion of any specific companies, commercial products, trade names or otherwise, does not constitute or imply its endorsement or recommendation by Springer Nature Limited.

Printed and bound in Lebanon

2023 2022 2021 2020 2019
10 9 8 7 6 5 4 3 2